animating films without a camera

By JACQUES BOURGEOIS

**LITTLE
CRAFT BOOK
SERIES**

STERLING
PUBLISHING CO., INC.   NEW YORK

Oak Tree Press Co., Ltd.   London & Sydney
SAUNDERS OF TORONTO, Ltd., Don Mills, Canada

Little Craft Book Series

Translated by Anne E. Kallem

The original edition of this book was published in France under the title
"Cinema D'Animation sans Camera" © 1973 Dessain et Tolra, Paris, France

Copyright © 1974 by Sterling Publishing Co., Inc.
419 Park Avenue South, New York, N.Y. 10016
Distributed in Canada by Saunders of Toronto, Ltd., Don Mills, Ontario
British edition published by Oak Tree Press Co., Ltd., Nassau, Bahamas
Distributed in Australia and New Zealand by Oak Tree Press Co., Ltd.,
P.O. Box J34, Brickfield Hill, Sydney 2000, N.S.W.
Distributed in the United Kingdom and elsewhere in the British Commonwealth
by Ward Lock Ltd., 116 Baker Street, London W 1
Manufactured in the United States of America   *All rights reserved*
Library of Congress Catalog Card No.: 74-82324
Sterling ISBN 0–8069–5304–7 Trade   Oak Tree 7061–2011–6
5305–5 Library

Contents

Before You Begin

If you have been under the impression that animating film is a tedious and costly process, you are mistaken, and this book will prove it to you! Actually, drawing directly on film not only costs very little, but provides a fresh and spontaneous means of expression that is completely different from other animation techniques and is quite easy to do.

You do not have to learn complicated technical terms, such as focal lengths, depth of field, and so on, because there is no need for it in the simple technique of animating film without a camera. What you *will learn* is how to draw and color directly on film—not only images, but sound, too. This does not mean that you have to be an artist. As a matter of fact, because of the small scale of film drawing, only the simplest of forms is required and some films are completely non-representational—simply the interplay of lines and colors. No matter how complex a subject you choose, you can still break it down into basic forms.

You can produce animated films that tell a story or you can just amuse your viewers with something as simple as putting a group of dots through some zany antics.

You can produce films by yourself, with a movie "crew," or as a class project, and project them on a screen. Using just your own imagination and creativity plus, commonly-available materials such as pen and ink, soft-tip markers or a scratching implement like a needle, you can produce figures that move and transform themselves into other objects, designs that seem to appear from nowhere and then disappear again, or compositions of moving lines and color. If you have a sound projector available, you can add this dimension to your films.

Here's your chance to be your own producer, scenarist, director, projectionist, editor—in other words, a jack-of-all-trades film-maker. You will have hours of pleasure using your hidden creativity to produce a film and hours of entertainment watching your productions on the screen in your home or classroom.

This book does not attempt to cover the complexities of the work you see in a professionally made cartoon. All of the projects and films here have been experimented with by youngsters in schools so that the techniques have been considerably simplified. Nonetheless, the results are exciting and prove how easy film animation can be. At the same time, all of these projects provide you with an excellent basic foundation for going on to more complex techniques, for example, producing films from photographs made with a still camera. The completed films in the illustrations are not models for you to imitate exactly, but they will serve as a point of departure, or a "jumping off" place, for you to go on experimenting with your own ideas.

Here, on these pages, are all of the vital steps you need to know in the preparation and production of a film. When, after just a few hours of "work," you see your own creative efforts moving across the screen, you will be amazed and wish you had tried it before. So, get started and make up for all that lost time right now!

What Is Animation?

Following are three very simple experiments for you to make which, although not really part of the technique of animating film without a camera, will quickly provide you with a thorough understanding of the basic principles of animation.

Breakdown of a Movement

In order to render a movement by means of static drawings, you must "break it down." It is easy to do this with a form with moving parts—such as an articulated puppet.

First, make a sketch of your puppet figure on a piece of paper. Then transfer your drawing to a piece of heavy cardboard. Cut out the various parts of the body one by one—the torso, head, upper arms, lower arms, upper legs, and lower legs—so that your figure resembles the one in Illus. 1.

Now, using paper fasteners, assemble the parts in such a way that the parts move easily. Take a sheet of paper and draw the basic outline of your puppet on it. Then move the puppet slightly across the paper, change the position of the arms and legs, and draw another outline. Change it again and outline the new position. Continue in this way until you have a succession of slightly

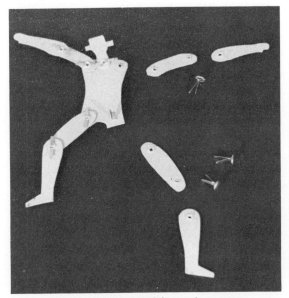

Illus. 1. A puppet with moving parts.

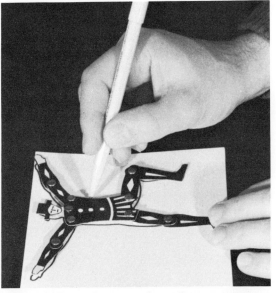

Illus. 2. Trace the puppet's outline onto paper.

Illus. 3.

overlapped drawings as in Illus. 3. *This series of drawings represents the breakdown of a movement.*

Make a "Flip"

A flip is a small pad containing a succession of stacked drawings, or drawings superimposed one upon the other. Each drawing is a "snapshot" of one part of a movement. The first drawing shows the start of the movement, and the last shows the final stage of the same movement. Each drawing differs slightly from the one preceding it and from the one following it.

By rapidly flipping the pages of the pad between your thumb and index finger, you "animate" the figure—a puppet raises his arms or kicks his legs, a ball bounces up and then down, and so on.

Let's make a flip breaking down a simple movement with the help of the puppet you made.

Choose a pad that has semi-transparent paper so that you can easily see the drawing that precedes the one you are making, but do not use very light tracing paper, or the effect of the individual drawings will be spoiled.

You must first determine the limits of the movement—where the figure will be at the start of the movement and where it will be at the end. The next step is to decide how many drawings you will need to reconstruct the movement. Although this number is variable depending upon the speed at which you riffle the pages, for the purposes of this experiment, you should make 24 drawings for each second that you want the movement to last. (The reason for this, as you will find out later in more detail, is that the standard speed for most movie projectors is 24 frames per second.)

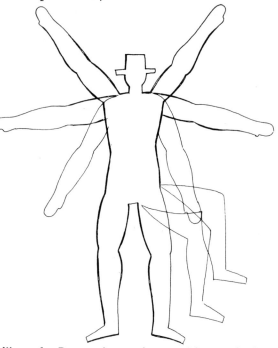

Illus. 4. Draw the major positions of the movement first.

6

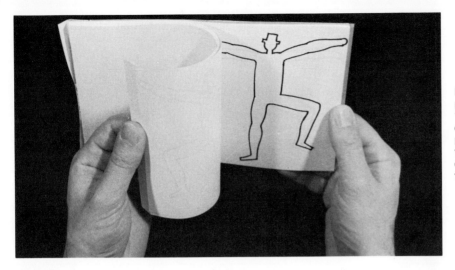

Illus. 5. Use your puppet to make a "flip." By riffling quickly through the pages (from back to front preferably), you can make your puppet figure move.

To simplify the production of your first flip, plan to have only the arms and one leg of the puppet move. You will find it easier to first trace the *fixed parts* of the puppet—the body, the head and the stationary leg—on each piece of paper. Now, on the first drawing and the last drawing, trace in the arms and leg that are to move and which will, of course, be in different positions on each. In the first drawing, both arms and both legs are at rest. In the last drawing, both arms and one leg will be raised as high as they can go.

Your next step is to draw the positions of the arms and the leg half-way through the flip, as shown in Illus. 4. Now you can easily calculate the positions for all the in-between movements and complete your drawings. Number the pages of the flip so that you can gauge the positions as you go along.

When you are finished, riffle the pages quickly, but carefully, and watch your puppet come to life.

Breaking Down a Movement with Slides

You can do another simple experiment in the fundamentals of animation with the aid of a slide projector that has a tray or carousel for holding the slides. This will allow you to move a succession of slides quickly enough to create movement from a series of broken-down steps. The actual reconstruction of the movement, however, depends upon how rapidly the slides can be moved.

Make a series of drawings, breaking the movement into parts. You can make these preliminary drawings large. When you are satisfied with the series, take tracing paper and, using either a soft-tip ink marker or pen and ink, render the drawings on a smaller scale of either 24×36 mm. (about $1 \times 1\frac{1}{2}$ inches) or 40×40 mm. (about $1\frac{5}{8} \times 1\frac{5}{8}$ inches).

Mount each one of the drawings in a standard

7

Illus. 6.

8

2×2 inch (5×5 cm.) cardboard frame. These frames are available at any camera shop.

Number your "slides" so that you will not get them out of order and place them in the projector tray. Then project them as rapidly and smoothly as possible.

Now that you have gone from merely drawing on paper to actually projecting your images, you have reached the threshold of film animation.

Speed of the Images

The standard speed for movie projectors is 24 frames per second but Super 8 runs 18 frames per second. This number of images per second is recognized as the best to allow the eye to reconstruct a movement easily. If your drawings are not lined up just right in making a film, the projected picture seems jumpy when shown on a screen. To give the animated movement some stability, each drawing is projected twice.

In the production of an animated movement *with* a camera, there are 24 frames of film per second, but only 12 different drawings, since each drawing is reproduced twice. In other words, the same drawing is produced on two successive frames.

In drawing directly on blank film stock, as you will do to animate films without a camera, the breakdowns of movements are rather more difficult to render because of the small scale of the drawings. If you attempt to modify your drawing so as to show a very slight movement on each frame rather than making a somewhat greater movement every two frames, you run the risk of

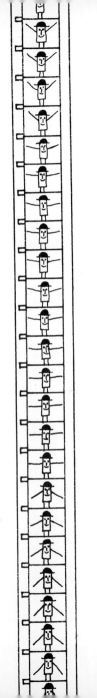
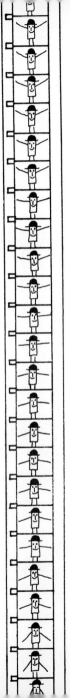

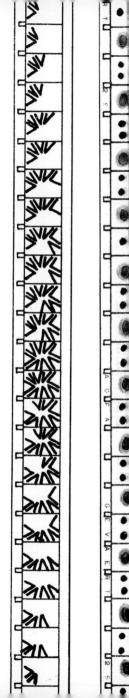

uneven movement when the film is projected. The jumpiness is due to small errors in the relative placement of the drawing within each succeeding frame.

For better stability of the projected image, therefore, it is advisable for you, as a beginner, to repeat each drawing six times even though this means that each movement will be broken down into fewer steps. You will soon be able to reduce the number of times you repeat each drawing and correspondingly increase the number of stages. Also, with experience, you will be able to take advantage of what is called "persistence of image" on the retina and leave a blank frame now and then. (Persistence of the image simply refers to the fact that every image that the retina of the eye receives is retained for a short time or until it is replaced by the next image.)

Note: Although the standard speed for projectors is 24 frames per second (f.p.s.), some projectors can be regulated to run as slowly as 16 f.p.s. This feature allows you to project the film of a movement that seems poorly broken down at 24 f.p.s. at a slower speed which usually succeeds in making it more acceptable.

Techniques

There are essentially two techniques for working directly on blank film:

1. Drawing on clear film with colored inks or dyes, using a pen or paintbrush, or using soft-tip ink markers.

2. Drawing on dark or fogged film by scratching into the emulsion with a sharp-pointed instrument, such as a heavy needle or a hatpin. (Fogged film is regular film which has not been exposed, but has been developed. It can also be purchased at camera shops in 100-foot rolls.)

Characteristics of Film

For drawing directly on blank film, you can use any of the three standard-size motion picture films—8 mm., 16 mm., or 35 mm.

Your choice of film is naturally tied into the kind of production you are planning, the size of your budget and the kind of projector you have available. The larger the frame of the film, the easier the drawing and the more faithful the reproduction on the screen. The larger films are also the most expensive. The kind of projector you have available may be the determining factor, however. You will find that 35 mm. film is easy to work with, but 35 mm. projectors are for the most part restricted to professional use and are not always available, even for rental.

Even though you will not be using the film in a camera, you still have to send it to a developing laboratory. You have to do this before you start to draw.

If you want clear film for working with pen or paintbrush, you must first expose the film by unrolling it in sunlight. Send it along to a laboratory with an explanatory note attached stating what you did and what you intend to do

with it. You will receive a developed, but clear film. For scratch drawing on fogged film, just send the roll along as is without exposing it, also with an explanatory note. They will return a fogged (opaque black) film to you.

You can avoid sending film to a developing lab by buying transparent leader at a camera shop. This comes in the three standard sizes. You will find it very easy to draw on, but because it is a little bit stiffer than regular film, you might find it slightly more difficult to splice during your later editing, but not enough to cause any trouble.

To clearly understand the use of the basic tools and equipment for drawing on film (film-holding block, light box, and so on), you need to be familiar with the characteristics of the three common film sizes. The techniques presented here are actually adaptable to any existing or possible future film sizes (Super 16, for example). The important thing for any film is to determine the size and placement of the frames (that segment of the film that is projected onto the screen at one time) and to reproduce an outline of that film on an actual-size scale on a strip of paper. This strip of paper, set in proper relation to the sprocket holes of the film, will serve as a guide-strip underneath the film.

The film stock, which is completely transparent, does not show a frame line, that is, a line separating one frame from the next. You can tell where one frame ends and the next begins, however, by referring to the sprocket holes. With 16 mm. film, for example, each perforation is exactly at the frame line (see next page).

11

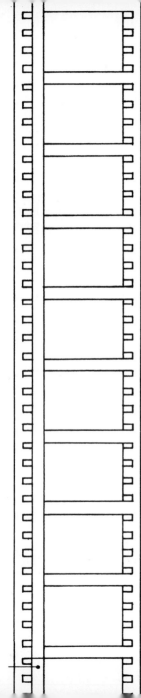

35 mm.

This is the largest of the common film sizes and is, therefore, ideal for drawing directly on blank film. You will probably find it difficult to locate a 35 mm. projector but it is possible to do your drawing on 35 mm. film and then send it to a lab to have a print made on the smaller 16 mm. or 8 mm. film. These reduced-size prints are expensive, however, and so is the 35 mm. film.

The 21 × 15.3 mm. frame size does allow you to make well detailed drawings. As you can see in the actual-size drawing of the piece of 35 mm. film, each image, or frame, has four perforations alongside it, and there is a blank space between each frame which is equal to the distance between two perforations. The sound track (dot in drawing) on 35 mm. movie film is wide enough to allow you to make a very precise co-ordination of sound and drawing (see pages 45 to 47).

16 mm.

Contrary to the situation with 35 mm. projectors, 16 mm. projectors are used extensively by schools, clubs, and cultural groups. Serious home-movie makers may have them also. This size is available for rental and they are easily carried, so that you can view films wherever and whenever you please.

The 16 mm. film is available both with and without a sound track and there are both sound and silent projectors. The film for silent projectors has a double row of perforations, one along each edge. Sound film has only one row of perforations,

Illus. 7. Actual sizes (from left to right) of 35 mm., 16 mm., and 8 mm. film. The sound tracks on both of the larger sizes are indicated by a dot.

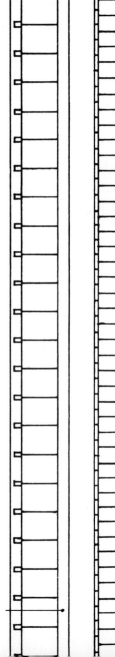

with the sound track running along the opposite edge. If you are planning a film with sound effects, these will be recorded or scratched in along this track.

The frame dimensions of 16 mm. film are 9.5×7.1 mm. (about $\frac{3}{8} \times \frac{1}{4}$ inch), which allow less freedom in your drawing than with the larger 35 mm. frame. You can represent only a single form at a time. Since each sprocket hole indicates the start of a frame, this simplifies the marking of the drawings on the holding block which you will be using (see next page).

In spite of the smaller scale of 16 mm. film, it is recommended because of the availability of projectors.

8 mm.

This size, especially the Super 8, has become very popular, especially for home projecting. Projectors are inexpensive, and their adjustable speed (usually from 16 to 24 frames per second) is useful for improving the effect of a film on which the movements have not been broken down as smoothly as you might wish.

On the other hand, it is probably the least interesting size for the animator to work on because of the small area of each frame—5.5×4 mm. (about $\frac{3}{16} \times \frac{1}{8}$ inch). Nevertheless, you can make very simplified drawings on 8 mm. film with the aid of a magnifying glass. It is particularly easy to carry out a film project on this size if it does not require frame-by-frame drawings. Films that consist of continuous lengthwise lines, random scratches, bands of color, etc., can be produced very easily on this size film. Detailed drawings on 8 mm. film require great manual ability.

Viewers

If you do not have a projector handy, you can use a film viewer or editor. A viewer is less expensive than a projector and has the advantage of allowing you to stop at any frame you choose. Viewers do not have a sound-effects system.

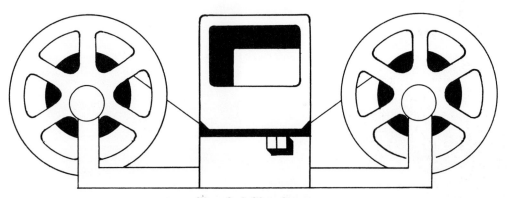

Illus. 8. A film viewer.

Drawing on Clear Film

In order to produce an animated film, even a very short one, you must repeat the same image a number of times, making sure that it is always spaced the same within the frame "line." Only the actual moving parts of the drawing should change position in relation to the frame.

These requirements mean that, as in the "flip" which you made (page 6), the images must fall precisely one on top of the other. The vertical arrangement of the frames along a length of film, however, as opposed to the arrangement of the pages in a book means that you must use a different technique than you used for the flip. The simplest method is using a film-holding block, which you can make yourself quickly and easily.

Make a Film-Holding Block

The purpose of the block is to hold the film in a fixed position while you are tracing your drawings on it. It must therefore have a groove or slot which is the same width as the film you are using. If you intend using different sizes of film, you will have to make a holding block for each size.

You can carve a slot in a solid block of wood, but this is difficult to do. It is easier to start with a piece of flat wood that is somewhat wider than the film, then add two strips to create a groove of the right size. Measure the width of the film and transfer the measurement to the wood block to make a "slot" that is only barely larger than the film. This means that the film must slip easily, but fit snugly, in the slot. Test it before glueing or nailing down the wood strips.

The length of your holding block should accommodate 24 frames of the size film you are using. This will permit you to gauge the projec-

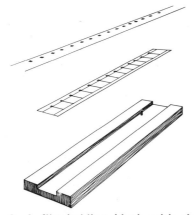

Illus. 9. A film-holding block with the paper guide-strip and the clear film ready to be put in place.

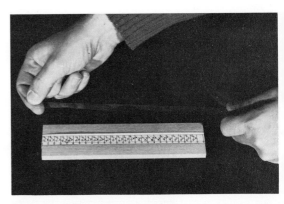

Illus. 10. When your drawings are ready, lay the film over the guide-strip in the holding block.

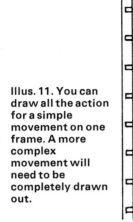

Illus. 11. You can draw all the action for a simple movement on one frame. A more complex movement will need to be completely drawn out.

For a *simple movement*, you can draw the entire breakdown on a single frame of the paper strip as shown in Illus. 11. Then simply place, first the paper strip, and then the blank film, on top of it in the slot. Slip one film perforation over the peg and trace the first frame. Shift the film, frame by frame, and trace all of the fixed portions of the design plus the appropriate part of the movement, using the peg each time to hold the film in place.

Now, for a more *complex movement*, you will need to break it down on several frames of the paper strip. Use a piece of tracing paper when you move from frame to frame to ensure that your figures maintain the same relative positions to the frame lines. Proceed to transferring the design to the film as above but watch carefully that you follow the sequence of drawings accurately.

tion time easily since you will know that the length of film in the block is equal to one second on the screen.

The next step is to attach a tiny wooden peg to the holding block in the position shown in Illus. 9. Since this peg will hold the film as you draw, make it just the right size to allow a perforation to slip over it easily.

Now take a piece of sturdy paper cut to the size of the groove in the holding block and draw on it the frame lines of the size film you are using. Use the perforations in the blank film as guides for your frame lines as shown in Illus. 9. Since you will need several of these sheets in the course of making a film, you might want to make a number of photocopies so you will not have to redraw the frame outlines time and again. You draw the figures for your movies first on these strips and then transfer them to the film.

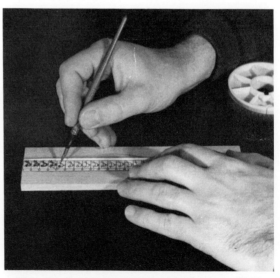

Illus. 12. Trace the design onto the clear film.

Using the Block According to Film Size

8 mm. and 16 mm.: These sizes are very easy to use in the holding block. You merely move the film one perforation ahead in order to change a frame when you are using a single frame as a guide—that is, when your movement is simple, as in Illus. 11. For more complex movement, where you have done a separate drawing for each stage of the frames, there is no need to shift the film until you put down a new strip of drawings.

35 mm.: In this size film, each frame has four perforations beside it and the space between two frames is equal to the space between two perforations. In order to correctly shift one frame of film from one drawing to the next, you must move the film ahead by four perforations. If necessary, place guide marks on the film with ink so you will not get mixed up. For a movement broken down on a number of frames, these marks are vital. (Be careful, however, not to place any marks on the sound track—they will cause sound effects during projection!)

Simplified Film-Holding Device

If you want to avoid making a holding block, you can substitute another very simple device. Fasten the strip of drawings onto a small board or drawing board. At the top and bottom of the paper strip, sink two headless nails at the exact location of two film perforations (Illus. 14). Engage the film on the two pegs and proceed as with the holding block. This device is just as stable as a block, but using it takes more time, since you must catch the film on two pegs instead of one.

Illus. 13.

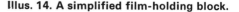

Illus. 14. A simplified film-holding block.

16

Materials for Drawing on Clear Film

Special Inks

Until recently, drawing on blank film was all but impossible without consulting an expert in the chemistry of dyes and colors. The main problem was to make the inks hold on the film, since all then-available inks had a tendency to retract, or shrink, on slick surfaces. The solution was to add ox-gall constantly to the inks and keep going over and over the drawings until the ink finally held. Then the problem would arise of running the film through the projector without having the inks stain the film track or other parts of the projector. The solution was the costly one of having a copy made of the original film—and this without your having been able to view it beforehand!

Today there are special inks that adhere so perfectly to the film that the film track of the projector stays perfectly clean—and these inks are very easy to apply as well. Made by a number of different manufacturers (Craftint, Higgins, Pelikan) these inks are sold as transparent inks or dyes for use with brushes and pen points for working on plastic sheet. They have the advantage of being erasable also—you can simply wipe them off with a damp cloth if you wish.

These inks and dyes not only come in bottles, but are also available in soft-tip ink markers. If you purchase markers, be sure they are for use on acetate or are labelled "permanent for projection."

No matter what you use, however, always be sure to test them on a piece of scrap film. Lay on the colors, allow a little drying time, and then

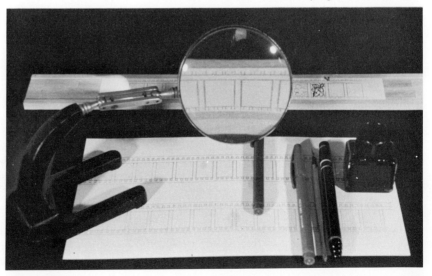

Illus. 15. The basic equipment for animating films without a camera: a film-holding block, paper guide-strips, soft-tip ink markers, paintbrush, pen, ink and a magnifying glass.

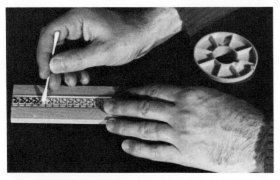

Illus. 16. Erasing a mistake with alcohol.

scratch them lightly with your finger-nail or with a pen point to check on their solidity. (Always apply paint or ink to what is called the "emulsion side" of the film—this is very obviously the *duller* side.)

Brushes, Pens, and Markers

Since all of your drawings are going to be quite small, choose implements with the finest points possible: the smallest paintbrushes you can find, extra-fine drawing pens, and so on. No matter what you use, always clean them well afterwards. For ease and speed in working, you might use a different implement for each color, so that you will not have to clean the points constantly.

You will soon find that soft-tip ink markers, no matter how fine, do not produce the delicate lines of a fine pen point. If your drawing does require very fine detail, use a pen, and then use markers for filling in color.

Since the light of the projector is very strong, you might find that your colors seem "washed

out." If this happens, strengthen them by merely going over them. Experience with your own projector will show you just how much you have to strengthen your colors.

To erase a poorly made drawing on transparent film, use 90° alcohol for alcohol-based inks and dyes. Apply it with a paintbrush or cotton swab. Use an ordinary blotter to absorb any excess alcohol on the film.

Accessories

Gloves. In professional film labs, cotton or nylon gloves are used to avoid leaving finger-prints on film. If you want carefully done work, use such gloves when drawing, or even handling, clear film. This is especially important when you are editing or splicing, since you will be constantly touching the film.

Magnifying Glass. A magnifying glass on a stand (Illus. 15) allows you to enlarge the drawing you are making, yet leaves both your hands free.

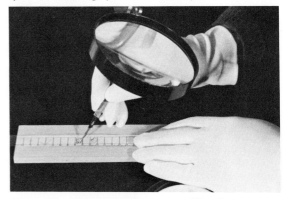

Illus. 17. Gloves protect your film from stray finger-prints.

Ideas for Fun Projects

Now that you have gained an understanding of the basic methods and materials, you can go on to master the technique of animating film through some simple and amusing projects. On the following pages are some ideas that you can draw upon to produce a film quickly and enjoy yourself while doing it. The drawings are more or less condensed, since showing the total unrolling of each film would take more space than a page of this book allows. The drawings represent only the important steps of a movement. It should be an easy task for you to imagine the intermediate drawings.

In creating a film, you must take into account two essential elements—*rhythm* and *harmony of colors.*

Rhythm

As you know by now, one second of projection on a screen corresponds to 24 frames on your film. This then is your basic unit for calculating the time for the reproduction of one movement, and from that the duration of the total length of a film.

If different movements follow one another with a consistent, regular speed, the result is likely to be boring. On the other hand, if you follow a slow movement with a quick movement, or vice versa, you will arouse far more interest in your viewers. This alternating of "weak" and "strong" time is called *rhythm* and it is one of the fundamental elements in animating film. To grasp the importance of it, notice in regard to the drawings on the following pages the indications of the duration of each movement.

A watch with a second hand, or a stop watch will be helpful in evaluating the duration of a movement that you want to transfer to the screen. You must remember that the eye has a difficult time perceiving the projection of too short a movement, even though the same movement, spread out to say eight seconds, seems long! Of course, there are some very rapid effects that *are* perceptible in a second, or even in a fraction of a second. They have a strong suggestive power.

Harmony of Colors

The second point to keep in mind is the fact that for a short moment your eye retains the memory of what it has just perceived. The image which is disappearing still affects the retina at the moment the following image is presented. This phenomenon is called the persistence of vision.

Thus, your impression of the colors of an image is strongly influenced by the colors of the preceding image. So, when you are working out the color effects of your film, you must plan in terms of the total color effect of the images rather than image by image or frame by frame. Experience will show you the best way to handle this problem.

Illus. 18.

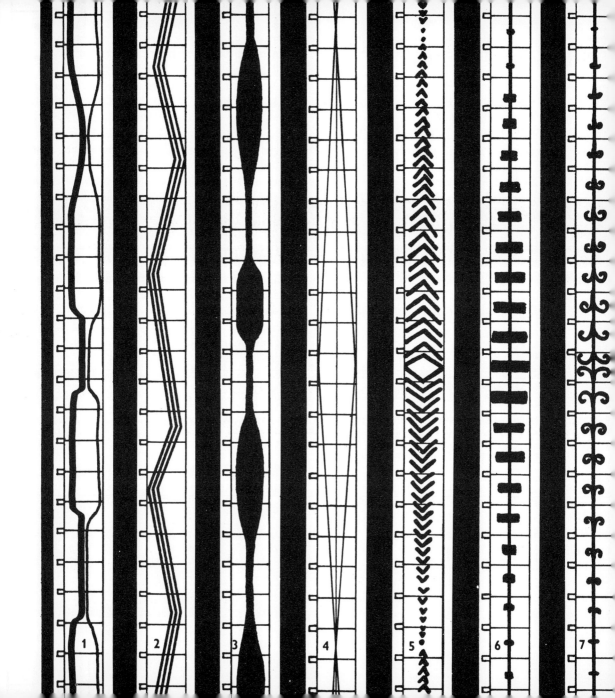

Play of Longitudinal Lines

1. Undulating lines.
2. Zigzag lines.
3. Thick and thin lines.

Plan the coming together of the lines on a triple-time rhythm—24, 48, and then 96 images.

4. Preliminary drawing made on paper to serve as a guide for film design No. 5.

5. Study for a design made without reference to frame lines.

6 and 7. Studies for designs centered on a longitudinal center line *and* within the individual frames.

Compare the effect of stretching the narrow-wide-narrow movement over 120 frames (5 seconds) to that of the same movement made very quickly over 24 frames (a single second).

8. Lateral shifting of a vertical line. The "jump" effect depends upon the shifting of the line from one series of frames to the next. Contrast one shift per second in one direction to a slower shift, perhaps one movement in five seconds, in the other direction.

9. Lateral shift of two lines of different thicknesses or different colors.

10. Preliminary drawing made on paper for film design No. 11.

11. Progression of a zigzag line shifting from frame to frame.

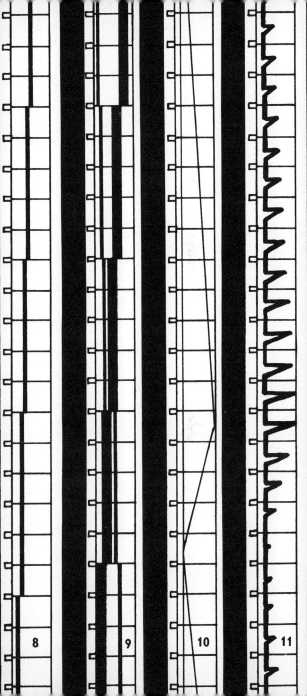

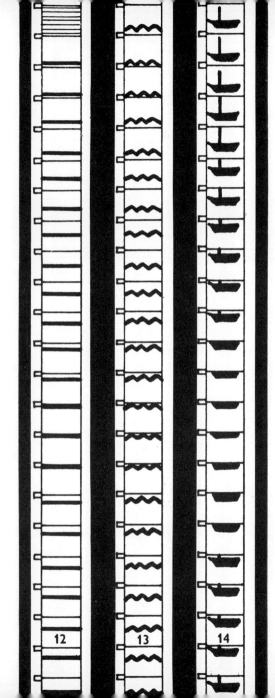

Play of Horizontal Lines

12. Vertical shifting of a horizontal line. In the first frame (at top) is the drawing to be made on the guide-strip in the holding block. Repeat each position on at least six frames of film.

13. Vertical shifting of a horizontal line to show the rising of a tide.

14. Same as No. 13, showing the rising and falling of a boat on waves.

Play with Dots

15. A network of dots of which you can vary the density, width, and colors. Develop your design by alternately changing different characteristics, for example, by the size and then the color (binary rhythm).

16. An undulating line broken down into dots. Set the rhythm by placing a very large dot every 24 frames or every 48 frames.

17. Construction of a shape with dots. On the first frame (at top) is the drawing to be made on the guide-strip in the holding block. Progressively fill up this shape with dots, repeating the same image 24 times.

Enlarging and Reducing a Shape

18. Plan the enlarging over 120 frames, the reducing over fewer frames (faster)—so that the rhythm is more interesting. Draw the profile of the enlargement and its important stages on a single frame of the guide-strip (shown in top frame here).

19. Enlarging and reducing a mushroom.

20. Enlarging and reducing a bird. The effect is to make the bird seem to come closer to you, then move away.

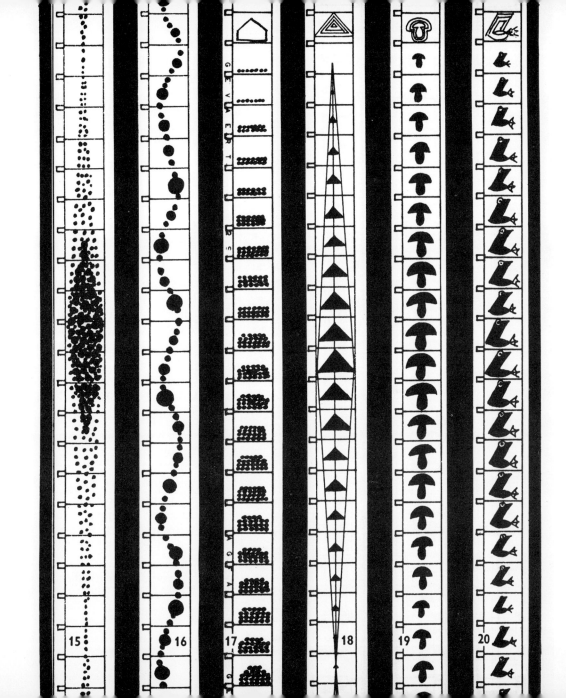

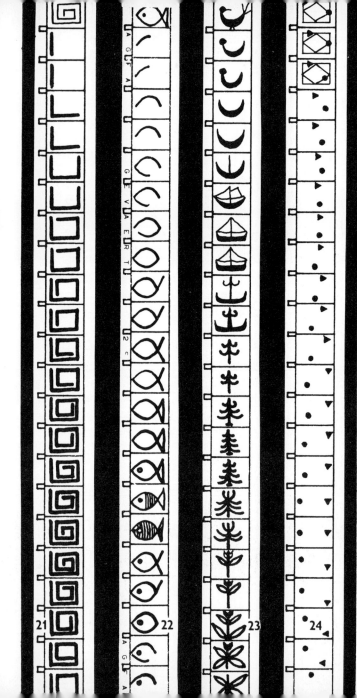

Construction of a Geometric Figure

21. On one frame of the guide-strip, draw the entire geometric figure. Then, on the film trace the figure at the rhythm of one line added every 24 frames. If you want, to help you maintain your frame line, draw longitudinal lines on the drawing in the holding block.

Construction of Simple Representational Objects

22. On the first frame of the paper guide-strip, draw the complete figure. Then, every few frames, add a portion of a line or element until the drawing is complete. Then go backwards, that is, "remove" lines until the figure disappears.

Transformation of a Shape

23. This is a very exciting process which is ideally suited to film animating. As you can see, our bird undergoes a number of transformations, changing into a boat, a tree, a bug, a flower, and finally into a butterfly. If your transformation is simple, draw the entire thing on a single frame of the guide-strip in the holding block. In order that a transformation is as clear as possible on the screen, you must spread it out over five or six seconds at the very least (120 or 144 frames).

Shifting of a Shape within the Frame

On the guide-strip, first draw the path that the shape will follow. When you draw it on the film, shift the shape every six frames following the path indicated on the paper guide.

24. Shifting of two elements on two different paths.

Repeated Movements

Again, make a preliminary drawing on one frame of the paper guide-strip, superimposing all of the stages of the movement.

25. A peacock opens up his tail feathers and then closes them.

Movement of a Silhouette Figure

26. Draw all of the movements on the first frame of the paper guide-strip. Trace the images onto the film, repeating each stage for at least six frames.

Facial Expressions

27 and 28. If the face is simple as shown here in 27, make all your drawings on the first frame of the guide-strip. Progressively modify the expression, tracing the identical image on at least six frames of film. Then move on to not only changing the expression on the face, but the position of the head as in 28.

25

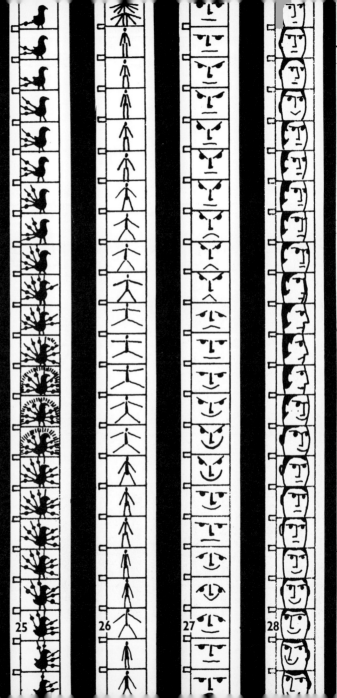

25 26 27 28

Animation of Simple Subjects

Breakdown of a Subject into Simple Form

Within the narrow limits of the frame of a film, the subject must be simplified to the maximum in order to "tighten up" the ideography. Ideography, put simply, means the conveying of ideas through graphic symbols.

What it means for you, a beginner as an animator, is that you must extract the geometric structure from every form you choose to animate. This may sound complicated, but actually it is not. For example, the drawings on this page were all made by 11-year-old children, and are based on simple geometric forms (circles, square, rhombus or parallelogram) which, when put together, represent certain people or animals (a mouse falls into an oblong; a giraffe into a succession of rectangles, and so on). To this "geometry" you simply add the breakdown of the movements. For example, it is very simple to

animate the head of a camel if you represent it by a triangle, as shown below.

Keep in mind, however, that the images you produce are going to be greatly enlarged when projected on a screen, so never sacrifice the expressiveness of your figures by oversimplifying them.

When you have decided upon a subject that you can break down easily into some geometric forms, you are ready for the next step—preparing a story.

The Story Board

Now that you have experimented with the various means of animation, it is time for you to tell a simple story. The first step that an animator takes is setting up a "story board," which is the plan of your film. It includes a brief description of the story, the duration of, and number of frames for each part of the plan, and the corresponding sound effects, assuming you have a film with a sound track and a sound projector available. The technique for producing these sounds is described in the last chapter of this book.

Story Board: "Adventures of a Red Woodpecker"

Subject	Duration (seconds)	No. of Frames
1. A red woodpecker descends the length of a tree, pecking as he goes.	5″	120
2. He arrives at the level of an owl.	15″	360
3. He continues his descent. A wolf awaits him at the foot of the tree.	5″	120
4. The wolf eats the woodpecker.	10″	240
Total	35″	840

Story Board: "The Oak and the Cattail"

	Duration (seconds)	No. of Frames	Sound
	8″	192	
	8″	192	
	4″	96	
	4″	96	Strong bangs.
	8″	192	Strong bangs.

	4″	96	Strong bangs.
	8″	192	
	4″	96	
	8″	192	Strong bang.
	8″	192	
	6″	144	
Total	70″	1,680	

Story Board: "The Thunderstorm"

Subject	Duration (seconds)	No. of Frames
1. Appearance of the sun and a cloud.	15″	360
2. The cloud darkens. The sun disappears.	10″	240
3. Two bolts of lightning.	5″	120
4. Rain.	10″	240
5. The cloud empties and disappears.	5″	120
6. Rainbow. The sun reappears.	10″	240
Total	55″	1,320

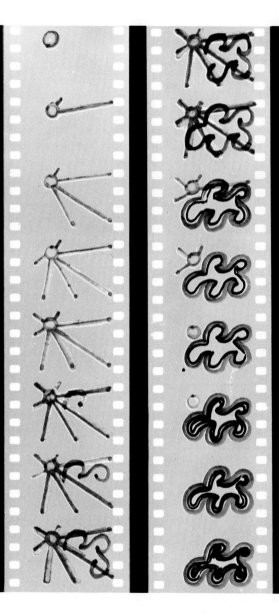

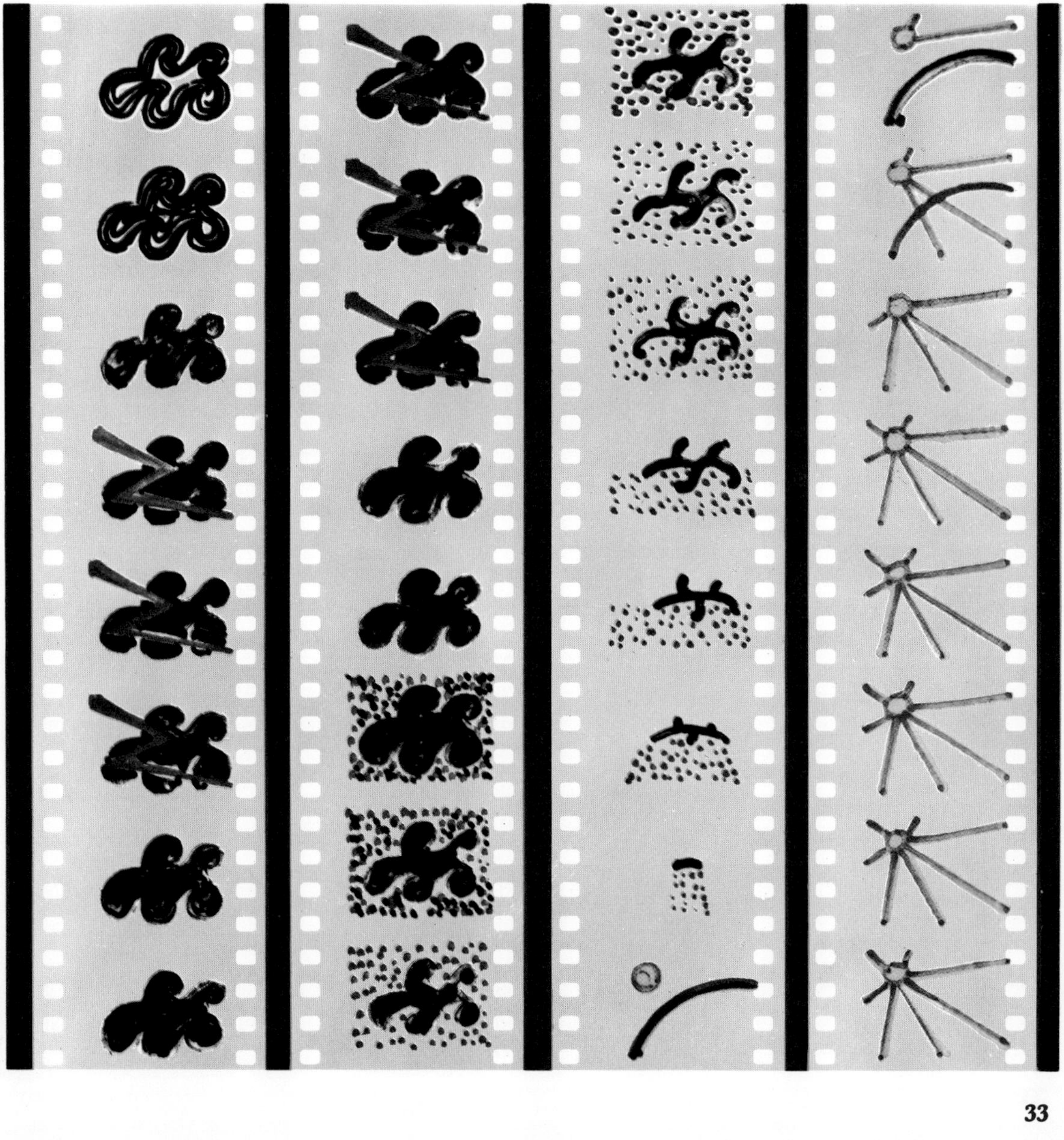

Illus. 19. Work at a slant if you are part of an animating group (see page 38).

Story Board: "Battle of the Black Dots and a Triangle"
(16 mm. production)

	Subject	Duration (seconds)	No. of Frames	Sound
	1. Presentation of the dots.	3″	72	
	2. Up pops a triangle seeking entry into the middle of the dots.	3″	72	Heavy vibration.
	3. The dots resist.	5″	120	Bangs.

4. The triangle returns to its place.	5″	120	Heavy vibration.	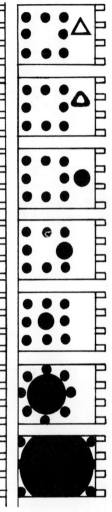
5. Transformation of the triangle . . .	3″	72	Shrill vibration.	
6. . . . into a circle.	5″	120	Shrill vibration.	
7. It finds its way then . . .	5″	120	Shrill vibration.	
8. . . . into the middle of the dots.	5″	120	Amplified vibration.	
9. It grows big to eliminate the dots . . .	5″	120	Bangs.	
10. . . . from the image.	5″	120	Bangs.	
Total	42″	1,008		

Story Board: "The Creation"

Scenario based on the principle of the transformation of forms.

Subject	Duration (seconds)	No. of Frames
1. Chaos.	5″	120
2. Transformation: the earth.	10″	240
3. Transformation: the sun.	5″	120
4. Transformation: the sea.	10″	240
5. Transformation: the plants.	5″	120
6. Transformation: the tree.	5″	120
7. Transformation: the fish.	10″	240
8. Transformation: the amphibian.	5″	120
9. Transformation: the bird.	10″	240
10. Transformation: the cat.	5″	120
11. Transformation: man.	5″	120
Total	75″	1,800

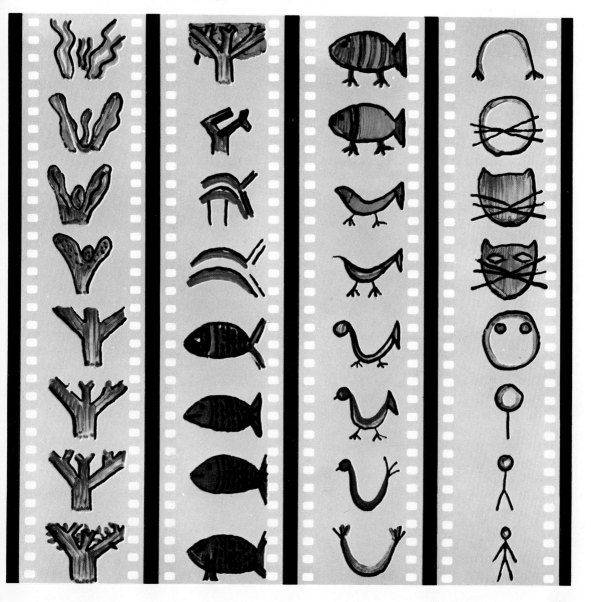

Group Work

Animating film without a camera is an ideal medium of expression for groups. Working together to produce a film has many advantages. First of all, a group of 30 people can produce a two-minute film in the space of approximately three hours if each person produces 96 drawings, or four seconds of projection time. In addition, by providing each person with a simple drawing to make, the results can be viewed within a short time, so that the beginner can see the end product of his efforts far more quickly than if working alone, and thus can learn the techniques more rapidly.

Distribution of Work

Depending upon how many people are involved and how long the film is to be, the amount of projection time for each animator's drawings should be from three to five seconds.

There are two ways in which the production of an animated film can be handled by a group. Either the film can be cut and have each animator work on his own piece, and then splice the pieces together, or have the entire group work on one continuous roll of film. The latter is preferable because of the problem of splicing the film together again, but it requires a special arrangement in the "production" room.

In order to unroll the film completely and to allow each person to work easily, you must set up the worktables in the form of a spiral, corresponding more or less to a film reel. At the middle of the spiral is the end of the film, and on the very outside is the beginning (Illus. 20).

As you can see in Illus. 20, the animators are using the holding blocks in a position that is parallel to them. For simple geometric shapes, this position presents no problem. However, for representational drawings where you must face the frame, you will have to place yourself at a slant in relation to the table and incline the holding block on an angle towards you as shown in Illus. 19. All of the animators should face in the same direction, from right to left, for example, as they are doing in that photo (see page 34).

If your film is done in individual sections, you will have to link up the parts so that you have a continuous, uninterrupted story. This means that each animator will have to use his imagination to form a transition of some kind from his last frame to the first frame of the next person. This can be done in any number of ways, of course, such as by a simple little play of lines.

You should choose a theme for your film which is adaptable for the group to execute easily. For example, you might select the idea of someone getting ready to go out in snowy or rainy weather. This would allow one base drawing which everyone can use—a figure. Then each animator is responsible for the donning of one article of clothing. The first animator will present, for example, the putting on of the coat, the second will do one boot, the third the second boot, and so on. You must, however, decide ahead of time

Illus. 20. For group work, desks can be placed in a spiral with the beginning of the film on the outermost desk.

how long the film will be and then how much projection time each animator is allowed for his particular movement.

A Painting in Motion

The simple play and interplay of colors put down even haphazardly on a length of transparent film create a painting in motion, the effect of which is enhanced by the light from the projector.

The beginning group will find this technique ideal since it requires only scratching and coloring and does not require editing. You must watch out for the apparent simplicity of this process, though, because it does require the observation of the rules of organizing and harmonizing colors and of rhythm.

Aside from that, it gives free rein to the imagination which will appeal to young beginners as well as to the experienced creative film-maker.

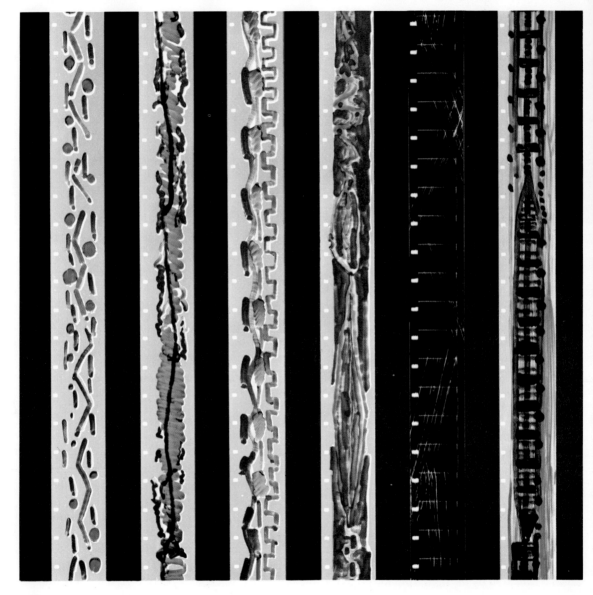

40

Drawing on Fogged Film

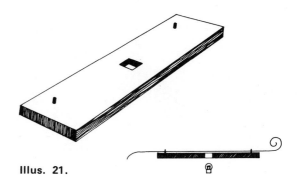

In drawing with pen and paintbrush on clear film, you must constantly strive to capture the fine points of the drawing in order to produce a really clear reproduction on the screen. However, with the scratch technique, you can obtain these effects much more easily. The ideal base for scratch work is fogged, or opaque black, film. By simply scratching the emulsion (dull) side of the film with a sharp-pointed implement, you will find you can create a fine white line with very little trouble.

This technique is even more exciting when you use colored fogged film. As you scratch, you reach the different-colored layers that make up this type of film. Experiment on a piece—first scratch lightly, then a little more deeply, and so on. Then project your test pieces to see the effects! Always be absolutely certain, however, that you scratch only the emulsion (dull) side.

Making a Holding Block for Fogged Film

Since fogged film is black, you cannot trace your drawings on the film nor find the frame lines using a paper guide strip as you did for clear film. However, by making a special holding block, you can manage regular spacing from frame to frame (Illus. 21). In the middle of a piece of wood, make a little "window" in the shape of a film frame as shown. Set two pegs for holding the film on each end of the block.

Illus. 21.

When this block is set over a light, it will show through the film indicating the area of a single frame. Move the film from frame to frame over the light just as you would with transparent film.

The best illumination to use under the holding block is a light table (Illus. 22). If you do not have one available, you can construct a substitute that combines the holding block and the light table.

Illus. 22. A completed holding block set on a light table.

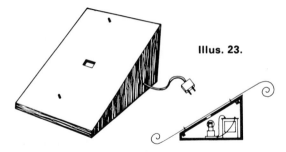

Illus. 23.

Making a Light Box

To make the light box, you will need $\frac{1}{4}$-inch (6-mm.) plywood. Make the box in the shape of a lectern as shown in Illus. 23. The slanted top will make it easier for you to work on. The box should be approximately 6 × 8 inches (16 × 20 cm.) at the base and 4 inches (10 cm.) at the tallest point in the back. In the very middle, cut out a little window the size of a frame of the film you are using, and then sink two headless nails to hold the film as shown in Illus. 23. You need to install a socket and cord of the type used for wiring a lamp. Use only a low wattage (not more than 40 watt) bulb inside the box.

Scratching Materials

Sandpaper. This offers a wealth of different effects. For an example, see Illus. 26. Sandpaper comes in a number of degrees of coarseness—try them all.

Needles. You can use any needlelike implement for scratching. Plain sewing needles come in a great variety of sizes, and depending upon how you scratch—whether with the points or the sides of the points—you can vary the effects even

further. Other pointed objects include hatpins, the corners of single-edged razor blades, X-Acto knives, and so on.

Projection of Scratched Film

One problem is likely to arise when you project your scratched film. Since you are actually scratching off the emulsion on the film, minute particles of the emulsion, or tiny shavings, are likely to remain on the film even though you may not see them until the film is projected. For this reason, it is generally advisable to have a copy made of your scratched films *before* you project them.

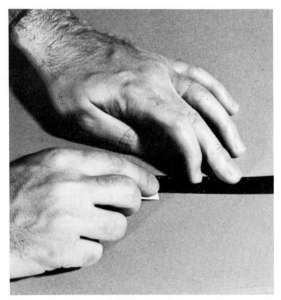

Illus. 24. Scratching on fogged film with sandpaper.

Mixed Techniques

An interesting possibility is to mix the drawing and scratching techniques. In the same way that you scratch fogged film, you can also smear colored inks on transparent film and then scratch them. Another experiment you might try is coloring with inks or paints the scratches that you make on fogged film with either sandpaper or needles. As you gain experience, many such ideas will undoubtedly come to you.

Optional Equipment

Light Table

If you want, you can make a light table just as easily as you made the light box on page 42. Again use plywood and form the box in the shape of a lectern (Illus. 25). A good all-purpose size for your light table is 17 inches (42 cm.) long, 14 inches (35 cm.) wide, $2\frac{1}{2}$ inches (6 cm.) high in the back, and $1\frac{1}{4}$ inches (3 cm.) high in the front. Use a piece of frosted glass or translucent plastic sheet for the surface. The dimensions for this would be $12\frac{3}{4} \times 10$ inches (32 × 25 cm.). As for the light box, a low-wattage light is advised.

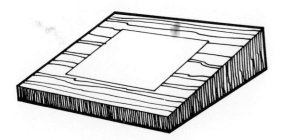

Illus. 25. A light table.

Illus. 26. The effects of scratching on fogged film with needles (left) and sandpaper (right).

Splicing and Editing Films

Splicing

Splicing is simply the fastening together of two ends of film. This can be done with a splicer (Illus. 27) which cuts the ends off smooth and allows you to join them together with special cement, at the same time preserving the normal spacing between the perforations.

Some splicers come equipped with a self-adhesive tape. If you use glue with your splicer, watch out! Film glue has a tendency to dissolve surface colors and you might have to reconstruct the drawing at the splice line.

Editing

Editing cannot be reduced to such simple terms as with the splicing of two ends of a film. Editing is a creative process. You may want to cut out some parts of your film, shorten others and re-arrange the sequence. No matter how carefully you plan a film, editing will improve it. One important thing to keep in mind is that you must edit before you work on the sound track, since in the editing the film will be cut and the sound-image will be displaced, causing a lack of synchronization on the final film.

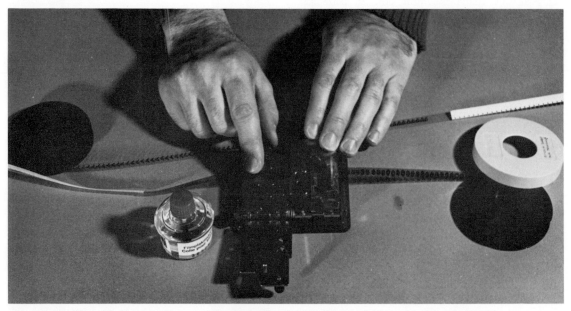

Illus. 27. Use a splicer to join the ends of two pieces of film together perfectly.

Sound Effects

Although animating film alone produces its own exciting results, adding sound will really make you feel like a professional! And, believe it or not, it is just as easy as drawing your images on the film.

Sound tracks, however, are found only on 16 mm. and 35 mm. film (see page 12). If you look near the edge of a 16 or 35 mm. sound film, you will see that the image does not occupy the whole width. A straight band is reserved for the sound track. On this track you will find a small continuous design which, when it passes before the electronic reproducer of the projector, creates the sound. By drawing on this track on your blank film, you can produce certain sounds which the electronic reproducer of a sound projector will convert into actual noises and sounds.

Synchronization of Sound and Image

Although film advances by "jumps" (24 per second) in front of the projector window, it advances with a very uniform movement in front of the sound reproducer. For this reason, the sound reproducer is not at the level of the projection window, but placed below it. To put it another way, when you place the film in the projector, the sound track unrolls *ahead* of the image frames. This sound-image displacement corresponds to a total length of 21 frames in 35 mm. film and to 28 frames in 16 mm. film. In order to obtain a perfect synchronization of sound and image, you must pay close attention to this displacement.

In order to do this, make a holding block the length of either 21 or 28 frames depending upon which film you are using. This will serve as your gauge for measuring the exact variation between the image and its corresponding sound.

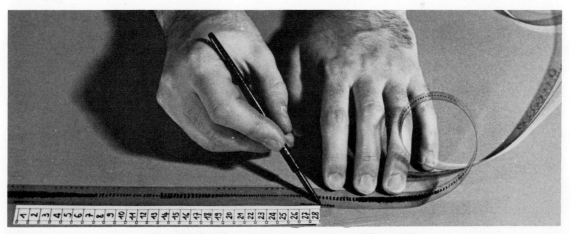

Illus. 28. Synchronizing the sound on a 16 mm. film.

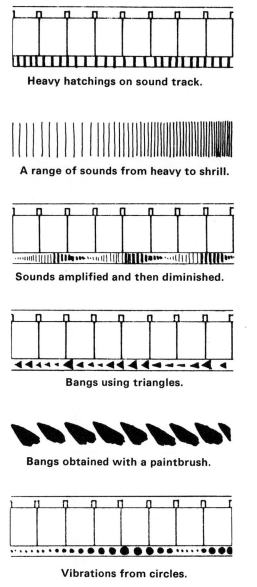

Heavy hatchings on sound track.

A range of sounds from heavy to shrill.

Sounds amplified and then diminished.

Bangs using triangles.

Bangs obtained with a paintbrush.

Vibrations from circles.

Drawing on the Sound Track

Because of the narrowness of the sound band, 2.13 mm. (about $\frac{3}{32}$ inch) in 35 mm. film, and 1.8 mm. (about $\frac{1}{16}$ inch) in 16 mm. film, you could never hope to reproduce, by drawing, a sound as perfect as a voice or the tones of a violin! However, this is not your aim, anyway. What you want to do is produce unexpected sounds, vibrations or bangs, and so on, that will illustrate your images. Here are some possibilities that you might try on your sound track.

Hatching. Perpendicular hachures or "hatch marks" drawn on the sound track make vibrating sounds. Tightly spaced hatch marks make a sharp vibration, while more loosely spaced ones will produce a heavy vibration. Between the loosely spaced and the tight hatching, you can obtain a whole scale of medium vibrations.

By varying the width, or thickness, of the lines, you can either amplify or diminish sounds.

Geometric figures. The sounds that geometric shapes produce on the sound track depend upon the size and the shape of the figures and on their dimensions. Figures such as equilateral triangles, squares, and circles, which have equal dimensions will produce bangs. By juxtaposing different geometric forms and making them as small as possible, you can also produce vibrations which, however, will be different from those produced by hachures.

Materials for Drawing on the Sound Track

You need only the same implements that you use for drawing your images. However, the sound track is so small that it is difficult to draw on this scale. You must use drawing instruments to produce the forms without preliminary sketches. For example, to make a triangle, use a small paintbrush; for a circle, the point of a fine pen; and for a square, a wide-nosed pen point.

Scratching on the Sound Track

By scratching on the emulsion side of the sound track, you can also produce unusual effects. Simply draw on ink lines with a fine-pointed pen, and then go over these lines with a needle or hatpin. Another technique is perforating the sound track with a needle, but this is tricky. The holes have to be absolutely sharp and clean which is not easy to achieve. But experiment anyway—you might have just the right touch!

Experimenting with Sound

The best way for you to obtain the sounds you want for your animated film is by trying out all of the various methods on a piece of test film, say, 20 to 25 feet (7 to 8 metres) long. When you have finished making one sound effect, leave a sufficient space on the film between it and the next effect so that you will be able to distinguish the sounds easily. When you have made a number of effects, put the film through the projector and select the drawings which produce the sounds you find most satisfactory and interesting. In this way, you can establish a whole gamut or range of sounds. Be sure to record in writing on a pad which effects make which sounds, so that you can quickly produce the sound you desire by referring to the record.

47

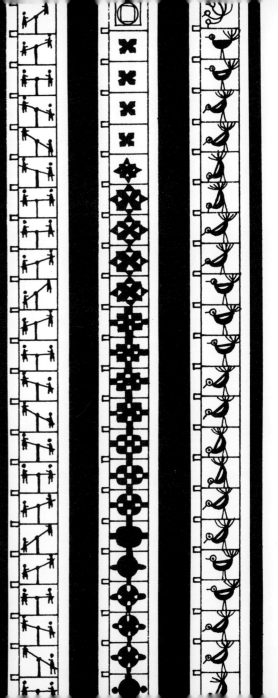

Index

"Within this winning portrait of a bicultural childhood
are a host of notable characters. . . . A rich and
compelling personal narrative."
—*Kirkus Reviews*

"Arana is like [a] bridge. She is North.
She is South. . . . She is both worlds. She is neither.
And for all the . . . dichotomy, her life is richer than most."
—*The Advocate*
(Baton Rouge)

AMERICAN

CHICA

Two Worlds, One Childhood

MARIE ARANA

DELTA TRADE PAPERBACKS

A Delta Book
Published by
Dell Publishing
a division of
Random House, Inc.
1540 Broadway
New York, New York 10036

Copyright © 2001 by Marie Arana
Book design by Jo Anne Metsch
Cover design by Royce M. Becker
Cover photo courtesy of the author

Delta® is a registered trademark of Random House, Inc.,
and the colophon is a trademark of Random House, Inc.
Library of Congress Catalog Card Number: 00-047529

ISBN: 0-385-31963-0

Reprinted by arrangement with The Dial Press

Manufactured in the United States of America
Published simultaneously in Canada
June 2002

RRH   10 9 8 7 6 5 4 3 2 1

To my parents,
Jorge Arana Cisneros
and Marie Elverine Clapp,
who taught me that there are
two sides to my America,
and two Americas in this world.

I am, seeing, hearing,
with half my soul at sea and half my soul on land,
and with these two halves of soul I see the world.

Estoy, mirando, oyendo,
con la mitad del alma en el mar y la mitad del alma en la tierra,
y con las dos mitades del alma miro el mundo.

(Pablo Neruda)

PROLOGUE

THERE IS LAUGHTER. There is the sharp report of a slamming door and the staccato of high heels crossing the ceramic tiles of the atrium garden. There is the reveille shout to the servants' quarters, the slap of sandals making their way to the animal pens, the *skrawk* of chickens as they are pulled from their cages, one by one, into the ink of night. It is three o'clock, before the light of day.

I rub the sleep from my eyes, swing my legs over the side of my bed until my toes touch the llama rug, and then sniff the air of a morning (like all my mornings) redolent of ripe bananas, raw sugar, rum—and the sharp, ferric odor of freshly drawn blood.

I cross the room, hoist myself onto the window ledge, pull back the heavy wrought iron, and lean out into the dark. The second-floor vantage offers me a rich display of the courtyard below. My mother is floating into view, her green dress billowing like a gossamer wing; her long, gold hair throwing light like a tungsten filament; her all-American, Hollywood face alive with expectation. At her side is my Peruvian father—black-haired, handsome, smiling and shouting Spanish over his shoulder, waving a bottle in his fist as if he were a carnival barker on opening day. His friends spill in behind them. Through the kitchen window I see the cook, yawning and plucking feathers from a chicken, letting the blood ooze from its neck into the frying pan for an early-morning *sangrecita*. I do not read omens in that. I do not yet know about signs.

My parents are young. It is their moment. Every marriage has one. When love seems infinite, the road feels free, and nights trip festively into day.

I was only four, but life had already had upheavals. The year I came into the world, five major earthquakes shook Peru. By the time I stood at that window, I'd lived through eighteen. I cannot recollect any one of them. Off in a geologist's lab, a needle was dancing, wild, registering one disaster after another.

Three days before I dangled my head into that courtyard, a quake ripped through the Peruvian seaboard, registering almost eight points on the Richter scale. It started shortly after five in the afternoon. The men were at work, the women in kitchens, their children at play. Where was I? The entire population of our hacienda must have heard the rumble beneath, felt the waggle in the stomach, seen concrete slabs wrench loose and skitter across ground. Across, then up, in fragments—belching gray dust. Walls usually rip before a mind can factor it, roofs fall, babies hurl through air.

I know it happened only because the World Data Center for Seismology tells me so. *Earthquake, December 12, 1953, South America: Latitude 4°, Longitude 80°. Magnitude, 7.8. Displacements: thousands. Deaths: severe.*

Shaky days. Yet all I can recall of them is a predawn tableau, my mother and father bursting into our garden with joy.

As I grew older and learned to register the ground beneath my feet, I saw that my parents' marriage was shot through with fissures. Something like earthquakes would come—geologic upheavals, when the foundations that underlay their union would rattle with dislocation and longing—but now, just now, in the eighth year of marriage, with three children upstairs and my father's engineering career in ascendance—in that quick freeze frame before dawn—the gulf between them did not matter much. They were full. They were one. And I, hovering above their world, was seamless and faultless and whole.

A South American man, a North American woman—hoping against hope, throwing a frail span over the divide, trying to bolt beams into sand. There was one large lesson they had yet to learn as they strode into the garden with friends, hungry for rum and fried blood: There is a fundamental rift between North and South America, a flaw so deep it is tectonic. The plates don't fit. The earth is loose. A fault runs through. Earthquakes happen. Walls are likely to fall.

As I looked down at their fleeting radiance, I had no idea I would spend the rest of my life puzzling over them: They were so different from each other, so obverse in every way. I did not know that however resolutely they built their bridge, I would only wander its middle, never quite reaching either side. These were things I was slow to understand.

I see such childhood moments in sharp relief now. The past comes slamming up like rock through earth, brought there by sights and sounds, sheer happenstance. Aftershocks, they are. One shivered through not long ago, on a winter afternoon as I lazed in the company of a friend.

She was a rain-forest woman. She'd never seen cleared land until the year before I knew her, when she stepped from the jungle onto a patch of dirt where a helicopter sat waiting to lift her out. She had never seen a road, a roof, a wheel, a knife. She was an Amazon nomad, a Yanomama, one of "the fierce people."

Spikes pierced her face. She was not used to possessions. There had been little reason to carry things—a string of beads, a sharpened rock, at most. No need for clothes. No need for walls to house them. Bed was a hammock of vines. But there came a day when an anthropologist from Philadelphia pushed through the undergrowth to tell her he had come to study her language and ways. Before her sixteenth birthday, he had made her his wife, given her three children, taken her out in that helicopter, back to his New Jersey home.

One January afternoon, as I sat with her on the floor of their Hackensack living room, watching an endless succession of her husband's research videos, my eyes happened to fall on their five-year-old daughter. The child was not looking at the screen. She had seen that particular film countless times: In it, a distinctly wobbly Yanomama headman puts a thick bamboo to his nose and gestures for someone to blow a little bomb of *ayahuasca*—a powerful hallucinogen—up the reed into his brain. The girl was not looking at that. She glanced from her mother, stretched out on the mauve wall-to-wall carpet, to her father in the other room. Back and forth she looked, then back again. The mother was fingering the spike holes in her face, staring raptly at the image of her headman in the electric box. The father was perched over a dining room table strewn with paper, scratching his professorial beard, scribbling into a book.

I suppose I could have thought of a million things at the sight of that girl, twisting about in her lime-green T-shirt, swiveling a pretty head from left to right. But what struck me was the look in her eyes. How anxious she seemed. How delicate a bridge she was between the northern man and southern woman.

What I thought of was me.

GHOSTS

Pishtacos

THE CORRIDORS OF my skull are haunted. I carry the smell
of sugar there. The odors of a factory—wet cane, dripping iron,
molasses pits—are up behind my forehead, deep inside my
throat. I'm reminded of those scents when children offer me
candy from a damp palm, when the man I love sighs with wine
upon his tongue, when I inhale the heartbreaking sweetness of
rotting fruit and human waste that rises from garbage dwellers'
camps along the road to Lima.

I am always surprised to learn that people do not live with
memories of fragrance as I do. The smell of sugar is so strong in
my head. That they could have spent the first years of their lives
in places like Pittsburgh or Hong Kong and not gone for the rest
of their days with the stench of a steel furnace or the aromas of
fungus and salt shrimp tucked into some netherfold of cortex—
how is that possible?

I had a friend once, from Bombay, who told how baffling it
was to travel this world smelling turmeric, coriander, and

cardamom in the most improbable corners of Nantucket or Palo Alto, only to find that they were Lorelei of the olfactory, whiffs of his imagination, sirens of his mother's curry, wafting in like she-cats, flicking seductive tails.

He chased after those smells, cooking up curries in rented houses in New Jersey, in tidy chalets in Switzerland, in motel rooms along the Shenandoah, mixing pastes from powders out of bottles with Scottish surnames, searing ghees in Sara Lee aluminum, washing out lunch boxes in Maryland rest stops, trying to bring it back. Bring it back. Up into the sinus, trailing down the throat. He was never quite able to recapture that childhood blend: mashed on stone, dried in a Mahabharatan sun, stuffed into earthenware, sold in an old man's shop, carried home in string-tied packages, measured onto his mother's mortar, locked into the chambers of his heart.

So it has been with me and sugar. I look back and see piles of it, glittering crystals of it—burned, powdered, superfine. I smell sugar everywhere. On whispers, in books, in the loam of a garden. In every cranny of life. And always—always—it is my father's sugar I am longing for: raw, rough, Cartavio brown.

Cartavio was the name of our hacienda: a company town as single of purpose as Akron or Erie or Turin or anyplace where pistons and steel drive residents' lives. It was the mid 1950s, boom days for sugar in Peru, and the American industrial giant W. R. Grace was making the most of it in this remote coastal hamlet, five hundred miles north of Lima. Cartavio was surrounded by fields of sugarcane, fringed by a raging Pacific, and life in it was an eerie mirror of Peru's conquistador past. On one side of the hacienda were the cinnamon-skinned indigenous in a warren of cinder block. On the other, in houses whose size and loveliness depended on the rank of their inhabitants, lived Peruvians of Spanish ancestry, Europeans, North Americans, the elite. There was a church on the square, a mansion for the manager, a Swiss-style guest house, a country club, and a clinic. But in the middle, with smokestacks thrusting so high there could be no doubt as to why the unlikely multitude was there: my father's factories.

Cartavio was nestled in the heart of the nation, just under the left breast of the female torso that Peru's landmass defines. But it was, in many ways, a foreign place, a twentieth-century invention, a colony of the world. Its driving force was industry, and the people who had gathered there were, one way or another, single-minded industrialists. The Americans had come with dollars; the Limeños with political power; the villagers with hands. Although their objectives were shared—a humming production of sugar and paper—Cartavio citizens lived in uncertain harmony. The laborers were willing to surrender themselves to the practicalities of an iron city by day, but under their own roofs by night they returned to ancient superstitions. The Lima engineers were willing to obey the gringo directives, but they suspected they knew a great deal more about those factories than any mahogany-desk boss in New York. The Americans soon learned that if the indigenous believed in ghosts and the *criollo* overlords resented gringo power, then Grace's fortunes turned on such chimera as phantoms and pride. They understood the social dynamic, used it, and with old-fashioned American pragmatism, made it work for them.

I knew, with a certainty I could feel in my bones, that I was deeply Peruvian. That I was rooted to the Andean dust. That I believed in ghosts. That they lived in the trees, in my hair, under the *aparador*, lurking behind the silver, slipping in and out of the whites of my ancestors' portraits' eyes. I also knew that, for all his nods and smiles at the gringos, my father believed in ghosts, too. How could he not? He faced them every day.

To the hacienda of Cartavio, Papi was *Doctor Ingeniero*, the young Peruvian engineer in charge of the people and the maintenance of this whirring, spewing, U.S.-owned mill town. He was a sunny man with an open face. Although his hands were small, they were clever. Although he was not tall, his shoulders filled a room. There were photographs my mother would point to when she wanted us to know she thought him handsome, but they were of a man I didn't recognize—gaunt and angular, black wavy hair, eyes as wide as a calf's, mouth in a curl. The Papi I knew was barrel-chested, full-lipped. His hair had receded to a V. His cheeks were cherubic and round. His eyes bulged. In the subequatorial heat, he wore his shirt out, and it flapped in the breeze, revealing skin that was brown, smooth, and hairless. He was not fat but taut as a sausage—*bien papeado*, as Peruvians like to say. Potato-tight. When he laughed, he made no sound. He would lean forward as if something had leapt on his back and held him in an irresistible tickle. His eyes would squint, the tip of his tongue would push out, and his shoulders would bounce vigorously. He'd laugh long and hard like that—silent, save for the hiss that issued from between his teeth—until he was short of breath, red-faced, and weeping. When he wasn't laughing, he was barking orders. When he wasn't doing that, his mouth was ringing a cigarette, sucking hard, his eyelids fluttering in thought.

Papi would not so much walk as strut. Not so much drink as guzzle. Not so much chat with a woman as flirt, wink, and ogle. He was clearly not the slender, soulful man in Mother's photographs. Not anymore. From the moment he registered on my brain, he was straining buttons, *bien papeado*—threatening to burst.

He was a machine virtuoso, improvising ways to go from desert to sugar, from burned plants to Herculean rolls of paper. He could take a field of sugarcane into his steel colossus, shove it through squealing threshers, wet it down with processed seawater, suck it dry of crystals, and feed it onto the rollers to emerge warm and dry from the other end as flying sheets of paper. He could take a faulty German turbine whose only hope for survival was a spare part eight thousand miles away in Stuttgart and, with a knickknack here, a length of wire there, make it hum again. He could pacify the gringos when they came from New York, matching them eye for eye on the intricacies of macrome-chanics or spherical trigonometry or particle physics. He in-spired fervent loyalty from his laborers, striding through his iron city in an impeccably white suit, teaching them the way to an in-dustrial future. The American way.

Every morning he would head for the belching beast long be-fore the whistle sounded. In late afternoons, he returned to sur-vey his pretty wife over lunch and take a brief siesta in his chair. But there seemed to be no end to his work. Even as he walked back through the gate for a late lunch or dinner and the servants fluttered into the kitchen to announce the *señor* was home, he was on call. Ready to pull away.

That he had to work with ghosts was a fact of life and every-body knew it. A worker's hand might be drawn into the iron jaws of the *trapiche* as it gathered cane into its mandibles and pulled the mass into its threshers. A finger, a foot, a dog, a whole man might be lost to that ravenous maw as it creaked and shook and thrashed and sifted everything down to liquid sugar and a fine bagasse.

Los pishtacos, the workers would say to one another whenever such tragedies occurred. *Pishtacos*, their wives and mothers would whisper the next day as they combed the market or pol-ished the silver services on the richly carved *aparadores* of the en-gineers. Ghosts. Machine ghosts. *Pishtacos norteamericanos*. And as anyone who knew Peruvian *historias* understood: They needed the fat of *indios* to grease their machines.

⁓

OUR HOUSE STOOD on the corner of prime real estate, behind the offices of head engineers but far enough from the factory to allow us to ignore the less pleasant aspects of a churning industry. Finished in white stucco and shielded by manicured rows of tropical botanica, the house loomed above its compound walls like a castle behind a barricade. Flowers cascaded from its ramparts. In the garden, trees pushed forth pineapples, lucuma, bananas, and mango. An iron gate shut out the world. Behind the gate and the wall and the garden, the house itself was impervious to vendors, to factory workers, to ordinary Peruvians, to the sprawl of humanity that struggled a few hundred feet from its door.

The house was skirted by a capacious veranda. Inside, it was filled with high-ceilinged white rooms, heavy doors, yawning keyholes, arched passageways, Spanish tile. The living room— the *sala*—was dominated by my mother's ornate ebony piano. The master bedroom lay behind it, on the other side of a carved double door, so that when those doors were thrown open, the entire *sala* was surveyable from my parents' bed—a bizarre feature, but houses in outlying haciendas were often capricious and irregular. Through an open arch, you could go from our *sala* to the dining room, which held two massive pieces of furniture—a table and an *aparador*, carved with undulating scallops and garlands. The kitchen was stark, a workroom for servants, stripped down and graceless. A cavernous enamel sink—pocked and yellow—jutted from the wall. There was a simple blue table where we three children and our servants took meals. The kitchen door led to a back atrium garden. On the other side of that, behind a wall, were the servants' quarters, a shabby little building that could sleep six in two spare rooms. There was a stall with a spigot where our *mayordomo* and *amas* could wash, a storage area, and a concrete staircase that led to their rooms. To the left of those stairs, under a shed of bare wood and chicken wire, were the animal cages. At four, I was told very clearly—as my older brother and sister, George and Vicki, had been—that I was not allowed in the servants' quarters. The cages were my demarcation line; they were the point beyond which I could not go.

Our own rooms were upstairs, well away from our parents' bedroom and out of the circuit of revelers when a party was afoot. After dinner, which we regularly took in the kitchen, the *amas* would trot us upstairs and bathe us, struggling with their small arms to balance us in the tubs. We would loll about in our pajamas thereafter. There never seemed any urgency to get us to bed, which was just as well because all three of us were terrified of the dark, afraid to look out the windows at tree branches, so well had our *amas* taught us that *pishtacos* were perched there, slavering and squinting in.

Had we overcome our fears and looked out those windows onto Cartavio's main residential street beyond our own house, we would have seen five other houses of the first rank, equally grand, equally walled. Behind them, a row of modest ones for the lesser company families. Our immediate neighbors were the Lattos, freckle-faced Scots whose brogue-filtered Spanish made George and me horselaugh into our hands. Their eight-year-old son, Billy, was the undisputed object of Vicki's affection. He was a straight, good-looking boy with an easy smile. He would direct his grins freely to Vicki, but George and I—who thought ourselves far more appealing than our prickly sister—had to work hard to draw his charms: We'd stand on our heads, swing from trees, make fools of ourselves if we had to, for the incomparable joy of gazing on his teeth.

As a young child, my days unfolded in the garden. It was, as every garden in that coastal desert is, an artificial paradise: invented, deceptive, precarious. Without human hands to tend it, the lush vegetation would have dried to a husk and sifted down into an arid dune. For years, I did not know how tentative that childhood environment was. Walled in, with green crowding our

senses and the deep sweetness of fruit and sugar in the air, I felt
a sense of entitlement, as if my world would ever be so richly
hung. But it was an illusion, and many had labored to create it:
to make us feel as if we were emperors of a verdant oasis on the
banks of the Amazon just north of the Andes, where the green
was unrestrained.

Fooled, happy, ignorant, George and I would splash in the
duck pond our father had built for us. Or we would play with the
animals we kept in the cages out back where the servants lived.
We'd pet the rabbits, feed them fragrant verbena. We'd put
chickens on the backs of goats and shriek with laughter as the
bewildered creatures scrambled around in circles, the goats
wild-eyed under their unruly riders, the chickens pounding the
air.

George was my hero, my general, my god. He was as bright
and beautiful as I was fat and slow. He could prance and swagger
as well as any cowboy in Mother's storybook litany of Wild West
valiants. He would hector; I would follow. He'd do mischief; I'd
do cover-up. He'd get caught; I'd confess to everything. He'd be
spanked; I'd yank down my pants. He'd yawp; I'd bawl louder.
And so we spent our days, crawling under the house, devising
schemes to scandalize the *mayordomo*, scare Claudia the cook
out of her wits, or pester Vicki, whose prissy ways cried out for
redress and revenge. If only to force her to look at us over an
eternal rim of books.

After lunch, after my father had come home, gazed at his
wife's Hollywood face, dozed off, and gone back to work, Mother
came to the kitchen looking for us. First she'd put George in bed
for his nap, then she'd lead me to her room for a musical siesta.

My mother did not tell us much about herself beyond the fact
that she had been a violinist when she and Papi had met in
Boston. She was different, odd, that much I knew: porcelain-fair,
near translucent, throwing off a kind of shimmer wherever she

went. She spoke a halting Spanish, every bit as strange as that of our Scots neighbors; I recall peering into other people's faces to see if it would make them laugh. Often, it would. But she did not mix much with Peruvians if my father was not about. She was not a social person. She seemed more inclined to spend time with her children than with women her age. Then again, she was so unlike any other woman in Cartavio. What distinguished her most from them was the way she moved, like no Peruvian I'd ever seen—straight ahead, gliding—a motion that led from the rib cage, not the hips. It was the kind of walk that tells you little about a body. Her clothes told less: They were loose and silky, more likely to drape from her shoulders than reveal her essential lineaments. She did not own a tightly belted, bust-hoisting, hip-flaunting dress, like those the Peruvian *señoras* wore.

Very early, somehow—I don't recall exactly why—in the same way that I dared not imagine what was beneath her frocks, I learned not to ask about her life before she married Papi. The sweet mildness of her demeanor, like the silk of her clothes, masked some indeterminate thing beneath. There was a hardness behind her glow. An ice. I felt I could quiz her to my heart's content about music, which came to be the language between us. But beyond that—like the point beyond the animal cages—lay a zone I was not supposed to know.

Her past was the only thing Mother was stingy about. Attentive to her children to the point of obsession, she doted on us, worried about us. Every headache was the start of some dread calenture of the brain. Every bellyache, the possibility that we were teeming with tropical parasites. I could make her ooze with love by telling her that I had eaten a wild strawberry from the roadside: She would be anxious for days that I had contracted some rare, Andean disease, taking my temperature at every opportunity, padding into my bedroom at night to lay a cool hand on my brow. Nowhere was her love more evident, however, than in the way she imparted her music to her children. It was, for her, a constant vocation. Any drama, any spectacle, any mathematical conundrum had a corresponding phrase of music, a melody that might frame it more effectively than words. It was as if she needed to convey the vocabulary and syntax of music to us as urgently as she needed to impart English. She would teach all three of us the language of music to some degree, but with time it became clear that I was the one she had chosen to be the beneficiary of this particular gift, and it was through music that she ultimately spoke to me most directly.

At siesta time, she'd recite long strings of poetry from memory for me. Or she'd try singing me to sleep—hopeless enterprises, since I found her poetry and songs more seductive than any prospect of slumber. Outside her room, I spoke Spanish. But inside, we were range-roving Americans, heirs of the king's English, and Mother unfolded that world in verse: Whitman's "Leaves of Grass," Coleridge's "Rime of the Ancient Mariner," Gilbert and Sullivan's pirates and maidens, Stephen Foster's dreamers and chariots, Robert Burns's banks and brae, George M. Cohan's flag and salute, Irving Berlin's moon and champagne.

I would lie big-eyed, starstruck, as she spun visions of a faraway country where cowboys reigned, valleys were green, wildflowers sprang from the feet of great oaks, water was sipped—unboiled—from streams, opera houses were lined with red velvet, and sidewalks winked with radiant flecks of mica. "You'll see it all someday, Mareezie," she'd say of her melody-filled *historias*. "You'll see it for yourself."

She would sing, then peek to see if I had drifted off. Into the fifth or sixth song, I knew to pretend. I'd burrow my ear into the place between her shoulder and her large, firm breast, reach an arm across her white throat to feel her corn-silk hair, and feign a deep, heavy breathing. When she stopped singing, I'd open one eye and see that she was asleep.

She was a beautiful woman. Big-boned yet slender. Her forehead was deep, unlined, nearly browless, which gave her the look of a perpetually startled doll. She painted her lips to a fullness they did not have, and, when they were in repose, you could see their thinness beneath the color. It was a beguiling mouth, sloped slightly to one side, so that if you positioned yourself to her left you saw someone pensive, to her right, someone playful. "My slop-pail mug," she called it, leaving me to wonder, in my narrow Peruvianness, what any one of those inexplicable American words—*slop*, *pail*, or *mug*—could possibly have to do with that lovely face. When she smiled and showed the little space between her two front teeth, it was enough to break my heart.

I loved to watch her sleep, for there was a vulnerability in her face then that was not there when her eyes were fixed on me. Ordinarily, her stare was as hard as a statue's, unreadable, until something brought her to the verge of anger, at which point her blue eyes would turn a harrowing shade of green. It was a color I did not like to see. But her most disturbing features, by far, were her violinist's hands, which were large and square, with meaty, muscled fingers that seemed to belong to another body, not to the delicate queen who lay on the wide carved bed.

When I had had my fill of studying her, I'd slip carefully out of her arms. I'd tiptoe off to wake up George, and in no time we were out in the garden with pockets full of bread—free of parents, free of the snoring *mayordomo* and the *amas*. Alone. Ready for our daily ritual with *El Gringo*.

More vivid than any other sound in memory—the crow of the cock at dawn, the cooing of mourning doves—was the rhythm of his advance. A tap, thump, drag—ominous and regular—as he made his way down the street. We would stand under the lucuma tree and listen for his step, cock our ears toward it, feel the hairs rise against our collars as it approached.

El loco, we'd whisper—the madman—and watch the black grow large in each other's eyes. By the time we'd made it under the verbena, he was rapping the white stucco with his knuckles, bone-hard and sharp as weapons. When he reached the gate, we'd see the whole man. Eyeless. Rags like leathery wings. A purple stump where a foot should have been. Dried sugarcane for a crutch. When he threw back his head and let the sun fill his eye sockets, a wail would rise from his chest like the keen of a wounded animal. And then a stream of words, sliding at us in a high whinny so that we'd have to strain to catch it. *Out, you little bastards!* And he'd wham the fence with his makeshift staff. *Out! Or I'll call on the* pishtacos! *They'll pluck you from that bush and eat your pygmy hearts!*

El Gringo, people called him. The American. Somehow, we believed he was one, although all evidence was to the contrary. He was small. Almost as small as we were. Dark. Like us.

Weren't all Americans as big, blond, and clear-eyed as our mother? We had serious reservations about her—she was so otherworldly, so ill-at-ease, so unwilling to conform, so *mad* in her own way—but it was terrifying to think she'd end up crazed and blind, staggering through some remote Andean backwater looking for her luminous land. Holding our breath against his stench, we crept out with our bread, dropped the offerings one by one into El Gringo's grimy sack—buying our mother's future, keeping the *pishtacos* at bay. Then we raced away, gasping and squealing, to our crawl space under the house. From there we would watch as he hobbled off to the neighbors. And we would worry.

But there were afternoons when my mother would sing and I'd actually fall asleep. Then it would be her turn to slip away.

One day, I woke to see the double doors wide open and her sitting in the *sala*, cameolike, her profile outlined against the wood of her piano.

She was not alone.

She was poised on one side of the sofa—its back toward me—
her arm stretched out along its spine. Across, in the other corner
of the same sofa, was a man. I did not know his name. His arm,
like hers, was stretched along the back, and it was long and
ruddy, with a halo of down against the skin. Their fingers were
close. But did not touch.

The *casa de solteros*, the bachelors' quarters, was across from
us. There, a rotating corps of young Americans and Northern
Europeans came for Third World adventure and a shot at the
boom. They were rough-hewn, long-legged. Almost as golden as
my mother. More often than not they were war veterans—ex-
army engineers—rail-hanging habitués of the bottle, with tales
of hard-won battle.

"Over here, let me tell you how I nearly got greased at
Midway!" one would shout over a brimming glass of rum at one
of my parents' garden parties. Off they'd go, weaving legends,
each one braver than the last.

I liked these *solteros*. I liked them because they seemed to be at
the white-hot core of a kid-hearted craziness that overtook the
grown-ups from time to time. I liked them because of their laughter. I liked them for their sweet smell of Cartavio rum. I liked them
most of all because, when their long limbs ambled through our
gates, the sky would open and my mother's eyes would dance.

The man sitting with my mother was a *soltero*. Of that I was
sure. Whether or not they'd been talking, I could not tell. I
rubbed my eyes and focused closer. My mother had a sweet,
peaceful expression on her face. The man looked at her, perfectly calm, and said something I could not hear.

Suddenly, her outstretched hand flew to her forehead, and her
long, thick fingers rested there for what seemed a great while,
her eyes cast down. Then he stood, bowed awkwardly, and
walked away.

It was a fleeting gesture, that manual flutter from chair to brow, but I can see it still, engraved in memory like some irrevocable omen. Up, press. *Presto, fermata.* A passage that sounds again and again, as if its notes should lead to something else, some other movement. But that something else bows and spins and floats away. Off. Up. Out of sight, never to be explained.

My mother's hand floated down. She turned her face to the open doors of the bedroom and looked deep into my eyes. A pause, and then a radiant smile. "You slept this time!" she said. Her voice was so full of joy that my heart slipped a bit. There was no cause for joy in my napping. It had been a terrible lapse on my part: I had not awakened George. I had slept through our rendezvous with El Gringo. I had not given the beggar his sacramental scraps of bread. I had not kept the ghouls away. I had not protected my mother from a stone-blind fate.

Her blue eyes were looking at me now with such love, though, I had to grin back. I flung myself off the bed, slipped into George's old boots, and marched into the afternoon.

I asked about the stranger on the sofa many times in decades to come—even caused a harrowing scene with my questions— but she only shook her head and said she had no recollection of him. "I can't imagine who you saw there, Mareezie. I just can't imagine." Until I thought perhaps the whole thing had been a dream, and the man another ghost in my head.

FATHERS

Padres

TWENTY YEARS BEFORE I leaned out the window and saw my parents laugh their way into the garden, my father's father, the redoubtable Doctor Ingeniero Víctor Manuel Arana Sobrevilla, stopped coming down the stairs. He and his wife, Rosa Cisneros y Cisneros de Arana, and four of their six children lived five hundred miles away from our Cartavio hacienda in an old colonial house on Calle San Martín in Miraflores, a sleepy district on Lima's outer lip, where the city trailed out to the sea. Their home was dark and knit with steep, narrow staircases that led where we children were afraid to go. In room after room of musty armoires and heirlooms, life hung like a relic, like a bat in an airless cave.

No one acknowledged that there was something deeply wrong in this. That a brilliant man, highly educated, traveler of the world, would progressively trim back his life until he no longer stepped foot outside his house, until he was a specter up the stair.

My father cared for his father, did not dare to wonder at the strangeness that had driven him up into a little room, far from kin. He was attentive to his mother, quick to assure her that her pantry would not run dry and humiliation would not drag them under. In the '30s, at the height of the global Depression, when it was clear that somebody had to be sent out to work, my father, the eldest of the six children, was the first to volunteer. For years, my grandfather stayed on the second floor, venturing down only for a special lunch, a family tea. Otherwise he was high up, behind a door: seldom seen. Meanwhile, perched on the wine-red brocade downstairs, my grandmother—my *abuelita*—sat and worried about how she would pay the maids, raise a family, face Lima.

She was a black-haired diva, a bantam hen on four-inch heels, clicking through the house as if she were making her way onstage. Abuelita was a Cisneros y Cisneros, a New World aristocrat with an Old World pedigree: five centuries of paper, through the viceroyals to Spain. She was as warm and funny as my grandfather was cut and dried. As much a lover of parties as he was a captive of books. As charged with high voltage as the miles of wire he had sketched out for the electrification of Lima. Insofar as anyone knew, she loved her husband, respected and admired him, deferred to his authority. But when it became clear that her husband had gone into retreat, it was as if part of her had been pulled away with him. That traction was never evident in the adoration she showed him, or in the humor she displayed to the world at large, but it was deeply engraved in her face, where everything—lips, eyes, nose—had begun a relentless plunge south.

Abuelito was the essence of compunction. He was consumed by the idea of honor, pricked by some unnamed remorse. A former professor at Lima's College of Engineers, he was cautious with family, aloof to associates, Olympian with students, and hyperborean with the rest of the world. But for all the importance he was accorded in his household, it was almost as if he wasn't there. If he was not standing at the top of the stairs in his three-piece suit, cravat, and cane, looking down on our upturned faces, he was alone and forgotten in his study—poring over one of the arcane science columns he wrote for *El Comercio*, formally attired in a vest, tie, and smoking jacket, which no one outside his family would see.

He was a small man and moved in small ways. He carried his head as if it were a fragile vessel, nestling it between his shoulders, turning it cautiously. He had lost much of his hair, most of which was confined now to a tuft of white mustache beneath a long, straight nose. When he peered over the banister, his eyebrows pulled into a high interrogative as if he were scanning the surface of a pond, on the lookout for danger. If he decided to descend to tea, he would then shuffle down, lost in thought, carrying a pad and pencil, scribbling words and formulas no one could fathom. He was at work on something, we were told; we were not to disturb him.

At table, he would lean over his food and eat slowly, his eyes seldom leaving the limits of the porcelain below. While my grandmother took the host's place at the head, where she would hold forth brightly about the news of the day, my grandfather sat to one side—a sullen island of solitude—and dispatched whatever she placed before him. No one addressed him directly, although from time to time Abuelita would demand it—"Tell your papa now about that party you went to last night," she would say to one of my aunts, or to us, "Tell your abuelo that amusing anecdote about" such and such—at which point his eyes would flicker and look around the table, momentarily stunned, before they dulled with whatever was being told him and he sank into reverie again.

He had been handsome once, as was clearly evident in the

portrait that hung in the *sala*. It showed a dashing young man, smartly dressed in high starch and a neatly pinned tie. His hair was shiny black and copious, parted in the center to reveal a broad, intelligent forehead. His eyes were deep and vibrant; his chin smooth and strong; his enigmatic smile shaded by an elegant mustache, turned up and twisted on either side.

I would stare long and hard at that portrait and wonder at the disparity between the man it depicted and the man I knew—or didn't know. For me, my grandfather was defined by neverness. I never saw him drink. I never saw him smoke. I never heard him raise his voice. I hardly heard his voice at all. The rest of his household—a fizzy menagerie of irrepressible females and hyperkinetic young men—tiptoed about, hissing and shushing and pulling the draperies down, so that the *señor* could think.

He had started out to be a force in the country: an engineer with a will to drive Peru out of Third World poverty and into the modern age. He was the son of a prominent politician, educated abroad—as many in the upper class were—at the University of Notre Dame. But somewhere along the way, his star began to dim. He withdrew from his work. Few knew why, and among those who did, no one wanted to say. Come the '30s and a worldwide Depression, he stepped into his study, switched on the lights, and sat there for forty years.

At first, in the years between 1910 and 1920, he had established a consultancy, tried putting his erudition to work. He had rubbed elbows at the exclusive Club Nacional, was called on for major electrification projects. But just as a sixth child was added to his table, his career rumbled to a halt. He had no stomach for politics, no patience for hypocrites. He stopped looking for work, began having disagreements with clients, resentments against cohorts, a general falling-out. There was one further thing about him, infinitely more crippling: an extravagant sense of pride. His

children were well aware of his pridefulness, but they learned
never to question it. My grandfather's demeanor was lordly: He
walked with his chin in the air. But it was a backward trajectory,
a voyage inward, a solemn recessional, as if something had
cankered his heart.

For nine years he was a professor in the Colegio de Ingenieros,
but he was a hard grader, insular, difficult. He had no taste for
the intrigues of academia, was doggedly loyal to the world he
knew, not least his own college education in the United States.
When one of his intellectual adversaries, Doctor Laroza, an
equally dignified man who had studied in Paris, was made head
of the Colegio, my grandfather wrote his employers a brief letter
announcing his resignation. It was untenable, he said simply, to
imagine that he could work under someone with whom he seldom agreed and who had trained—of all places—in France.
Although my grandfather could hardly expect to support six children without a salary, his wife never questioned his withdrawal.
The children were told not to bring it up. Abuelito rose every
morning, dressed, retired to his study, descended for one meal,
spoke little, and wrote for the rest of his life. He produced scientific treatises; trenchant articles; one book about the future of
Peru, a copy of which sits in the United States Library of
Congress; a valuable, unpublished thesaurus—all without ever
leaving that room, tucked away at the top of the stairs.

As a result, my father, by the time he was fifteen, understood
that responsibility for the family had fallen to him. He was an excellent student, ranked first in every school he attended, but
when his schoolday was over, his workday would begin. He
hopped the Lima tram to the Negri foundry, where he took attendance, paid the laborers, drew designs. He helped make the
streetlamps that line the Plaza de San Martin. When Jorge Arana
graduated from university in 1940 at age twenty-two, with a full

scholarship and honors, he'd been the family wage earner for seven years.

⁓

MY FATHER'S FIRST job pointed him toward the Amazon jungle, the vast expanse of rain forest that lay north of the Andean cordillera. He was hired by Peru's Department of Public Works as a bridge engineer—a good calling for a twenty-two-year-old. There was a bridge going up on the new road from Lima to Pucallpa, but its cables had snapped and the frames collapsed into the Previsto River. His job had been to recover the twisted beams, straighten them out, continue the foray into the jungle that the Spaniards had begun five centuries before.

He was living in his father's house, shuttling to the north and back, helping support his five siblings, keeping company with a woman who was too often found in bolero bars, too easy to bed, too many shades darker than his own skin, when a chance came to change his course. Doctor Laroza, the director of the Colegio de Ingenieros, Abuelito's former rival, offered him a scholarship to the graduate school at the Massachusetts Institute of Technology in Boston, all expenses paid by the U.S. Department of State. The war in Europe was devouring gringos; American schools had been drained of young men. Peru had declared itself against the Axis, and it seemed the U.S. government was grateful for that. The country and the university were offering one place to a Peruvian engineer. *Em Ay Tee?* my father said to Laroza— MIT? Never heard of it.

A year passed. The war in the Pacific intensified, changing the very face of America. The heavy deployment of young Americans had not only depleted the gringo schools, it was shrinking the gringo workforce. Whatever jobs women were unable to fill were now being offered to foreigners. Peru itself was little fazed by the war, except for Japanese Peruvians, who were rounded up and shipped off to internment camps in the United States—among them a family named Fujimori, whose ranks forty years later would produce a president of Peru.

In Lima, my father continued to come and go from the Peruvian interior, paying visits to his coffee-colored lover, appalling the family. Abuelita expressed disapproval. *La mujer no es gente decente!* She's not the right kind!

Here is the point, I often thought as a child, when the gears might never have shifted, that I might never have existed, that my father might have taken another path. But four little cogs changed everything: The first was my grandmother's censure of his woman. The second, the growing ennui of her charms. The third, a renewed offer of the scholarship. The fourth, a conversation at the Department of Public Works: His bosses promised to continue to pay his salary while he studied in the United States on the assumption that he would return to work at the same department. *MIT?* one of his *compadres* said. *Caramba!* That's the best science the gringos have!

MY FATHER LOVES to tell the story of coming to America and will tell it to anyone who will hear it, in an urgent present tense. He narrates it now so that I can write this book. It begins this way: In early June of 1943, just as General Patton is planning his leap from the African shore, Jorge Arana flies to Panama City. But he finds himself wandering that capital, wondering whether he'll ever get out. The planes are full. Panama is crawling with soldiers, and all flights to and from the isthmus are preempted for military use.

He spends days looking over the airstrip, lining up, waiting for announcements, loosening his collar against the furnace of the sun. At dusk, he is told to pray for luck, come back on the following day. Nights are tolerable, in town with other Latinos, young men lured north by the promise of bigger careers. They go

down to the sailor dives, perch on stools, sway to mambos, eye
women over tankards of rum.

Seven days pass and civilian travel remains paralyzed. The dollars he's hoarded thin to a precious few. MIT has sent only what
is necessary to get him to Boston, and each day in that way station is a drain on his future.

One morning, as he sits in the roiling airport—a suitcase at his
side and his parents' photographs in his pocket—an airport official emerges to bark at the crowd. *The day's plane to Miami is
light,* he says. *We're one hundred ten pounds short of mail.
Anybody weigh fifty kilos or less?*

My father steps forward: a stringy man, a tight bundle of
energy. They can see that he isn't much heavier than a sack of
mail. They weigh him, rush him through the gates, strap him in.
He comes to America as a letter might: with no more than a
destination and a sliver of hope. There, beside the green of
young soldiers and the dust of old burlap, he feels his fortunes
rise.

The Miami he flies into is jittery, quick with street life and
cash. War is everywhere evident—in the uniforms, the monger-
ing slogans on walls. He stays for two nights, dodges his way
through the mayhem, tries to get on a train. There are other
Hispanics headed for universities. Much of South America has
taken the side of the northern colossus; foreigners are being welcomed in. It's a liaison of convenience, between a country at war
and educated young Latino men. They're coming just long
enough to learn what they can from the gringos, woo a blonde,
man the machines awhile.

At the end of June, he steps off a train into a gray, late night in
Boston. He walks through the concrete city to a building he's
been assured will be home. A chain of head-scratching cicerones
point the way. The dormitory looks stony, imposing. A uniformed

man sits inside. *Yes, sir?* the sailor says, snapping up brisk under a pale crew cut.

Good evening, says my father, pronouncing the English words slowly, nodding politely. He rifles through his pockets and draws out the letter that has led him there. The military man scans it quickly, shakes his head.

This was an MIT building last week. Not tonight, he says, thrusting the paper back into my father's hand. *It's the headquarters for a V-12 navy training program now. There'll be a full crew by morning.*

My father's face darkens, the sailor's softens. *Here, let me look at that again,* the gringo says, and reads the worn document a second time. When he looks up, the eyes have a different intelligence. *Well, I don't see why you can't stay here one night.*

With that simple sentence, Jorge Arana takes a liking to America. Its food is bland. Its women rattle on incomprehensibly. Its afternoons rumble with thunder, torrents gushing from the sky. Its streets are all car horn and elbow. But there's a wartime goodwill in the air: a winking camaraderie, a link with the hemisphere at large.

Within a few days, my father is registered in MIT's graduate division, paying two dollars a day for a rented room and two meals, struggling to decipher Boston's expletives, sitting in a classroom with no idea what the professor has said. He has studied English for years in Lima, but he finds himself unable to produce it, helpless before the machine-gun fire of American slang.

Jack Coombs, the man in whose apartment he lives, is a working-class Irishman with a colorful vocabulary and a powerful thirst for ale. Coombs is short, square; so is his "missus." Together, they're a monument to chance. The Coombses are gambling aficionados, their conversation focuses on horses and hazards, jockeys and odds. My father sits at their table with a dictionary at his side, puzzling over the lexicon, marveling at the luck of his draw.

What's it like down where you come from, Horrr-hey? Coombs shouts between slurps of beer. *Y'all wear feathers and stomp around barefoot?*

We wear shoes, Mr. Coombs. Nice leather ones. We've been ordering them from Paris since the sixteenth century, before your people ever set foot in this country, he bandies back. But only after he's roared merrily and looked up the words in his book.

Graduate school is hard, and his English isn't good enough. His professors are direct: If he doesn't get a perfect score on his engineering project, he won't be granted a degree. The project is to be an invention, something no one on the faculty has seen before. Within the first weeks, he decides the form it will take. He'll build an instrument that will gauge the load on a bridge. Not burdens on spans as they're being erected; there are plenty of those contraptions around. No, his tool will test a suspension bridge that has gone up before anyone has had an opportunity to test it—a cable deemed unsteady, a structure everyone figures will fall.

More than five decades later, I ask him about it. He is over eighty now, paunched and grizzled and gray, nearly blind in one eye, but I recognize an intensity, the deliberateness he must have had as a young man. He takes out a pencil, sketches it for me: a bridge cable and a delicate instrument that squats on it. The next time I visit, he has constructed a model. *Here it is*, he says, setting the device before me. There is a metal cable between two pulleys, weighted with burdens on either side. A triangular pincer presses down from above, displaces the cable in increments, mathematically measures the load. The model is made—as everything he now makes is—out of something altogether practical: a wooden fruit crate, neatly painted, smoothly sanded, clearly labeled with equations. He explains it meticulously. My

eighty-six-year-old mother leans forward, engrossed in its fragile
balance. She's platinum-haired, lovely. She's holding a tangerine.

~

THE FIRST TIME I SEE HER, he tells me, *is through the frame of a
window*. He is inside a dormitory, she is walking along the
Fenway, a gaggle of women around. He registers her as a color in
a rainbow, one swift stripe on a variegated field. She is stately in
her fern-green suit, hair smoothed into a golden roll, a brown
feather quivering somewhere above. Her companions are fresh-
faced girls. She is a decade older, seasoned, a different flux in
the well of her eyes.

He sees her often after that. Every day into winter. He is in a
houseful of Latinos now, three stories of them, in a building
rented out by the Boston Conservatory of Music. In the spirit of
wartime frugality, the musicians are sharing a basement dining
room with the MIT men.

She comes up the stairs of 24 Fenway with her violin wedged
under one arm, shakes the snow from her fur coat, steps into a
roomful of dark-eyed lotharios, darts past to a table in the back.
She marks the din and the laughter but is removed, discon-
nected somehow.

She's unmarried, he can see that from the unadorned finger;
she's sleeker, more studied than the rest. She has the preened,
perfumed air of a woman who has been in the world for a while.

At first he sees she's well-courted, walking briskly from the conservatory with a series of suitors. He notices only in passing. There
are more-pressing concerns on his side of the window. Science has
swept romance from his prospects, into a far corner of life. Others
like him are washing dishes, waiting tables, taking odd jobs, earn-
ing money for a weekend jink. He spends his days in a library, in a
laboratory, between a dictionary and a stack of books. Some
Saturdays he puts on fiestas, mixing punch in a bathtub, ordering

up rhumbas and mambos, navigating the dancers with his drink in the air. The Latins at MIT are known for their parties, for scoring champagne, for serving it up in shoes. Mostly, however, he sees the world from a third-floor window, decoding gibberish he's copied from a blackboard, digging his shoulder into a wall. Everyone knows how America rids itself of Latino students who do not make the grade: They ship them to Ellis Island or, worse, to holding camps, before deportation home.

Between sirens and blackouts and rations of horse meat, there's a night of conga and rum. *Come here,* he beckons, when to his surprise she appears at the doorway. *Let me teach you.* He puts one hand on her waist, draws her in. She's warm with a strange phosphorescence, with a glow on the nape of her neck. She tilts her head to one side and laughs back at him, and then there's a point when the air is still.

Who can say when the first strand crosses the arroyo? The filament is flung. A fragile span arches down on the other side. The stories differ on the fine points of timing: Is it when she brings him ice cream on a late night before examinations? When he sits waiting for her on the steps of the conservatory building? When he asks for her help with a puzzling phrase?

His letters home say Americans are clever, industrious, admirable in every way. But they are an alien form of life. He cannot imagine himself with a woman of this dryasdust, pallid race. By spring he can imagine it. They are together, sunning themselves in the park, listening to the Boston Pops, stretching out on the grass, imagining life together in Peru.

Now, tell me about your family, Marie, he says, stroking her hair.

Nothing to tell, she answers simply. *My name is Campbell. I was born in 1921. I have a mother and a father, that's all.*

Well, start at the beginning. Where are you from? he says, piling bricks from the bare ground up.

Seattle. The conversation stops there. She's from Seattle. By way of Canada. From out there. Down the road. Away. She gets up and dusts off her clothes.

I'm spending time with a pretty gringa, he writes to his mother, *but as you know I'm not one to sniff after mysteries or wager on horses. These women are a chancy thing.*

In truth, he finds himself wondering at her mystery, confused about signals. In Peru, things are simpler. There are two kinds of women: the kind you meet on the town and the kind you join at the altar. The kind you court is no random stranger, strolling down the Fenway, taking meals in a basement hall. She's introduced by family, seen in her father's home, in the presence of a chaperone. Not in a college dormitory, drinking champagne from a shoe.

The woman you marry is a genteel creature with just enough of an education to patter over a dinner table or steer the schooling of a child. Chief among her virtues is chastity, an unwavering commitment to one man and his children and, by association, to his family tree.

The gringas of the conservatory, on the other hand, are perplexing. They seem reasonably cultivated, decent *señoritas,* but self-reliant, brash as men. There is an unattached quality, a freedom that would be taken as scandalous in Lima. Maybe it's a difference in cultures. Maybe it's the nature of a nervous time.

War has become the explanation for everything. There's a sense that your time is short. Each cigarette is a miracle. Every song a seduction. A party stumbles along for days.

The women are different; I don't know how to judge them, he writes to his mother. *There's a code at work here; I don't know what to think. In restaurants, you say what you've eaten and the waiter just trusts you and writes up a bill. It's an upside-down country. A labyrinth of mirrors. Whenever I think I understand it, I find out I'm wrong.*

He is wrong about much when it comes to her. He thinks she is twenty-three, three years his junior. She is thirty-one. He thinks she is rich. She only looks as if she might be, in her fur and her charge-account cabs. He thinks that she shuttles to Seattle and back again because parents await her. What is there is not family; it's a past of her own.

In June, as Hitler limps out of Italy and American boys march into Rome, he finishes his thesis. The bridge apparatus works; he takes a master's with honors. But by then, he is deep into a curriculum of a different kind. He is in love, looking for a way to stay. When a General Electric executive from Schenectady offers him work inspecting turbines for tankers, he takes it.

That winter he takes a wife as well. As he tells the story, he and my mother had spent many months apart: she in Manhattan, studying with the distinguished violin maestro Emanuel Ondricek; he in Schenectady, driving steam through a throttle. One weekend, they meet in Boston. By Monday, they are looking for a judge.

This is where the story unravels. Where the string wafts off into unfinished sentences, like a thread into February wind. It is she, after all these years, who fills in the gaps. It begins with her going to a Catholic priest on a Sunday, she tells me. She asks the holy man to marry them, but after a short conversation, he turns her away. When she reports to my father that the priest has refused her, she doesn't tell him why. The next morning, they find a justice of the peace who agrees to do it. He takes down their information, tells them to return with their documents.

They come back another day, ready to make their pledges, but there are unexpected questions on the judge's mind. *Where's your birth certificate?* he asks my father. *You can't marry without one.* My father holds out his passport, but the lawman shakes his head.

And you, young lady, he says to my mother in her teal blue dress. *The information you gave me on this application is incorrect. Your driver's license says you were born in 1913, not 1921. And Campbell must not be your maiden name. You've been married before.*

My father looks down at the page as she takes out a pen and amends it. She draws a line through the year and writes above carefully. *1913.* Then she skims down to the place at the bottom. Previous marriages, it asks. She checks it off, answers it. *Three.*

Fine, says the judge. *That's more like it.* He is softening, like the crew-cut sailor on that first Boston night. *We can go ahead now,* he tells my flustered father, reading shock as impatience, *but you must promise to bring me a copy of that birth certificate eventually, won't you? Shall we call in two witnesses and do this?* He waves in the direction of the stragglers in the hall.

Yes, my father says, pulling himself together, and the wedding is on. The bridge goes up.

⌒

PAPI DECIDED TO accept my mother's mysterious past in that one split second just as surely as I have come to accept it over the years. I have puzzled over my mother's heart for almost half a century. She has told me so little about its workings. But now that I am older, I know she has a right to her secrets. I am content to understand that my mother has had real love, hard love, heartbreak, and to know that while my father has given her the first two, he never will give her the last.

Not until I was in my forties and she in her eighties did we finally bring the question into the open. We had traveled to New York together. I hadn't planned it, hadn't rehearsed it, but after a few glasses of wine at a Manhattan trattoria, there it was.

"Mother," I said, "I've spent a lifetime trying to ask you one question."

She looked at me with her steady blue eyes and nodded her

silvery head. Her thumb and fingers were tilting her glass back and forth, as if she were seeking balance in a violin bow. "You're asking me about the marriages?"

"Yes, I am. Yes."

She put down her wine, knit her fingers. "There were three before your father," she said simply.

I was flabbergasted, amazed. She was talking without any hesitation, coolly, frankly. As if we were talking about rooms in a house. "There were *three*." She had three fingers up now, and she was pressing on one with a finger of her other hand. "In the first, I eloped. Or, I should say, a group of us eloped. I was sixteen. My sister Erma talked me into it. Made me do it. On a dare. On a lark. I never realized how responsible Erma was for that miserable first marriage until I was an old woman, until Erma was dead. Until now."

She paused there and studied me. I strained to remember Erma. She was the only one of Mother's three sisters I'd ever met, but all I could summon was a shadowy figure on a childhood visit. I was pulled more to the image of my teenage mother getting married on a dare. It was as if I'd never known her. As if I were seeing her for the first time through a telescope, from another planet. She had allowed me to grow up, it suddenly dawned on me, nothing like her. I was cautious, hesitant, mindful of mores, of my own virginal image, of *como se hace*. The way good Latinas *ought* to behave. It was why she had never talked about her past to me. She had recognized the limits of my circumspection, the essential Peruvianness of my soul.

"That first one's name was Gerardy," she said quickly. "The town postmaster. He'd always had an eye on me. So we got married, and that was that. I was a silly little girl. But Erma should have known better. The second was out west, in San Francisco. He was a foreigner who didn't want to be sent to war. I did him a favor. He needed papers, citizenship. It was a marriage of convenience. There really isn't any more to tell."

I shook my head yes, fine, let that one go.

"The third one," she held up a lone forefinger now and moved it through the air, "the third one had love in it." She stopped there. I waited for several beats to pass.

"Campbell." I said it.

"Yes," she said, "Campbell. That one. He was killed in the war. And that is all I'm going to say." She pushed the glass away, across the white tablecloth.

"That is all you're going to say?" I blinked.

"Yes," she said, "that is part of my life I keep separate. It has nothing to do with the part I'm in now. It is sacred, do you understand that? Sacred. I do not want to go into it. I do not want *you* going into it. It is not for cocktail conversation. It is not for talk over casual dinners in New York." She stopped, and I could see her shoulders tense with familiar steel.

It was clear why she had to get herself on a train, head for another coast. Thank God Papi had been there. That's enough, Mother. God knows it's enough, and I will leave it. I didn't need to know more.

The irony is that I came to know more anyway, proving the gringo rule that if you shut up, mind your own business, people may tell you a thing or two. In a telephone conversation several years later, I learned from a cousin I'd never met that Gerardy, her first husband, was a hard drinker, brutal. That he'd wanted to get at her father's fortune. That he threw my sixteen-year-old mother around like a doll. When he wasn't tossing mail sacks around as the town postmaster, he was punching her face in and flinging her down the stairs.

That's the reason my mother needed a different direction. Hers was a road that had led from a cruel postmaster to a draft dodger in need of a favor, from a heartbreaking war casualty to a

plane with my father on it—to the mail route from Panama to
Miami, with a cargo that was one sack short. She was drawn to
my father's foreignness. He responded by dismissing whatever
past she brought. When she reached down to correct the judge's
document—*previous marriages, three*—anything might have happened. But in that pivotal moment, my father didn't dither. He
shot out a sturdy span: To another life. To another world. To a
point she might never have touched.

~

YES, MY FATHER says to the judge, pulling himself together,
and the wedding is on. The ramparts sink in.

When they return to a Boston apartment as man and wife,
their friends are there to raise a glass. It's when they're finally
alone that the masonry wobbles. *Yes,* she says, *it's true. I didn't
want to lose you. There were others.* She weeps. The cables so
shredded, they could snap.

Never mind, he says. *It's behind us now. That part of your life is
over. Please don't say more.*

He weighs the choices, knowing what would be the full im-
pact of the truth on his family. Their marriage is impossible in a
Catholic society, unacceptable to a faith that damns divorce as
devil's work and remarried women as tramps. But America is so
different. For all he knows, his new wife is nothing more or less
than typical. He writes to my abuelito and abuelita. *I've married
the pretty gringa,* he tells them. *We're coming to Peru. Send out
announcements: Seattle is her city. James B. Campbell is her father's name.*

He does not broach the subject of the three marriages with
her again. To this day. Even as I move between them now, trying
to paste together this story, it is something they do not discuss.

Somewhere in Denver, a city my mother has never mentioned
to my father, Elver Reed receives a telegram from my mother,

and the old man's heart sinks with the news. Uncle Elver is her uncle, a rich Denver lawyer, a pillar of his community. He's been paying for her studies in New York and at the conservatory, giving her a chance to reshuffle her life. But there's something he doesn't like about the news of a Peruvian husband. *God made those people different. Not like us Anglican folk.* It's understood that the money will stop.

Even as my father arranges their sea voyage to Lima, all he knows about my mother is what he has heard in an American courtroom. He thinks his in-laws are in Seattle, but they are really in Wyoming. Though he knows their name is not Campbell, he doesn't yet know it is Clapp. As for his wife's former marriages, he makes a conscious effort to forget them. And so, although he is wending his way home to Peru, he has taken his first step toward becoming an American: The future interests him more than the past.

ANCESTORS

Antepasados

Y ES, BUT IF you are a Latin American well along the way to becoming a North American, your past is a heavy load of what you carry into your future. That was true for Papi as he brought his pretty young gringa to Peru, and it has been true for me for as long as I can remember. This is not just because we are and always will be Latinos, but because we are Aranas, and for us history is even more inescapable than it may be for other Latin Americans.

I'VE STOOD IN Venice, on its Bridge of Sighs. It is monumental, rank with history. It is where the tourists go. I've lined up behind the Piazza di San Marco to see its stone thrust from one side of the canal to the other. It is a covered span, ornate, with two small, grated windows that look out over the water, and it joins the Doges' Palace to a dungeon on the other side. They say condemned Venetians were made to walk that chute from judgment to execution. As they crossed and peered through the grating, they would look out beyond the canal, the lagoon, and sigh for their lives, sigh for their sins, sigh at the beauty of that one last view.

It is this bridge—steeped in yesterday, wrapped in guilt, shut in stone—that brings to mind my father's deep history. Like Mother, he had been molded by the past, but his was a past he had not made and was unaware of, a legacy inherited before he'd seen the light of day. It was the Mark of Arana: as real as a shriveled leg, a maimed hand, a welt from shoulder to shoulder. It had reverberated from jungle to mountain, from one side of the Aranas to another. It had spun into every branch of the family, stung his grandfather, stifled his mother, chased his father up the stair. Nobody spoke of it, no one acknowledged it, nor did anyone really care to track the circuitry, but for Aranas the past had been toxic, and shame spilled through generations like sap through a vine.

All my life, strangers had asked me about the rubber baron Julio César Arana, and I'd always given the rote response: no relation, no connection, not me. So a shadowy figure had been responsible for a human hecatomb in the jungle? Well, that story had played out at the turn of another century, at the hearth of another family; it had little relevance to me. But Julio César crept into my life anyway.

In the summer of 1996, I was granted a fellowship at Stanford University's Hoover Institution, where I intended to study the problem of Peruvian women and poverty. I had decided to focus on the doughty survivalism that persisted at the hardscrabble edges of Lima. I had returned to Peru with my father for the express purpose of combing Lima's slums for a newspaper story I might produce during that fellowship. I took my notebooks, a camera bag, and headed for the dunes that embrace the city. I sat in mud huts with mothers who were determined to put the terror of the *Sendero Luminoso* (Shining Path) guerrillas behind them, listened to men who had seen their babies dismembered, talked to children with stony eyes.

One day, I asked my father to go to the *barriadas* with me. We rode through the shantytowns in my rented car, coiling down the dusty roads to the house of a crippled priest whose legs had been whacked by terrorists' machetes. Papi was seventy-eight years old and had never seen a *barriada* in his life. He rode in the backseat wordlessly, gazing out the windows, staring at the filth. When I took him home to his sisters, he was sick for a week. I wrote about poor indigenous Peruvians for my newspaper. In the luxury of a Stanford office, I got the job done. But even after I'd put all my notebooks away and sent the piece off to the editors, Peru's sorrows sat on my desk like a stone.

It was then that I decided to throw open a window on my own past, delve into Arana history. I thought it would be a pleasant enough recreation for a sabbatical: sorting through Stanford's rich Latin-American collection, finding out who my forebears were. Each morning I'd descend to the library stacks, pull out every book that mentioned Arana, and cart it dutifully to my quiet little office overlooking a picturesque square. What I knew about the Aranas until that point was only what I'd been able to glean from my immediate family.

I knew that my great-grandfather Pedro Pablo Arana, who had graduated from Peru's finest schools and gone on to a distinguished career as governor, senator, and revolutionary hero, was mysterious and given to secrets about his family ties. He was a proud man with a Napoleonic temper, impatient with curiosities like mine. But his arrogance had nothing to do with lineage, as so much of arrogance can. He did not talk about relatives.

I also knew that when my grandfather—my abuelito—was six, Pedro Pablo had sent him to a boarding school in Lima, then gone off to pursue his political career. Abuelito's mother, Doña

Eloísa Sobrevilla Diaz, was a dreamy woman who despised the pretense of city life. She preferred to spend her days with her daughter, Carmen, in the hills of her estate in Huancavelica, where she became obsessed with the plight of the *indígenos*, remote from her husband and son. By the time Pedro Pablo Arana was made governor of Cusco—Qosqo, navel of the world—his son was so entrenched in the hermetic world of Catholic schools, from Lima to the University of Notre Dame, that he had little contact with other Aranas. His mother's family, the Sobrevillas, lived part of the year in Lima and looked in on the boy—but his father's family was a null.

I found mention of my great-grandfather Pedro Pablo Arana in the first book I looked at—a Latin-American encyclopedia. *Peruvian hero*, it said, *led the last known populist uprising against the military in 1895*. Pedro Pablo had been secretary of war in a revolution against the military machine of General Andres Caceres, president of Peru. "The rule of law over the rule of force!" was his battle cry, and he led three hundred rebels on horseback—springing unexpected from the cordillera—in the 1895 insurrection at Huancayo. But the card catalogs led me to far more mentions of another Arana, Julio César Arana—row upon row of references with provocative rubrics attached to them: *atrocities, London investors, trials, dungeons, human-rights organizations, Mark of Arana*. And so, although I'd never gone looking for Julio César, his ghost beckoned me to the task. I decided to learn why his name never failed to raise eyebrows. Why, every time I asked my family to tell me about Julio César Arana, the answer had been unequivocal: "Oh, there are so many Aranas, Marisi. He has nothing to do with you."

The facts, as I came upon them in that Stanford library, were as follows: Julio César had been born in 1864 in Rioja, a town in northern Peru, on the cusp of the cordillera and the Amazon jungle. The year he was born, my great-grandfather Pedro Pablo

Arana was a university student, graduate of a prestigious Lima school, bound for a career in law. In 1882, as my great-grandfather made senatorial declamations from podiums in the southern highlands of Huancavelica, eighteen-year-old Julio César decided to try his hand at fortune in Yurimaguas, a musty little jungle outpost on the Huallaga River. He began forays into the rain forest, searching for *cauchos*, rubber trees. Rubber was on the verge of a boom—black gold, *oro negro*, they called it—and the Amazon was thick with it.

As some accounts have it, Julio César was the son of a jipi-japa-hatmaker and spent a barefoot childhood hawking hats from the back of a mule. The real history is far more complicated. His father did own a straw-hat business in Rioja, but the Aranas were a network of pioneers, capitalists, and politicians. Our part of the clan had originated in the historic city of Cajamarca, where Pizarro and the Incas first came face to face. One Arana remained in Cajamarca and started a business in precious metals. Another—Julio César's father—settled in Rioja and made his fortune in the Panama-hat boom. A third—Benito Arana—went to Loreto, to try his hand in politics. A fourth—Gregorio Arana, my ancestor—went south to the highlands of Ayacucho and Huancavelica, to the silver and mercury mines.

By the time Julio César was three, an Arana was already cutting a path through the jungle for him. Benito Arana, governor of Loreto, Peru's Amazon state, opened the way for rubber fortunes by navigating the Ucayali, the Pachitea, and the Palcazu. The governor was not thinking of rubber only. He was on a mission to dispel the notion that the Amazon was unsafe for commercial development. He decided to make a show of that point by going downriver himself.

There was good reason entrepreneurs were wary of the jungle. Two young sailors by the names of Tavara and West had been lost in the land of Cashibo cannibals, and Benito Arana decided to find out exactly what had happened to them. In the company of a journalist, Governor Arana made his way to the heart of Cashibo territory. He strode into the camp, searched out the largest hut, and called for the fearsome chief, Yanacuna, to come out and say what had become of the boys. Yanacuna's wife ran out of the hut in a fury, accusing Benito Arana of invading sacred territory. Two intruders *had* come into Yanacuna's village, she cried to him. *Dos hombres de hierro!* Iron Men, toting their iron torches. They had cooked up quite nicely, in thirteen clay pots, over thirteen fires. The chief's wife flung down two jawbones—two sets of teeth—at Governor Arana's feet. *There are your "boys,"* she snarled. *Take a look. The same could happen to you.*

When Benito Arana returned to Iquitos, it was as Moses descending from Mount Sinai with commandments: The rainforest Indians were beasts, not people. They were less than simian, incapable of real, human feeling. Henceforward they would be dealt with as animals. And with that, a road was paved; two decades later, my ancestor Julio César would travel it.

He was a charismatic man, Julio César: a ringleader, a schemer. He was straight-backed, with powerful shoulders, a high, arrogant forehead, and a weakness for elegant clothes. By eighteen, he'd decided to make a career in rubber. He married Eleonora Zumaeta, a small-town aristocrat, and with her brother established an enterprise called J. C. Arana Brothers, Inc. By twenty, he'd recruited an army of foremen. By twenty-five, he was buying up land from Colombian adventurers, putting rainforest Indians to work—forcibly—by the thousands, running a business from Iquitos to Manaus, two medullas of rubber that would drive the automobile into the industrial age. By the turn of the century, Julio César had finagled enough leases and staked enough claims to master the rubber-rich Putumayo, a lush stretch of jungle between two tributaries that echoed his name: the Igaraparaná and the Caraparaná.

Precious rubber, white latex, *caucho*: The Amazon was pulsing with it, and nowhere in that jungle was it more copious than the Putumayo, the ungovernable border where Colombia faces Peru—the very point at which the cocaine plant now flourishes. The finest rubber—Para fine hard—was to be found in twelve thousand acres of land no flag had laid formal claim to: the territory between Peru and Colombia that Julio César Arana had established as his. His armies of slaves hacked their way into the green, sending caracaras and marmosets screeching back in retreat. The *cauchos*—"trees that weep white tears," as the Omagua call them—were slashed, drained, their desiccated trunks left to creak in the wind.

The entire Putumayo was under the rule of this one man: The "Casa Arana" had a monopoly on Para rubber, and treasure hunters from as far away as Pakistan and Australia streamed to Peru to work for its founder. Julio César had put Iquitos—a jungle outpost that was unreachable by land—on the map of the civilized world. He had made it one of the wealthiest cities on the planet. He had six hundred gunmen scouring the jungle for slaves. *Hombres de hierro*, the rain-forest Indians called them: Iron Men, for the dread guns they toted. They would sweep into the villages, make bloated promises, lead able-bodied natives away. Julio César had forty-five centers of operation at strategic points along the border with Colombia, an area that was too feral for either country to defend. By the turn of the century, he had the Peruvian military helping him hold on to it. *I have six hundred men armed with Winchesters*, he cabled the president. *Essential you send me a supply of Mannlichers.*

By 1902, when Abuelito, my grandfather, was twenty years old and moving the tassel from one side of his graduation cap to the other at the University of Notre Dame, Julio César had thousands of rain-forest Indians making him rich. They were the Huitoto, the Bora, the Andoke, the Ocaina: from fierce head-hunters to doe-eyed forest folk. They would rise at dawn under the vigilance of overseers, head for the trees in the gray light of morning when the latex flows freely, score V channels in the bark, and let the white milk well into little tin bowls. Each tree could yield a hundred pounds of rubber before it shriveled into a husk. When a stand of *caucho* dribbled all day, a rain-forest Indian might gather enough to roll a cable the size of a human leg.

Julio César's henchmen recruited *flagelados*, scourged ones, fugitives from the great dust bowl of Ceará. Hundreds of thousands were making an exodus from the wasteland of Brazil's northeast. The streets of Iquitos and Manaus were full of them—gaunt, toothless desperados, willing to board ships for the promise of work and food. By the time Arana got them to Iquitos, they were in debt to him for passage, for food, for buckets, for bullets, for Winchesters. It didn't take much to get them to drive slaves.

By 1903, when my great-grandfather was governor of Cusco, campaigning for the vice presidency, dreaming of a fine, democratic republic, Julio César had become one of the wealthiest men in the hemisphere, and his domain—twenty-five million acres of it—stretched from Peru to Colombia. Two years later, he incorporated his business in New York and London, under the name of the Peruvian Amazon Company. He hired a British board of directors, put the company on the London exchange, and began making the gringos rich.

In the space of a decade, the Casa Arana had become a towering enterprise. Julio César and his brothers ran it from his palace, a sprawl of red and white magnificence overlooking the Amazon, not far from the point where the river splits. He called his boulevard Calle Arana and lined it with royal palms. From his raised balconies, he could survey his dominion. From his oleander gardens, he could stride out to a triumphant balustrade that abutted the gray-green water and watch his barges approach. Out in the jungle were the armies of four hundred, the overlords, the guards, the weighers, the tappers. Out they would go, on trails they could run blindfolded, knowing instinctively which trees would bleed. Once the bundles were brought into the camps, the workers would weigh them, cure them to a smoky charcoal, then ship them downriver on flotillas of armed barges.

Some overlords decided to breed their own workers, in shacks where slave girls were kept for that purpose, six hundred women at a time. The Huitoto children born in those camps were taught to kiss the overlords' hands, worship them as deities. By the time they were seven, the natural Huitoto gentleness was bred out of them: They were an army of diminutive *guerrilleros*, wielding rifles, shooting trespassers, trained to kill.

Eventually, Arana decided to import black men from Barbados to consolidate his empire. He needed disciplinarians, punishers. The Caribbeans were tall, imperious, dark as onyx, and they terrified the rain-forest people. He hired two hundred of these colossuses, put whips in their hands, and promised to pay according to how much rubber their Indians could haul. It was a masterful plan. The Barbadians were British subjects, hired into a firm he was making increasingly British: incorporated in England, traded in London, paid for in sterling, ruled by him in the heart of a no-man's-land. When he saw that the British directors did not object to having British blacks involved, he sent representatives back to Barbados to hire several hundred more.

By 1905, Arana's Peruvian Amazon Company was exporting one and a half million pounds of rubber a year from the rain forests. Michelin tire factories were screaming for rubber. Gringos were riding it into the motor age. They were buying it up, laying down highways, racing to factories with machine dreams in mind. And the jungle kept right on trickling. The Amazon River and its one thousand tributaries became thick with steamships, gorged with barges, packed with black gold. By 1907, it was impossible to enter and exit the Putumayo without a permit from an Arana agent. The monopoly had become complete—and its operations legally sanctioned.

⌒

THE REPORTS OF the atrocities began in the early months of 1907. Detailed testimonies from Arana's former employees appeared in Peruvian newspapers with small circulations. Then, in September of 1907, two articles on the Arana monopoly appeared in *The New York Times*. The news was largely about money. Peruvian rubber was flowing through Liverpool and New York, according to reporters. The money through London and Park Avenue banks. But the most interesting news was how rich the company foremen were getting: One had earned forty thousand dollars from three months in the jungle. It was equivalent to almost a million today.

Sometime later, further details about the Casa Arana appeared in a memo from the U.S. consul in Iquitos to the American secretary of state. In that longish description was a single scene, chilling for its simplicity. A Barbadian guard employed by the Aranas had reported to the consul personally that he had been fired for not punishing one of the female tappers under his supervision. The ex-employee—a tall, black man who spoke good English—said he had refused to strike the woman when his foreman had ordered him to do so. She had a baby strapped to her back and was paying more attention to it than to her work on the trees. The foreman became angry—at the woman for not attending to the rubber, at the guard for not obeying his orders. He grabbed the baby, dashed its brains out against a tree, and screamed at the woman to go back to work. Then he turned and whipped the Barbadian until the man ran for his life.

Days after the American secretary of state received that

memo, Walter Hardenburg, a twenty-one-year-old American, pushed his canoe off the banks of the Putumayo. Eight months later, he stepped into a London press office to send news of the carnage into the breakfast rooms of the civilized world. The young adventurer had been gliding downriver from the Colombian frontier, making his way toward Manaus, where he hoped to find work on the Madeira-Mamoré Railroad. What he stumbled into on his way changed the lovely, bosky image of the Putumayo forever. No one could call it a paradise now.

The Putumayo as witnessed by Hardenburg was a cauldron of violence, a human hecatomb: Rain-forest Indians moved through it in shackles. Their lives could be snuffed out at whim.

The Indians were not paid for their work. They were herded together at gunpoint by the Iron Men, at which time each was offered a can of food, a cooking pot, a mirror. *Comisiones*, these wholesale sweeps were called. In exchange, the captives were told they would have to work to pay off the gifts. Chained to one another, naked, they were led down jungle trails or transported upriver to Iquitos, where they would be sold to overseers for twenty to forty pounds sterling. After that, they were simply working to stay alive.

Slaves who dawdled were made to pull kerosene-soaked sacks over their heads. They were told to wait quietly until the Barbadians set fire to them. Seeing a father burn tended to make a youth work harder. Seeing a little girl run shrieking to the river, her skin melting, tended to make mothers concentrate on the trees.

When slaves ran away, the foremen found ways to track them. One runaway guard told of a tracking party that was trying to locate the whereabouts of a dozen or so fugitive slaves. They ran across an old woman who hadn't been able to keep up with the others. When she refused to tell them in what direction her people had gone, they tied her hands behind her with a rope. They cut a post, secured it between two trees, hauled her up and hanged her from it, so that her feet hovered above ground. Then they set dry leaves on fire under her. Even as her feet cooked and her thighs blistered, the woman refused to talk. Finally, the foreman, disgusted with the smell, kicked the pole down and hacked off her head.

In the camps, on airless, mosquito-clouded afternoons when work was finished and foremen were feeling good, the rum would come out, then the Winchesters and the Mannlichers, and target shooting would begin. This, just for fun: Send an Indian running to the river, riddle him with bullets before he gets there. High points if you kill him. Higher still if he never gets wet. Stand a woman out in the clearing with her baby; make her hold out the child while you aim for the round little bull's-eye of cranium. Brag about it, take a swig, stagger around cackling, until you pull the trigger, explode the skull, splatter the trees with brain.

The first worldwide report on what was really going on in the Casa Arana was issued by a London magazine called *Truth*. The headline read: THE DEVIL'S PARADISE—A BRITISH-OWNED CONGO. The reference was to the genocide twenty years before in the Congo, where ten million Africans had been slaughtered under the watch of the Belgian King Leopold. In the text, Walt Hardenburg was quoted: *"Now that the civilized world is aware of what occurs in the vast and tragic forest of the Putumayo, I feel that I have done my duty before God."* The article in *Truth* was followed by a lightning streak of revelations across world newspapers from Europe to the Americas, North and South.

It was in this very year, 1907, that Pedro Pablo Arana, my great-grandfather, was made governor of Cusco. He had campaigned fervently for a civilian government, certain that the country had invested its army with too much power. He despised the tin-pot tyrannies that self-satisfied generals were prone to, and he believed they were likely as not corrupt. He had fought militarists on horseback, been elected senator many times over, had run for the vice presidency of the land on the basis of those convictions. The civilian president, Manuel Pardo—the very same man who, ironically, was approving shipments of Mannlichers for Julio César— wanted to reward my great-grandfather for his contributions to the cause of the *civilistas* and so made him the prefect of Cusco. Just as my sixty-year-old great-grandfather was setting his inkpot on his desk in the Cusco prefecture, just as he was ready to reap the rewards of an illustrious political career, a *New York Times* piece about the Arana atrocities was printed, and British pulpits began to resound with his name. When his twenty-five-year-old son unfurled a newspaper in a faculty room in Maine one morning and read about the Mark of Arana, a chill must have mounted his spine.

I imagine my great-grandfather, Pedro Pablo, reeling, stunned, back and forth from Lima to Cusco to his estate in Huancavelica, trying to get a grip on his life. He had been a patriot, a warrior, a hero, a public servant, no more than a cousin to the rubber baron; he had not been prepared for the blot on his family name. He had not anticipated the jungle splatter. Not on his perfect shirts, shiny spats, satin sashes. Not this. His son was writing him desperately from America: *Why don't you answer my letters?* Querido Papa, *what is going on? Where is the money?* Finally, Pedro Pablo sent his son a telegram. *Come home,* it said. *On the next ship. Money is gone.*

Pedro Pablo began trying to salvage what good name he had. He cut off all contact with his extended family in Iquitos. He stepped down from the Cusco governorship and retreated to Huancavelica. He refused to take questions about the "Devil of the Putumayo." When asked, he responded simply: I have no siblings or ancestors. Not one.

"Judge *me* as you *see* me," he'd say from that moment forward, "not as you see others who bear my name," and all attempts to learn of parents, siblings, or a larger family would be stopped at the first question. But to divorce himself from his clan made him an aberration—a spontaneous generation in a society that nurtured family histories as if they were precious instruments, radar nimble, eggshell fragile, unfailing in their power to triangulate the truth about a man.

The jungle poison seeped through his circle anyway. Pedro Pablo's wife—my great-grandmother—who had worked tirelessly to help improve the lot of the *indígenas* in the mountains of Huancavelica, had a heart attack and died. Peru's newly elected president, Augusto Leguía, a landed capitalist who was a personal friend of my great-grandfather and a defender of Julio César Arana, was wounded in an attempted assassination. He slipped off to London to convalesce.

~

WHEN MY GREAT-GRANDFATHER summoned his son home and quit the governorship of Cusco, he descended from the Inca omphalos in a state of high anxiety, spinning into Lima with a double vertigo: It wasn't only his name that made him feel like a criminal—he'd been inspired by Julio César. As the rubber baron's empire had grown, Pedro Pablo had tasted ambition: He'd tried his hand at capitalism, too.

He owned a good stretch of land in the highlands, including a vein of mercury that cut along the cordillera of the Andes. They were rich mines, old mines, with a wretched history he hoped to amend. The largest was the Santa Barbara, an ancient deposit the Spaniards had mined since the late 1500s. *Las minas de muerte*. The mines of death.

Just as Julio César was consolidating his power, Pedro Pablo published a book called *The Mercury Mines of Peru,* in which he proposed that the old mines of Santa Barbara—which now lay on his land—be reopened, so that the country would no longer be dependent on foreign imports. It was a proposal for investors, a ticket to the Arana boom, and he was ready to create an empire of his own. His book did not shrink from the truth about the abuses Indian workers had endured in earlier centuries. His own venture, he insisted, would be a model for the enlightened world, a leap into gringo modernity. He posed the program to the president of the country and got no reaction. Then he posed the question to his cousin in Iquitos and got the encouragement he desired.

He had fully expected to enter the mercantile world when his duties in Cusco were over. He had not expected the chaos that ensued: the news about the atrocities; the freeze on all Arana bank assets; the realization that beneath his own ambitions, speeches about progress, and attempts to mimic a gringo efficiency, there lurked a terrible, inescapable truth: The mercury would leave his mines the way rubber had left the jungle, the only way hard labor ever got done in the Americas—as when the Incas enslaved the Chimu, the Spaniards enslaved the *cholos*, the half-breeds enslaved the *negros*—on the backs of the darker race.

Pedro Pablo did not need to look far to see that he would never mine Santa Barbara, that he would not match the lucre the northern family had in abundance, that if he could just hold on to his good name, it was all the wealth he would ever want.

His good name. The world was telling him he couldn't have even that. Imagine a family, the gringos intoned, who put *Indians to work without payment, without food, in nakedness; with women stolen, ravished, and murdered; with Indians flogged until their bones are laid bare, left to die with their wounds festering with maggots, their bodies used as food for their dogs.* Imagine what lower hell those monsters might dig, unchecked.

When Julio César Arana protested the allegations of human-rights abuses and the Peruvian government sprang to defend him, the charge then shifted from Arana to Peru, and then to all

Latin America. *To deny the truth is part of the Latin American character, a* British parliamentarian thundered. *It is an "Oriental" trait they possess, the curious belief that sustained denial is the equal of truth, no matter what the real conditions.*

Eventually, Reginald Enock, a London barrister, took it upon himself to issue a final denunciation, tracing the evil back to its root, which, as he explained it, was Spain: *The occurrences on the Putumayo are, to some extent, the result of a sinister human element—the Spanish character. The remarkable trait of callousness to human suffering which the people of Spain—themselves a mixture of Moor, Goth, Semite, Vandal, and other such peoples—introduced into the Latin American race is here shown in its intensity, and is augmented by a further Spanish quality: The Spaniard regards Indians as animals.*

A Peruvian judge took offense and barked back in a Lima newspaper: *Quite funny, don't you think,* he wrote, *that England, a country whose debt to history is the massive eradication of redskinned people; a country that has commandeered plots, assassinations, rapes and assaults on Ireland for centuries and has released convicts and predators of the lowest level to mete out horrors in colonial Australia; a country that has dealt inhumanely with Jamaicans and Boers, conducted abominable witch-hunts in New England, and erected abominable camps in America; England, a country that today is forcing the venom of opium on Chinese people; that has obtained that substance with much violence and murder; that is perpetrating these very acts,* this very hour, *against the Hindus—I repeat, is it not funny that such a nation should elect itself an arbiter? That it should pretend to judge the work and destiny of a people who may be naive, but have high ideals of justice, who have never hidden behind hypocrisy and false Puritanism?*

But it was like shouting into a wind; the campaign was too loud, too broad now.

My great-grandfather could not answer for the whole of

Iberia, the whole of Spain, the whole of Peru, the whole of Latin America. He could, however, answer as Pedro Pablo Arana: He was not one of the evil ones. It was a lie that would define us into the fourth generation. *We are not those people.*

⌒

HOW COULD SOMEONE feel so tainted by a cousin a cordillera and a river away? The gringa in me asks that in disbelief and wonder. Why did my great-grandfather feel such shame? When the scandal erupted and Julio César's empire was exposed, Pedro Pablo left his governorship and called his son back from his northern idylls. Whatever money he had, and he had had plenty—enough to keep a mansion in Cusco, a hacienda in Huancavelica, a fine residence in Lima, enough to maintain my abuelito like a prince in America—his money was gone.

When Víctor Manuel Arana, twenty-five years old, hurried back from Maine, he set up an engineering atelier in Lima with the hopes of using his *yanqui* expertise, but he was on his own. There were no family coffers to help him get established. Worse yet, there were few customers at his door. Time did eventually bring one interested party: Rosa Cisneros y Cisneros, my abuelita—a mere thirteen and oblivious to the intricacies of the Putumayo scandals. As years passed, she became fascinated by the startled-looking young man with the dapper American clothes who came and went from the offices across Quemado Street. When my grandfather noticed the bright-eyed, bird-faced girl peering out her window, he returned the curiosity. Shortly after her eighteenth birthday, he approached her father, introduced himself, and was met with the question: Was he one of those Aranas? No, certainly not! Following Pedro Pablo's directive, Abuelito pushed his relations away with such force that one day it propelled him in the opposite direction—out of society, out of career, up to a second-floor limbo.

I don't have to look far to see how that force has had its effects on me. I am forged by family denials, fed by that long vine of history—a vine I'd one day be warned to examine. My great-grandfather was so ashamed to be an Arana that he disowned the entire extended family—a grave act for a Latin. My abuelito was so mortified by his father's shame that he drove himself into the rafters. My father, knowing none of this, was so bewildered by his father's quirkiness and his mother's long-suffering acceptance of it that he reached for another life altogether. As for me: I ended up so divided between the two sides of my hybrid family that I boomeranged with a burning curiosity. The dominos clacked around—effects spilling from one generation to another—until they clacked round in a circle. Until I found Julio César. Until the last chip hit the first.

~

DENIALS ISSUED FROM all quarters, not just from my family. Everyone rushed to wash their hands of any responsibility. The British and American investors in Julio César's company claimed they had nothing to do with the slavery, the importation of Barbadian overlords, the killing, the maiming, the scars.

Julio César, in turn, claimed that the blood of thirty thousand rain-forest Indians was certainly not on him. The horrors, if any, had been played out far from his desk. How could he be blamed for the excesses of deputies who worked far below him? He hadn't killed anybody. If he was responsible for anything, it was that he had brought Peru rubber glories, that he was defending the country's frontiers.

The denials worked to a degree. The case against Julio César Arana fizzled. A decade after the scandals broke in the gringo world, the jungle state of Loreto elected him senator and sent him to Lima to work to keep control of the Putumayo. My great-grandfather Pedro Pablo by then was mired in poor health. He had had to suffer the indignity of having his assets frozen. He had had to work hard to deny a business association. He had had to hear the news that Julio César was not only surviving the arsenals of a mean gringo justice, the man was advancing to the Peruvian senate, where Pedro Pablo himself proudly served. It was more than my great-grandfather could bear: He crashed down the family gate, lopped the tree off at the trunk, and insisted he had no relatives at all.

Pedro Pablo's enormous effort to rid himself of the stain eventually did him in. He died in the care of my abuelita, the vibrant young woman who had bought the lie willingly, who had forfeited all social ambition, who would live out her days with his brilliant and brooding son. For a while, Pedro Pablo's efforts succeeded. It seemed he had washed Julio César right out of the picture. The *cauchero* was not part of our lives. But he couldn't erase history.

History eventually pulled Julio César Arana under, as one might expect the freight of thirty thousand dead souls would do. He left the senate, watched Peru lose control of the Putumayo to the Colombian army, and spent the last twenty years of his life in a wretched tenement in Lima's Magdalena district, staring at walls, listening to the angry sea. His body grew emaciated, wraithlike, but God did not reach down to claim it. Over the years, it withered to a wisp.

Julio César died in 1953, neglected and destitute, never imagining that his son would make a quick bid for power a scant decade later. In 1960, Iquitos, that jungle capital with an itch for perversity, made Luis Arana its mayor. At some point during his tenure, a rumor started that the Mark of Arana had come back to claim even him: He was suspected of filching funds from the city coffers. One quiet morning in his gilded office, the mayor took a gun from his desk, lifted it to his temple, and blew out his brains.

MOTHERS

Madres

So THAT IS the burden of history that weighs upon the Aranas in the first half of the century. It is the burden that weighs on them still when, on August 6, 1945, just as Hiroshima disappears beneath a swiftly banking cloud, Jorge and Marie Arana land in the port of Callao. Mother is telling me the story of her arrival now, and I can see her old eyes grow deep green at the thought of that morning.

The two of them are standing on the deck of a homebound Argentine freighter, looking out at the swirling crowd. Mother's belly is large with my older sister, Vicki, her face chalked with anxiety. She holds on to my father as she searches the landing, scanning brown faces for features like his. *There!* yells Papi, but when she wheels around to see, she cannot tell what he's pointing at. A throng of strangers surges forward, waving arms at the floating steel.

The Aranas are there: Abuelito in his hat and cane, Abuelita in her waisted silk, all five of my father's siblings trussed up in their teatime best. When the young couple descends the gangplank,

Abuelita steps forward to reach for the gringa across the swell of her first grandchild. She greets her warmly, moves her firmly to one side, and flings herself hungrily on my father. It's perfectly natural—that show of partiality from a mother—but the message is unmistakable.

The house on Calle San Martin is another indication of how different Mother's life will be. It is walled off from the street, its front door at the top of an ornate staircase, its interior a seemingly endless warren of rooms. There's an atrium at its center; a chapel with a crucifix. The living rooms are dark with Victorian furniture and relics of a venerable past. Papi's five brothers and sisters—all adults by then—still live in this colonial town house: children minding their parents, South American style.

These rooms are for you and Jorge, says her mother-in-law, addressing her in the well-enunciated Spanish one reserves for a child. What is being shown her is my grandparents' own bedroom, with an extra room on the side.

They move in, set up a nursery. It is, at first, a pleasant task. Clearly, my father is loved beyond measure. His progeny will be received with all the honor that an eldest male's firstborn deserves. For Mother there's the immediate problem of language: the wall of incomprehensible chatter that rattles from dawn until dusk. Papi is sympathetic. He's lived through those puzzlements himself. But in the case of my mother, the social pressures are more acute: Here is a round pink foreigner with the verbal capacity of a backward child in a society that prizes, above everything, the turn of a graceful phrase.

Qué hiciste hoy, Marie? What did you do today? The family's eyes shift onto the gringa's face at the dinner table, and her head whirls with the little Spanish she knows. She wants to say that she organized her drawers.

Limpié mis cojones, she attempts, putting one vowel where another should be. I cleaned my balls. She wonders why they squirm in their chairs.

She's as spoiled as a princess, as scorned as a cretin, and before September is upon them she moves through the house like a rabbit through flames. Her husband is back at his desk in the Department of Public Works, and she is marooned, untongued, expatriated, alone.

Abuelito speaks English, as do some of the others, but he rarely appears, and besides, a clear proclamation has been made in the house: The only way she'll learn Spanish is if she's made to speak it, by everyone, all day. An exception is made the day the United States claims victory over the Japanese emperor, bringing the war to a close: They congratulate her in her own language. She excuses herself, ducks into the bedroom, sits on the bed, and cries.

VICTORIA IS BORN in Lima's Clínica Franco. My grandmother had expressed a preference for that hospital, where they allow long visits from the family, as Peruvians are accustomed to having. When Vicki enters this world, she enters it as a princess during the Conquista might have, with family courtiers in an adjoining room.

Abuelita sits by Mother's bedside, holds her hand, and as the contractions intensify, so do the festivities on the other side of the wall. The birth of an Arana Cisneros is no private affair. More like a family extravaganza. It's 1945, a decade before women's suffrage comes to Peru, and the principal duty of a woman is to bear and raise children. The responsibility of her relatives is to see that she gets it done. A child is the finest expression, the ultimate bond of an extended family. To that end, courtships need to be vetted, the union of two families consecrated, and when the fruit of that marriage drops, the family attends as if it's a party. It's as simple as that.

These things may make all the sense in the world to a

Peruvian mother, but to mine—an Anglo-American of free-spirited pioneer stock—they are more vocabulary she doesn't have. It doesn't occur to her that an act she considers private will be a spectacle for people she's only just met.

From the instant Vicki exits her mother's womb, she is family property. The Arana Cisneroses break out the champagne. Abuelita longs to hold her, teach my mother all she's learned about babies in having six of her own. Mother, on the other hand, is nervous: wary as a feline dam. In her mind, this child is not the cumulative handiwork of a complicated Peruvian family. It's her only blood relative in a bewildering land.

She digs in, marks her turf.

When Papi brings Mother back to my grandparents' bedroom, the struggle begins in earnest. The Aranas may not realize it. There's no reason for them to suspect a new calculus at work: They're in their own country, their own culture, their own home. But there's an American card in the game now. Mother, too, does not reason through differences. She only knows she wants what her instincts tell her she has every right to have: both hands on her infant child.

As days wear on, the tug-of-war becomes more evident. In the mornings, my grandmother asks for the child. Mother reluctantly hands her over. By week's end Abuelita delegates her daughters to carry the babe out to her. Mother's face twists into a snarl. By month's end, the household is sending in the squealing *ama: La señora de la casa is anxious! She wants the baby right now!*

My grandfather's sister, Tía Carmen, visits. She's a serious woman who fancies herself a writer but is, in my grandmother's view, a weird little crone with a meddlesome side.

That gringa is the very picture of sadness, Tía Carmen pipes up. *Her little face breaks my heart.*

One day, months into the ground battle, when Vicki is already cooing and crawling, Mother decides she's had enough. The women in the family are playing with the baby in the other room. Their laughter tinkles through corridors, brittle as mockery, skittering under the door like shards. When she hears it, she glowers into a corner where her maidservant huddles. The girl stares back at her, fighting the tears.

Qué pasa, Concepción? my mother asks.

Your eyes, señora. They make me want to cry.

That's the thing that begins it. Mother bangs out of the room, shuttles down the corridor, hell-bent for the laughter. She swings the door open and stands there, large, in the frame.

Le toca? Feeding time? Abuelita asks her, and the faces all turn up to see. She is a mammary gland, a biological necessity. That is all.

It's an account she recites over and over, like the bead of a penitent's rosary, like the point where a frayed string is broken: They have no gauge on her feelings. It's a family of strangers. Her child is Peruvian. And a gringa in this country always stands at the door.

She is old now. She sits at a wooden table my father has made for her in their sunny kitchen in Maryland, recounting a moment that is more than half a century, half a world away, and yet her voice is shaking with indignation. Her account involves far more than woman and mother-in-law. Whole cultures are in dispute. My gringa mother had assumed that her baby was something between her, her husband, and God. My abuelita had assumed that her grandchild was the first of a new generation, the next row in the family cloth, an offering to the family matriarch. Hers.

They say that motherhood everywhere is the same. That mothers give birth and mothers give milk, and up and down the animal kingdom real differences do not exist. I know it isn't so.

I once met a Mexican woman who returned to Monterrey with her three children after many years as a migrant laborer along the southeastern United States. She had picked apples, strawberries, tomatoes for years alongside her husband, borne him three healthy children, followed him wherever their hands were wanted. That she was a loving mother, loyal wife, was never questioned by anyone. Until one spring day, when she found herself on the steps of a school in Danville, Virginia, listening to some wattled gringo tell her that if she were a better mother she would understand that her fourteen-year-old boy shouldn't be so worried about the family coffers. He shouldn't be working the orchards after school, helping her harvest peaches, minding his baby sister. He should be on the soccer field, playing with boys his age. It was the American way, he said, and her boy was an American boy. *Lady, you must raise these children up. Make them walk. Be somebody.* The mother looked down and saw her son slumped on the school lawn, cradling his sister between his knees, tears sliding down his cheeks. He was a good boy, an honor to his mother, and the man was misunderstanding everything, twisting her motives and her family traditions into something they were not. She was not taking advantage of her son, exploiting him to pick a few more peaches, enslaving him to another child; she was teaching him a responsibility to something greater than himself. The next year, she and the children stayed in Mexico. Her husband hit the migrant road alone.

I tell this as if I agree with that mother. The truth is: I do not know. The principal may have been right. The Mexican woman may have been right. As I sit in my mother's kitchen in Maryland listening to her angry recollections of my grandmother, I do not know what to think about the two of them. I'm on my mother's side one minute. I'm on my abuelita's side the next. I am an ark of confusion.

In the Lima house, my mother issues a letter of grievances. She sits down with her worn dictionary and composes—in ridiculous Spanish—a declaration of her rights. *If I say something to you*, she writes to her mother-in-law, *I'm doing the best I can. I*

*say it as an American. Don't take my words at face value. They may
not say what I mean. Allow me to make mistakes.*

*As for the baby, she is Jorge's and mine. I want her with me at all
times. Not just for feedings. I am not a cow.*

I had always sensed the antagonism between my mother and
my grandmother. I knew there were variances in the ways they
lived, things they believed. But only in later accounts—told by
both of them—did I understand the gulf of their divide. My
grandmother was wary of my mother's independence, of her unwillingness to have her life pried into, of the utter rigidity in her
upper lip. My mother was caught off guard by the family, surprised to find it commandeered by a matriarch, taken aback by
her rein on so many lives. Abuelita drew her clan with a magical
charisma, funneling their energy toward her, deep into the sanc-
tum of that hearth. Not out, not away, not in the typical vector of
a Yank.

Mother's list of grievances is received like a low-grade detona-
tion. Abuelita shows it to others, then folds it into a drawer. She
has tried to make the gringa feel welcome: She has given up her
bedroom, moved her estimable husband into a side room, given
the woman advice on her disastrous ways: *For God's sake*, hijita, *I
don't care what you did during the war in Boston. You can't slather
your calves with makeup and go out bare-legged in Peru. People
will assume you're something you're not.*

She has, above all, tried to initiate her into the art of motherhood. She has given the gringa everything and has had it flung
back in a coolly penned note.

The letter begins a standoff Peruvians call *pleito*: that inching
toward fury, that lingering grudge to the grave. There's no word
for it in English. It's more than a simple resentment, less than an
all-out war. It's coal fire beneath a prairie, hell under the vista.
You come, you go, you chat in the *sala*—the exterior looks perfectly normal—but a fire is reaming your gut.

Mother asks that dinners be sent to her room, sends kind regards through her maid. Abuelita sews dresses for Vicki, sets them out for everyone to see. But unless etiquette demands it, the two do not talk at all. They bristle, walk wide arcs around each other, scowl from behind beatific smiles.

I can't play this charade much longer, says my mother to my father one night. *I can't fake it like she can.*

It's late July. They've been there for almost a year.

My mother doesn't fake anything, my father responds. *She's an honorable woman.*

A cable tightens. She's expressed pique. So has he. There are more words along these lines. Her anger escalates. So does his. She is barefoot, in nightclothes, in no condition to leave their room, but she snatches Vicki and heads for the door. *Where on earth do you think you're going?* he says, the first time he's ever used that tone with her.

Out, she says. *The hell out.* Parrying with a new tone of her own.

Out. The direction she knows best. As in *out* for all those other Americans like her, who reach thresholds, vault fences, hurl themselves out, out, out, in a centripetal rush away.

She bolts down the stairs with the baby (*thwap, thwap, thwap*) on pink feet, and my father follows. Past his parents' door, past the eyes of his mother's ancestors peering from canvases, trammeled to walls. She opens the front door and hesitates in the frame; the baby looks back at him, rubs her eyes under a curl of golden hair. He rushes up, spins his wife around by her shoulders, and slaps her across the face.

When she tells me this part, she says, *He spun me around by the shoulders.* When he tells it to me later, the story acquires a detail—the smack on the head. He is full of old anger about it. Not against her, not even against himself, but against the wavering in the bridgework, the tic in the colonnades. I doddle my head at the both of them. *I know what you mean*, I say.

He manages to get her back up to their room again. He makes her some promises, vows the situation will change. The next day he secures an invitation from prim Tía Carmen. *I can see what you're going through, Jorge,* she tells him. *Look, I spend so much time on my hacienda. Why don't you move into my Lima house?*

Mother goes about my grandparents' rooms quietly, retrieving her things: a toy here, a teacup there. Abuelita is heard intoning from another room, *La gente tiene boca para hablar!* Mouths are for speaking! But neither says a word.

The next night, my father inaugurates a protest all his own: He staggers in well after midnight. High as a spire.

THE DIFFERENCE BETWEEN my mother and my grand-mother—I know it now after all these years—was not one be-tween woman and woman. It was the difference between an Anglo's daughter and the mother of a Latin male. It was a differ-ence between men and men.

The mother of a Latin male is the mother of a Latin male no matter what her class or education. The Mexican migrant worker was not about to surrender her boy to some clutch of strangers from whom he would learn alien notions of bonding and inde-pendence. No. A Latin *macho* must be gradually nurtured, sedu-lously cultivated, carefully groomed. It doesn't fall to the father or some other *hombre* to shape him, as it does in Danville, Virginia, where, in all likelihood, that well-meaning gringo prin-cipal is still shooing boys onto a playing field to learn a thing or two from a man. In the *mundo Latino,* the task falls to the mother.

Latin man. Latin lover. The Anglo world doesn't have a clue. Ask a North American to imagine the Latin lover, and she will conjure a priapic lothario, an inexhaustible inamorato with the brain of a bullock. She will imagine—because this is the northern equivalent—a man nudged to those arduous heights by other men like him, a kind of clubby, winking acceptance of goatishness passed down from grandfather to father to son.

Ask any Latin woman who has walked down an *avenida* in Buenos Aires or a dusty *barriada* on the outskirts of Caracas, and she will tell you a Latin man doesn't need a gaggle of like-minded males around to make a *piropo* to a woman. A construction worker on the streets of Lima will follow her for blocks, sing in her ear, tell her how her face is breaking his heart. He doesn't sit by the side of the road, whistle from a distance, make catcalls in a chorus.

In its proper Latin context, a Latin woman does not begrudge a man his street flirtations. They are inevitable, harmless, easily ignored—in ways, reassuring. Love, seduction, *amor proprio*: these things are taught to men by women in Latin America. It is the mothers who do the teaching. And, in the tutelage, a fabric is maintained.

The myth of the Latin man is all about lovemaking. About libido. In truth, there are subtler motivations at work. Latin men worship women. They are trained to. Mothers admit sons to secrets, pamper them, teach them to cherish babies, prize beauty, pray to the madonna, wear perfume. A love of the feminine is a mother's legacy to her son. Boys learn to use it. Fathers understand its importance. A Latino is admired for revering his mother. He is sent from mother to wife, strutting, preening, adored. He is allowed vanities few men on this earth enjoy. But a bargain is struck in the process: A man is bound fast by women, tied back to family, held tight by obligation. It is the core of the Latin soul.

So it was in my family. Men were coddled, their petty narcissisms encouraged. My grandmother had learned it from her mother, had taught it to her daughters, and had expected an orderly transition of it through the ranks. In this, her husband had

been an unexpected quotient: a Latin man who, for some un-
known reason, had had the starch bled out of him, who no
longer pranced and preened as custom required. My grandmother may have understood him; she may have learned to toler-
ate him. But there was no way she could have predicted him.
His own father had been the very model of a Latin male.

After the death of his wife, my great-grandfather Pedro Pablo
Arana lived in the Hotel Bolívar and took his meals at the exclusive
Club Nacional for eighteen years, from retirement until his own
death in 1926. Even after the shock of the Casa Arana disclosures,
he was still a peacock of a man, regal in his London finery, stiff shirts
buttressing his airs. He was high-handed, haughty, skilled in the art
of oratory, a master at stonewalling inquiries. But in old age, he
made it a point to pay attention to his descendants. He began visiting his son's house, throwing my grandfather's household into a
nervous bustle, making my grandmother quake. When he arrived on
the first of these visits, he brought an ancient crystal goblet laced
with silver filigree and asked my grandmother to serve him a *refresco*
in it. Every Sunday thereafter, at eleven in the morning, the senator
would appear, staying only long enough to consume one beer from
his glass and confer with his son about the state of the republic, the
follies of the president, and the future of his mercury mines, the
Santa Barbara deposits in the highlands of Huancavelica.

One day, he arrived before the appointed hour, and my
abuelita found herself waving him in early, taking his hat and
cane. Her babies were mewling in the next room and her hair
was in disarray. My grandfather pulled on his waistcoat, secured
his spats, smoothed his mustache, and rushed out to meet his father. Abuelita went off to fetch the *señor* his beer, unwilling to
entrust the precious chalice to less-cautious hands. But she was
harried that day, made nervous by her father-in-law's hyperpunc-
tuality and the fuss in the other room. She opened the doors of
the *aparador* and reached up for the glass. It wobbled back from

her fingers, skipped off the edge of the shelf, and crashed to the floor, scattering into a hundred bits of twisted silver. When the woman realized that she had destroyed the old man's goblet, she wept and shook but pulled herself together, brought out an ordinary flagon, and poured her father-in-law a beer. She carried it out on a silver tray.

Ah, the guest said, lifting it to his lips. *Gracias.* He made no further remark. He continued his pontifications to his son, and she sighed and excused herself to see about the children. When he finished the last of his *cerveza,* he set down the provisional glass, rose, wished them farewell, and left. But because his chalice had been shattered, his Sunday covenant broke, too. He never came back again.

No one was much surprised.

There were other men as fearsome as Pedro Pablo Arana in the family, but if we knew about them they were on my grandmother's side, in the Cisneros line. Whereas Arana seemed to have materialized from nowhere, with no forebears, no ancients, the female side—the Cisneros tree—flourished like an overgrown banyan, its roots deep into medieval Spain.

The male ancestor I found most captivating was Joaquín Rubín de Celis de la Lastra, my abuelita's great-grandfather, who had fought for the Spanish crown at the decisive Battle of Ayacucho, the bloody struggle that won Peru's independence on December 9, 1824. A yellowed cameo still sits on my grandparents' mantelpiece, and in it, the tiny countenance of that birdlike warrior. His daughter's face stares from the opposite wall, smiling wanly as she draws a diaphanous shawl over one shoulder. She and her father had never met in real life, and that fact fills the room with ineffable sadness. Rubín de Celis had been the first Spanish general to charge against the rebel forces at Ayacucho, and the first among generals to fall. When he'd mounted his steed to ride into that bloody struggle, his wife had been pregnant with the dark-haired beauty on the wall.

That daughter was Trinidad Rubin de Celis. She married a Cisneros. Her son Manuel Cisneros—the high treasurer of the province of La Libertad—married one, too. That is to say, a cousin married a cousin. Abuelita was their child.

Not all Cisneros women were defined by the males of the family. One bright Cisneros spinster with a mind of her own fell in love with a Spanish priest, Padre Benjamín. He was seen coming and going from her house in Huánuco. Before long, the spinster's house rang with the cries of baby boys, and they all had the open, intelligent forehead of her robed visitor. They were given her name, but everyone knew they were sons of the *padre*. The fact was whispered in salons and bruited about on the street. All the same, the priest went on with his mission and the babies continued to thrive. Eventually, the wide-browed youngsters produced the brilliant, silver-tongued Cisneroses of Peru: the poet Antonio, the orator Manuel. The gossip began to seem vapid, ridiculous, beside the point. So what if the priest had turned out to have a little *macho* blood in his veins? There were mortal appetites few of Eve's children could control. Genius was the thing. Could a union that forged it be wrong? These Cisneros men were extraordinary, superior, far better than the rest of the clan. So the rumors about them became irksome, easily quashed.

There was more than one way to be a Latin male.

HOW COULD MY mother know, when she pledged her love to my father on the Fenway, that she would be dropped into the heart of a *familia* where what was wanted of her was not her American stock in trade—independence—but a clear understanding of three things: the primacy of a Peruvian family, a young wife's role in it, and the dominion of the Latin male?

Confused, angry, friendless, as soon as she heard about Tía Carmen's offer, she could hardly wait to leave my grandparents' house. When Mother, Papi, and Vicki finally moved into Carmen's spacious house on Avenida Mariátegui on the other side of Lima, they had all the comforts of an established home. There was Mother's maid, Concepción, a sweet-natured mountain girl, to assist with the concerns of an active baby; the furniture inherited from my haughty great-grandfather; the appurtenances of a good city life.

Independence remained my mother's forte. She took Italian lessons, studied Russian, memorized poetry, read philosophy with the fervor of a hermit sage. She had not brought her violin with her to Peru. In some strange unwillingness to transport all of herself to her husband's country, she had left behind the one thing she had always professed to love most: her music.

When Tía Carmen would return to Lima from the estate she had inherited from Pedro Pablo Arana in Huancavelica, the rest of the family came to visit. This would happen in the afternoons, while Papi was still at work. During these visits, my mother retired to a back room and listened to her husband's family through the walls. Two years went by like this, and Abuelita and Mother did not speak, the *pleito* was so thick between them.

Papi saw his parents, caroused with friends into morning, did as he pleased in the city of his birth, and the seeds of a compromise were sown. Mother retained her distance, wandered Lima on her own terms, learned its language and customs, and sealed a bond with her firstborn that has fastened them to this day.

Old Tía Carmen came and went less and less often. She stayed up in the hills, on the hacienda where her mother had hidden away. Eventually, she married an ill-tempered fortune hunter with expensive tastes and a greedy heart. With his fangs deep into her inheritance, he was drawing out all the rest of her: health, strength, the vitality of her remaining days.

Mother and Papi continued to live in Tía Carmen's languid corner of Lima, where the streets were lined with shade trees, bougainvillea spilled from rooftops, and fog smelled of jasmine. There was a grocer nearby, and a coffee shop. Mornings brought a procession of vendors: the knife grinder with his high, sad whistle, the bread man with gold-rimmed teeth, the fruit ladies with their brightly striped skirts and braids. In the afternoons, a russet-faced girl hawked tamales. There was a sleepy aspect to this life. One might have assumed there was peace of a kind.

But the truth was a different story. Just as the world slid into its version of a *pleito* and the Cold War bit in, Mother began greeting the mornings with panic. She was pregnant again. She had never been one to look back, but she was thirty-four, about to be a mother for the second time, and her independence had turned into bewilderment. She felt forsaken, alone. At twenty-nine, Papi had left the bridge-building position at the Department of Public Works. He was working three jobs to meet the high cost of living: as rookie engineer for the American company of W. R. Grace, as greenhorn professor at the Colegio de Ingenieros, and as an instructor at the Academy of Police. He had no time to dote on her.

A letter to her parents struck a plaintive note. *I'm expecting another child,* she wrote, *and am dreading the humiliations of another public birth in this city. I'm walking the streets like a banshee. All I can think of is you.*

In the spring of 1948, when the answer to that letter came, for the first time in two and a half years my father noticed the postmark. It was not from Seattle. It was from Rawlins, Wyoming. He swallowed hard, said nothing. She opened the envelope, drew out the contents: Two tickets home. Two one-way passages.

For three months, Mother and Vicki were gone. The first two

months were spent awaiting the birth; the third, recovering from its ordeal.

Mother's second child entered this world not like a descendant of *la Conquista*—crown first, courtiers all about—but like a ferret with its teeth in her entrails. It was a difficult birth, breech. In Lima, when Papi received the telegram about his boy, he celebrated many times over, with multiple corks on the fly.

It would be different if I were with Jorge's family now, Mother said to her mother one afternoon when the two of them were alone. *You can't imagine how difficult his mother is.*

Yes, dear? her own mother said simply, tugging spectacles down her nose.

She kept taking Vicki away from me, making me feel as if I were some barn animal. She doesn't like me. I don't know why. She's not like any mother I've ever known. More like a jealous girlfriend. I think she'd be happy to drive me out and get her son back in her clutches again.

Aw, come on, said my grandfather, walking in from the other room.

Darling, said my grandmother to him, *listen to her. Hear what she has to say.*

No. I'm not listening to another word. Takey, he said to my mother, using the name he had called her since infancy, *that woman is related to you now.* He nodded toward the children. *She is part of your life.*

Later that week, Mother boarded the plane to Lima with three-year-old Vicki clutching her skirt. A violin nestled in one arm, a male infant in the other.

GODS AND SHAMANS

Dioses y Brujas

THERE'S MORE TO this world than it tells us. I've always known it. I'm haunted by an unseen dimension in which everything has roots, logic, and reasons—a tie to another point in time. I believe this with a child's certainty: That there are demons and angels. That there is kismet. That stars command us. That a past we may never have heard of can poison a future we cannot foresee. That we are travelers on an ancient spool, iterations that trundle around again—since time immemorial—from bone to dust to bone.

Connections are everywhere, if I can track them. Here's one: A geological force called "man" fashions a rocket from minerals on the side of a hill. There is iron, a little nickel, a bit of potassium, some zinc. The minerals are the residue of his ancestors' bones. He shoots them skyward, opens a hole in the stratosphere, and hundreds of years later the dust of his forefathers—with its ancient loves and antipathies—rains down on his descendants. They don't see it, they don't know it. But it sifts gently over them; it settles.

As a child I saw the obvious parallels: Jesus and sun gods, witches and Buddhas. What was Jesus if not *inti*, the Inca thresher of earthly light? What was a witch if not hunger, a longing for order, a hand in the dark? What were the New Testament, the Torah, the Koran, the Upanishads if not guiding legends, *historias* to lead us through? Even Gautama Buddha, in his infinite wisdom—in the shade of a tree, on another side of time—practiced the magic of the Inca: Take in the evil, shoot it into a stone. Breathe it in, breathe it out. Until enlightenment comes.

I had equations for everything. If my grandfather was not descending the staircase, it was because a force was pulling him up. If I was drawn to a *loco*, it was because madness tinged my blood. If I could feel both gringa and Peruvian, it was because I juggled two brains in my head. If the image of my mother and a stranger was burned into memory, my mind was trying to show me something my eyes couldn't see. The possibilities of connections were legion, and they set me to staring at ceilings with plans. There were inheritances to track. Ramifications to hunt. Vines to follow.

Little wonder that for the rest of my life I have studied the string that ties my parents together and shackles them back to their pasts. I want reasons for what drew them together, for turns they took from the roads they'd known. As a teenager, I was lured by their story in the way any child would be. But in the years of hearing and rehearing it, I have seen that it holds more than logic: There is a prayer in its recitation, and a lesson at the end of the prayer.

WHEN MOTHER RETURNED to Lima with her three precious charges—Vicki, George, and her violin—she found Papi living with a monkey and an anteater. They were occupying the roof of the Avenida Mariátegui house, clambering down the stairs from time to time to scare the maid, Concepción, or to send one of my father's drinking buddies howling out the door in a hallucinatory rant. The monkey was dun brown, tall as a seven-year-old, with beady black eyes and a bark like the squeak of a hinge. The anteater was an aging caudillo, surveying the rooftops of Lima with an attitude, flicking his tongue from his snout.

It had taken no more than a month for a manly mayhem to overtake Tía Carmen's place. A gathering spot for Papi's companions—his engineering students from the Colegio, police initiates from the academy, and solitary gringos from W. R. Grace—the house had become more drinking establishment than home, more fraternity than the sleepy colonial address my mother had left behind.

Papi's uncle, Tío Salvador Mariátegui, a tall, gloriously whiskered, bemedaled naval *comandante*, had brought the monkey and anteater from one of his forays into the Amazon. It was said that he had conquered the tributaries of that great river as thoroughly as he had the hairs of his extravagant mustache, a magnificent handlebar that swooped out and back with rococo flourish. Less than a decade later, in 1958, Tío Salvador would pack up three hundred years of his ancestors' armor, pin innumerable medals onto his admiral's uniform, and set out to become emperor of Andorra, a tiny principality in the east Pyrenees. But for now, it was jungle animals he ruled. The unlikely twosome he'd brought onboard the ship had entertained the sailors on the long trip down the Ucayali; Tío Salvador's plan was to truck them up to his mountain house in Chaclacayo, where he imagined they would make an even more entertaining sight in his garden, in the company of his huffy peacocks. When it was clear he wouldn't have time to execute the whole plan, he decided to deposit the monkey and anteater at least part of the way there, in Lima, with my father. Promising to return for them, Tío Salvador disappeared up the Ucayali again.

The duo was irking the neighbors, drawing cold sweat from Concepción, but richly amusing Papi. Every time he stepped onto the rooftop and saw their absurd profiles, he'd throw back his head and roar. Day after day, as he tells it, he pulled on his forelock and listened to reports from Concepción: *The grocer across the street is complaining, señor. He says that the one with the long nose hangs out over the roofwork and scares away clients. But that isn't all, Don Jorge. The lady next door says she doesn't dare look out her own window, because if she sets eyes on the monkey, her unborn will come out ugly as sin.*

Muy bien, *Concepción,* my father responded. *Tell the grocer he's right, the anteater probably does scare his clients, but only those of the six-legged kind. His store is so full of* cucarachas, *the man should be paying me a fee. Tell the pregnant* señora *to take a good look at her husband. The monkey won't make one bit of difference. Her baby's already a freak.*

Somewhere during all of this, Mother walked in. It was the first of a lifetime of reconciliations: I have seen so many by now. It starts with an arch departure, a certainty that their life together is too much to handle; then come the months with my parents in different places, gazing silently from windows; a letter; a call; a telegram; and finally, a joy-filled embrace. My father swept his baby boy into his arms. The animals swung their nasal protuberances in the air. Vicki laughed.

Within a few days, Mother was on the telephone to Abuelita. *Rosa,* she said, *come meet your grandson.* My grandmother thanked her. She arrived with her daughters and sat in the *sala* awhile.

It was a checked conversation, in the clipped spirit of that uncertain time. Abuelita held George, cooed over him, but the occasion was only marginally festive. Mother served gringo-style hors d'oeuvres with melba toast, mint jelly, Philadelphia cream cheese. The family nibbled politely, remarked on the baby's handsomeness, then excused itself to go.

It was an era of paradox, even if no one was saying so. There was a tiny man-baby in the cradle, but there were also two beasts on the roof. Armed soldiers were posted on street corners, but the country was on the verge of an economic boom. My parents' marriage had nearly foundered, but it had also been blessed by a second child. Abuelita had paid Mother a visit, and stepped smartly out of her way. The bridge had tottered under the burdens, and settled itself with a sigh.

The monkey and the anteater moved on to join the peacocks in Chaclacayo. Tía Carmen's house bustled with our little family again. George grew round, *bien papeado*. And the neighbors admitted it was good to have the gringa back in town.

When Mother became pregnant with me the following year, Papi announced the most surprising shift of all. Once I was born, we were to leave Lima. He'd been offered a big job in Cartavio, he told her. In a hacienda owned by the gringos, where she was bound to feel more at home.

In March of 1950, my family picked up and headed north to Cartavio. Awaiting us there was the childhood of my memory: the garden below my window, the smell of burnt sugar, the yellow of floripondio, the animals with eyes at half-mast, the stones, the bones, the dust. There, too, were the *apus*—gods watching us from the mountains—and three shamans who would plow grooves into my heart: El Gringo, a witch, and Antonio.

BY THE TIME I was four, I was well-versed in the legends of the *pishtacos*. Why would I doubt that ghosts existed, when there were so many about? Our *amas* had taught us about the spirits that circled above us, howling when winds were strong, screeching when seas got rough. So that when El Gringo came hobbling around the corner one day, I never doubted that he was *un vivo muerto*, one of the living dead, and that he had the power to curse us. So that when I saw the old woman, the *bruja*, for the first time, I knew that she had come to speak to me.

Her eyes told us she was a witch. They were milky with too much seeing, marbled by sun, clacking around in her head as she wound through the streets of the hacienda, hawking fruit. When the *bruja* saw our faces behind the fence, she would stop, squint like a lizard, and flick her tongue against two yellow protrusions—more tusks than teeth—that drifted in the rolling sea of her mouth. *Ahí*, she would grunt. There you are. *Los duendes.* The dwarves. And George and I would step out and look in her face.

This was Cartavio. An oasis of cement, iron, and sugar in the long, gray sandlot of Peruvian coast. For children of privilege no less than for children of the poor in backwater towns like Cartavio, life was a dusty affair—an endless shuffle through dirt, punctuated by rapture and calamity, and encounters such as this, with mango-toting witches in multicolored skirts.

We emerged from behind my father's wall one day, my brother and I—now five and four—to find the neighborhood children trotting to her cart. There was Billy, the big Scots boy with the dazzling smile; Carlitos, the tiny, pinched son of the factory's accountant; Margarita, the flat-faced daughter of the cook across the street. We hurried out, knowing that the rush to the *bruja's* cart could mean only one thing: The witch was reading futures today.

By the time we reached her, she was addressing Billy, who, at eight, was almost as tall as she was. He was sober, grimmouthed, standing there with his chin thrust out, a pointed promontory in a freckled field.

"Come, gringo," she told him, "hold my braids while I see into tomorrow. One in your left hand, *papito*, one in your right. Good."

For the next few moments, Billy looked himself, a simple boy in a noonday game. He took the braids and his face relaxed, so that for a fleeting second he looked like his sweet-eyed mum, the gentle Scots lady who lived next door. Then suddenly it was as if a charge was shooting through him. His back arched. The *bruja's* braids undulated like snakes. Carlitos shimmied back into Margarita at the sight of them, but the girl pushed him away and stood erect, her eyes wide, mouth in a tight, thin line. Billy, too, seemed frozen from head to toe; only his arms moved tortuously, in waves that appeared to issue from the witch's hair. George and I shifted from foot to foot, turning nervously and searching each other's face to see who would cut and run. But we'd witnessed these things before, and though I could see George's face furrowed with worry, I could also see determination in his stance. He stood his ground in line. Quickly, I squirmed in behind.

"Ya, ya," the *bruja* said to Billy, her voice high and silky as a little girl's. "You have the face of a leopard, *papo*. Eyes of a puma. Heart of a bird. The spotted face will never change. The other two you yourself must change. See like the bird, gringito. Make your heart beat like a puma's. You must work at this. Work."

Billy dropped the braids, let out a grunt, and stumbled back against George. I took the big boy's wrist and pulled him behind me. He wafted back like a feather.

George stepped forward and grabbed the woman's braids. Her eyes focused and then squeezed shut. Her chin was still as granite. George did not move.

After a while, her lips began to pulse as she sucked on her delicately moored teeth. She ceased to look like a witch, more like a rag doll, her braids jutting comically from behind.

"Come another day, boy," she said at last, shaking her head. "I see night, I see stars, I see a path. But nothing more. The spirits in you are sleeping. We must not wake them now."

I loved George with every bone in me. He had a noble brow,

straight and clean, and hazel eyes that squinted up with a golden glow. His lips were full and rosy, pouting from his face like guavas. He was as agile and impish as I was lumpish and slow. He'd walk on garden walls like a trapeze artist; swing bananas from his pockets as if they were pistols; lob balloons full of water from a second-floor window. All I could do, in my fat little self, was look on his antics and giggle. If I could have had but one wish from the *bruja*, I would have asked her to make me like him. Seeing him now, disoriented and fortuneless, I could feel my heart slide through my chest.

"Marisi! Georgie!" I heard a woman's voice call out from our garden. It was Claudia, the cook; she was circling the house looking for us. Anxiously, I stepped forward and took the heavy hair. The witch's eyes were mantled with clouds, and I wondered if she could even see me. But she wasted no time in telling me what she saw.

"A root is stirring under your house," she whispered. "It is thick and black, with branches that grow while the condor sleeps. You will think the leaves pretty. You will pay it no heed. You will wake every day like the condor and fly. But, *chica*, someday that vine will reach your window. It will fly inside and grab you by the throat. Prepare yourself."

For days after that, the *bruja's* words played in my head. What could they mean? A *vine*? Under my *house*? The image crept into my dreams. I found myself reaching for my neck in alarm. I imagined black snakes, as fat and tense as a witch's braid, making their way up our pristine walls in the cover of dark, reappearing each night infinitesimally longer, imperceptibly thicker. Up, with no one believing it but me. Up, with everyone draped on their beds in slumber. Up, and there, before an open window, the sorry wretch of a girl, clenching the covers, gaping at shadows, fighting off sleep to keep the thing back.

Eventually, I had to tell. My mother seemed to take the news in stride. She listened thoughtfully to what I had to say, opening her eyes wide to ingest every word. None of this is true, she told me quietly, after all of it was out. None of it. No such thing will ever happen to you.

But that night I heard her pace my parents' bedroom and shout the whole thing out to my father. *These people* this! she said. *Those people* that! *Those people* were demented, sick, obsessed. Wasn't it enough to pass their *brujerías* on to one another? Why did they have to go around poisoning her children as well? Mother had sent my big sister's *ama* packing some months before when Vicki had recounted some of the stories the young woman had been spinning. Mother reminded my father of that now. "You remember what she was telling Vicki? That spirits of the dead crawl through the earth! That they enter the trunks of trees! That they slither through branches to grab at the living! She was saying it to our little girl!"

"Ah, *bueno*," my father responded, plumping the pillow and readying himself for sleep. "You fired that *ama*, all right, but you can't very well fire a street vendor."

"We'll see about that," my mother said, with a voice that made me shrink from the keyhole and slink to my bed in dismay. Getting rid of the witch wouldn't help me at all. Not at all. What I needed was someone to *get rid of the vine*.

The next morning, I slipped into the garden and scoured the perimeter of the house for anything that looked like a creeper. Pretty or not, I pulled it up, tore it to pieces, and threw it onto a wheelbarrow. George helped me, giving long opinions on whether or not a flower or a weed might pose a danger. Our house stood on concrete stilts, giving us good opportunity to crawl beneath and check the situation thoroughly. Apart from candy wrappers we had put there ourselves, there was nothing suspicious. Certainly nothing headed for my window.

At noon, Mother emerged from the house, walked resolutely

through the gate, and headed for the witch herself. George and I lurked behind the side walls, peeking through the gate to see our mother's blond head bob up and down in a rich display of anger. The neighborhood cooks and gardeners shuffled out to listen to the gringa speak Spanish: *"No mas brujería, m'entyenday?"* she said, wagging a forefinger. Next to her willowy heights, the witch looked small and harmless. "Take your fruit away," my mother said with finality. "We will not buy from you again." The witch lowered her head and stared at the ground. Her lower lip hung down and her teeth moved in and out, in and out. But when my mother spun around and marched back to the house, the witch's eyes clacked around again like dull balls in a pinball arcade. "Mango!" she screeched, finding our faces in the iron gridwork. *"Tráeme la boca!* Bring me that mouth! *Hay mango!"*

"Watch," I said to George, as we stumbled away. "This will only make it worse."

LOOKING BACK, I see that if I had a system of beliefs as a child this was it: the *bruja*, the *loco*, the look in any number of *amas'* eyes when they spoke about the dead reaching for us with long, green fingers. I do not remember attending church. If priests were disseminating the word of God—and there was every evidence that they were there in Cartavio, scurrying from barrio to barrio in long brown robes—those men were not speaking to us. If Mother was telling us stories of Moses and Jesus— and most assuredly she was, judging by the little booklets that still sit on my shelf, colored in by my childish hand—those men were not speaking to my soul.

I cannot speak for George, whose spirit has always been greater than mine. I only had to look at him to understand what I should be feeling about a wounded animal, a beggar, a stranger at the gate. I cannot speak for Vicki, whose brain has always been better furnished than mine. I only had to ask her to tell me more about the *pishtacos* to hear long disquisitions about how it was all poppycock, the unfounded ravings of ignorant minds. But for me, the Indian *leyendas* were religion. They were my church, my commandments, my faith. I worried them in the way my Lima aunts fingered their rosaries. I knew that my mother disapproved of those tales, and yet I suspected that, as with much she appeared not to know about the Peruvian world around me, this was simply a language she did not understand.

The *bruja*'s warning about the vine shot through me with all the urgency of a Virginal sighting at Fatima. There was a fat black root under my house and someday it would wring my throat. The admonition was far more vivid than any litany of saints my Catholic father could recite for me or any hymn about rocks my Protestant mother could sing. It would be a long time before I could laugh at the *bruja*'s warning. I was convinced I'd find the vine at my window. I was sure I'd look up one night and watch it twitch its little black head and fly in at me. I may have learned to laugh at the *bruja*'s words but, to this day, I cannot stand to have anything rest on my neck.

THE ONE WHO taught me how to use Peru's *leyendas* was Antonio. He was the most beautiful man I'd ever seen, eighteen years old, one of seven servants in our house. From the moment my conscious world had other people in it, Antonio was the one I wanted to look at, be with, know. He was tall for an indigenous Peruvian, high-browed, straight-necked, with skin the color of cinnamon bark. His forearms and shoulders were hard from years of heavy lifting. Since twelve, he had taken odd jobs in the factory and the hacienda: heaving cane, lifting vats, packing paper, working in the houses of the rich.

He didn't have the pocked face of a cane-cutter: no scars

digging into his nose and cheeks, no welts inflicted by high cane when a field-worker's machete slashes into the *corte* and angry stalks spring back like thorned swords. Antonio's face was smooth. His eyes, black as a monkey's. Ringing the straight, flat line of his mouth was a high ridge—almost purple—that I loved to look at, longed to trace with my finger, imagined from the window of my room whenever I heard him talking to our *mayordomo*, Flavio, or laughing with Claudia, the cook. His mouth was like a wale on ripe fruit.

But the thing I most loved about Antonio was the way he talked to me—as if I was someone worth talking to—and the way he listened. No matter how busy he was, no matter how many chores my mother gave him, he always had time for me, spinning about when he heard my voice squeak, "Antonio! *Espérame!* I have something to ask you!"

I asked him trivialities, concocted to allow me to cast my eyes up at him, stare at the trickle of sweat on his chest, ponder the contours of his face.

From the day Flavio had brought him to the house and introduced him as his nephew, my mother had singled him out as a bright young man. "That boy is smart," she would say, looking down at him from my window. "He has a future, and a mind for something better than this garden." I would watch her scratch her head and think what she might do for him: Teach him how to converse in English, do sums? Read to him from Van Loon's histories or Plutarch's *Lives,* as she did for us? Just as long as he doesn't go far, I'd pray. As long as he stays right there, by the window.

I loved him in the extravagant way children love grown-ups of the opposite sex. It is a need born early, our hunger for romance. We love our uncles because they are not our fathers, because they are familiar enough but essentially strangers: free, unpredictable, wild. We love our mother's friends because they have pretty faces, because their smiles invite us to, because their eyes seek us out whenever we enter a room. I loved Antonio because he was handsome; because he was good; because he appeared to love me back; because, when I considered the way he turned to look at this midge of a human being, when I saw the light in his eyes, when he put down his tools to pay attention, I knew that I was his; and that fact made him fully and incontrovertibly mine.

It was Antonio, as I say, who taught me most about the *leyendas*. But it hadn't started out that way. I had been his teacher first.

Sometime in my fifth year, during an endless afternoon while Papi was at the factory and Mother helped George and Vicki scribble words into notebooks, I skirted the kitchen and wandered back toward the animal pens. Antonio was there, cleaning out cages and sweeping out dung.

"Can I watch you, Antonio," I asked, "while you work?"

"*Sí, sí,*" he said, wiping his brow with his sleeve and turning a crate over for me to sit on. "But you must pay the price of admission." He put a finger to his chin. "Let's see," he said. He was sloe-eyed, tousle-haired, and the dirt on his face looked yellow. "I know what you can do, Marisi. Tell me a story." I frowned, thinking he was making fun of me. But his open-hearted smile told me he was not.

I sat on the crate, contemplated my white shoes, and tugged my cotton dress over my knees. On that day, I began the ritual that taught me everything. As Antonio heaved cages, pulled weeds, chased a renegade chicken, or wielded a wire broom, I'd repeat Greek myths Mother had told us at bedtime. I began, appropriately enough, with one about gardens: How Hades had burst through the earth into Persephone's garden, to drag the girl down into hell. I told him about Zeus's infidelities: How he'd turned a beautiful lover into a cow to avoid his wife's wrath.

Antonio chuckled at that, his white teeth glinting in the sun. "You have *chicas*, Antonio?" I asked him.

"*Ay, sí,*" he said, and shrugged. "But no jealous wife." He threw back his head and laughed.

Mother's face appeared at some point in the course of that afternoon, and I could see by her expression that she liked what I was doing. "Teaching is the highest form of learning," she told me later. And she told the other servants she approved.

"Where are you going, Marisi?" Claudia would ask shrilly from her perch in the kitchen as I trudged toward the servants' quarters out back, a place she knew I was not supposed to go. She was peeling potatoes, and Flavio bustled in and out, carting the day's dishes from the *aparador*. "To see Antonio," I'd say, as if I were the queen and he were my exchequer. "I'm telling *historias*. It's storytime."

I pretended to be Aesop one day, as Antonio raked the beds that lined the garden walk. I told him the one about the bird with the cheese. Then about the lion, the teeth, and the maiden. Last, with all the flourish of a rum-drunk *soltero*, I spun him the one about the fox and the crane. When I got to the part about the thirsty fox peering down the neck of the crane's pitcher, unable to reach the drink, Antonio looked up from his knees and shook a muddy finger at me.

"*Oye, chica!* That would never happen in Peru," he said. "A crane in Peru would know better than to do that to the fox. You know what happens to the thirsty, eh? You know about El Aya Uma?" A clod of dirt dropped from his hand.

I didn't know many *leyendas* at that point, but I knew about El Aya Uma. From quick, whispered accounts by my *ama*, from Vicki's long-winded disapprovals, from any number of frightened conversations with George. I knew all I needed to know.

Andean legend has it that if a man is allowed to go to sleep thirsty, come midnight his head will leap off his body and run out the door. Possessed by El Aya Uma, "The Thirsty One," the head will hop into the night—*tac pum, tac pum, tac pum*—out to the open road—*tac pum*—in search of anything to wet its throat. If the head encounters a traveler, it will chase him down, leap on his shoulders, tear off his head, and fix itself onto the bloody stump. Then it will ride to the river, take a long drink, and gallop home before dawn.

In the morning, the villagers will gather around to cluck at the carnage. There will be little left of the poor traveler who gets in the way of El Aya Uma: a rag of skin in the garden, a severed head on the road. Dregs of a demon thirst.

Antonio was right. A Peruvian crane would have poured the fox a drink.

I jumped off the crate and ran to where Antonio knelt in the dirt.

"Don't talk about El Aya Uma to me, Antonio," I said, putting my hands on his shoulders and making him look in my eyes. I loved this man. I couldn't bear the thought of his being sent away by my mother, like the *bruja* with her fruit. "If my mother hears you tell stories like that, she'll come out and tell you to go away. I'll never see you again."

Antonio looked startled.

"Promise you'll never do it again," I pleaded, "and I promise never to tell. Ever."

"I promise," he said. "I promise."

But come the next afternoon, I was daring him to tell me more.

"Listen to this one, Antonio," I began, dragging my crate close to the garden wall. He was scrubbing it with a long hemp brush.

"There was this woman, see? A queen. And when her husband went off to war and got killed, she was home with her three daughters. They were beautiful girls—*muy bonitas*, I'm telling you—big and pink with yellow hair and cheeks as full as papayas. All the men were crazy in love with these girls. And the queen loved them, too. Every night she would tuck them into bed, pat their pretty faces, and tell them *historias*, just like I do for you, Antonio. Maybe better."

"Impossible," he said, his back still to me.

"But then one day, an army of men swept into the city— *whoosh!* And they rode on their horses—*cataplún, cataplún*— right into the house, right up to the beds of the girls, and pulled 'em out. *Pah, pah, pah!* All three. Like that.

"The soldiers took the big pink girls out on horseback and galloped around until the girls couldn't breathe anymore. Then they threw them down on the ground like rag dolls—*splaaaa*—and rode away."

Antonio turned and looked at me as he dipped his brush slowly into a bucket of water. *"Ay,"* he said.

"Ay, ay, ay!" I barked back. "Because the queen got mad. She got so mad, she got out her chariot. You know what that is, Antonio? It's a fancy *carretón* with horses."

"Ya, ya," he said. "Go on."

"She put her three dead daughters in the front of her *carretón* and tied them in with ropes so they wouldn't fall off. And then she rode out onto the battlefield, shouting.

"You know what she said? This is the best part. She said, 'I am the daughter of mighty men!'" I pounded my chest for emphasis. "'And these are children of a very brave race! We are women! We are warriors! Fierce! And we fight not for kingdoms, or gold, or land. We fight for freedom! You think you can take us from our beds, ride us around, and flop us on the ground, *splaaaa?* Think again!'" I was standing on my crate now, crowing over the wall.

Antonio was staring.

I sat back down.

"And so?" he said.

"And so she went home and they never bothered her again, and all the queen's subjects stood outside the palace and sang 'Beautiful Dreamer.'"

He scratched his head. "What home? Queen of what?"

"Queen of the gringas, Antonio. Her name was Boadicea."

"And so she lived happily, et cetera, et cetera?" he said, waving the brush in circles.

"No, not really." I screwed up my nose. I knew that if my mother sang "Beautiful Dreamer" at the end of a story it was probably because it ended badly. At least in this case, I had found out the ugly truth. "Not really. After a while, Boadicea lost the war and took some poison and died."

Antonio burst into laughter, spraying the air before him. "Your mother told you that? And she doesn't like you to hear about El Aya Uma?"

"Actually, she didn't tell me that last part," I confessed. "Vicki read it in a book. She told George and me how the *historia* really ended."

"So the men win the war against the queen of the gringas, and the gringos keep the women in their place," Antonio said.

"But their gringa mothers protect them," I said, sticking a righteous finger into the air, feeling every inch a gringa myself.

"Well, mothers are always protecting their children, Marisita. That happens in Peru, too. Even *brujas* look out for their daughters."

The *brujas*. The witches. Antonio was in dangerous territory now. I knew the *leyenda* he meant. It was the one about the hungry crone who sent her daughter out to scoop out a warm heart for lunch. The girl didn't have to go far. She carved out the neighbor's and brought it home to her mother, who devoured the beating thing in one swallow. When the priest came to demand why the girl was staggering around town, crazed, the witch only smiled, picked her teeth, and said she had no idea. The child had just been doing her chores. So it was that a *bruja* could defend a daughter.

Antonio hadn't said a word about that *leyenda*. But he was

teaching me its applications. We were communicating in code now.

"Antonio?"

"Yaaaah?" He was concentrating on a patch of black mildew.

"Listen. This is really important. Do you think it would be a good idea to give El Gringo—you know, the blind *loco* who comes in the afternoons—a Coca-Cola instead of bread? George and I always give him bread, and I'm a little worried about that. I don't want him to go to sleep thirsty."

El Gringo, El Aya Uma, the *brujas*. I was thinking of little else anymore but forces of evil. Antonio spun around and looked at me with concern.

Not too long after that, he taught me the biggest lesson of all. Mother had taken over the kitchen one afternoon, tutoring Claudia how to make English marmalade. Flavio had gone marketing. The *amas* were doing the laundry. My father's *pongo*, Juan Diaz, had come to take George to the factory to watch sugarcane push through the *trapiche*. Vicki was doing some artwork. I darted through the house and headed out back for Antonio.

I found him behind the animal pens, by the servants' quarters, where the stairs led up to his room. There was something odd about the way he stood there, face to the wall, motionless, straight-backed, his hands out of view. He had on a dark blue cotton shirt with holes worn through to his skin.

I tiptoed closer, intrigued by the tableau of man and brick, not wanting to shatter its spell. As I circled around, I looked down at the object of his focus. He was holding himself, and from him, a long stream splattered the wall.

"You're peeing," I squeaked.

He turned suddenly and burst out laughing. "*Sí.*"

I drew closer to get a good look.

"You've never seen one of these before?" he said, wagging the hose back and forth so that it spat at the air.

I shook my head no. But it wasn't true. I had seen George's once, very quickly, before his *ama* ran in and covered it up. Nothing stopped me from staring now.

"Can I touch it?" I said, and stepped forward with one hand out.

He hesitated, then smiled and shrugged.

I lay my hand on the soft head and rested it there a moment, before it leapt and I jumped back and giggled, my hands to my face.

"*Bueno,*" he said, more soberly now, and tucked himself away.

"Now, look at me!" I sang, and with three brisk moves, pulled down my underpants, sat down, and yanked up my cotton dress.

He looked at the place between my legs, then at my face, and smiled.

"*Ya, ya, gordita. Ya.*"

"See it? See my thing?" I asked him, looking down at myself. "It's a *hueco.*" A hole.

"And here is another one," he said, pointing at my navel.

"*Sí.* But it's not the same. It doesn't do anything," I said authoritatively, my legs waving about.

"No, *mamita*, that's not true," he said. "Put the other one away and I'll tell you about this one." I scrambled to my feet and pulled up my drawers.

"That," he said, pointing to my midriff, "is the center of your being. The middle of your universe."

"Let me see yours," I said, and he pulled up his shirt and obliged. It was pushed deep, and the folds were brownish black. I raised my hand slowly, putting two fingers to its lip. The skin flinched. Then, I slid my forefinger into the orifice. He yelped and caved in, laughing.

"What's inside?" I asked.

"*Mi alma*," he said. My soul.

He squatted down and looked at me, eye level. "This is your *qosqo*, Marisi." His fingers tapped my belly lightly. "Your core. If you learn to see and feel with it, you will know the life force. This is where your power is, your energy. It is the greatest *leyenda* I can teach you. Learn to open your *qosqo* and feed on the world around you. Learn to eat the earthquakes. Learn to take in the chaos. Learn to pull it in to your *barrigita*. Then cast all the poisons out."

"The poisons?"

"The black light. The power of destruction."

"How do I cast them out?"

"First you bring them in. Open your *qosqo*. Let everything rush in, the bad with the good alike. If you walk through life afraid of the bad, you will walk hunched over, broken, defensive. Stand with your *qosqo* to the world. Straight. Proud. Open up. Open wide. Face the black light *de frente* and take it in. And then, when you are filled with the storm of life, let the poison pour away. Away. Away. Into the heart of a stone."

"And my other *hueco*?" I asked him provocatively, knowing that like the witch and the *leyendas*, that nether region of my self was important and forbidden.

"There is nothing wrong with it. It is fine. It is good. The body works from there. And it plays. Someday a man will teach you to play that game. But learn this much from me: It is your *qosqo* from which your life will flow."

He dusted off the back of my dress and we walked together into the garden.

~

I PRACTICED USING my *qosqo* after that. I pointed it up at the dark when nightmares startled me out of sleep. I stood at the window and aimed it down into the garden to stop vines from taking root. I scanned trees with it, on the chance that *pishtacos* were lurking there, waiting to spring.

Antonio's lesson worked; I became less worried about the *loco* and the *bruja*, and, for the time being at least, all the bad forces in the world seemed manageable, the chaos devoured, the black light spit away.

Four decades later, as I look back on that seminal lesson, I still wonder what concatenation of history and conscience predisposed me to be sure I was there to learn it. And to be drawn as I was to Antonio. These things cannot be attributed to chance.

Divine chance, perhaps. As in the story of my friend, Eddie, a "Blackamerican," as he likes to call himself, who set out a few years ago to find out who his ancestors were. Family lore had it that his great-grandfather had been a slave and had been manumitted in the courthouse of a little town in Virginia. Eddie made his way there cross-country on a motorcycle, filled with a wronged man's fury, determined to see the proof for himself. What he found took him by surprise. It was true that his great-grandfather had been a slave on a white man's plantation and that the master had taken the slave down to the courthouse to free him. But the words on the official document changed Eddie's life forever. There on paper, clear as could be, was evidence that the white man was not only the black slave's owner, he was his father, as well. The slavemaster had taken his black son down, acknowledged their blood tie, signed the papers, and given him his freedom. When my friend got back on his motorcycle for the ride home, he did it with the eerie understanding that he would never again feel something so simple as pure, racial anger. He was black. But he was also white. He was master; he was slave.

I am recalling that story now because it has everything to do with links and connections. Just as Eddie understood that he had been called to Virginia to learn an essential lesson about his anger, I was called to Antonio to learn a lesson I absolutely would need to know. It was a question only the *leyendas* could answer: Where does the evil go?

6

POLITICS

La Politica

W HERE DO THE poisons go? If it was a question for the spirit, it was one for the real world, too. The rage of the Second World War—the blood lust, the hatred, the killing—stopped, but its black light continued. Like amperage moving along the earth's surface, it galvanized air, tripped minds with a different fervor. In Peru there was an eerie escalation. The new president, José Luis Bustamante y Rivero, had legalized the long-vilified leftist party, the American Popular Revolutionary Alliance, and a socialist zeal quickened the air. Prices rose. Tempers mounted. The Peruvian military, which the Aranas and Cisneroses had always been wary of—which, from time immemorial, had seen itself as the guardian of prosperity—began clanking its guns.

By late 1948, Peruvian soldiers were taking to the streets to tamp down the leftist euphoria. It had not been the first time. In an uprising in Trujillo sixteen years before, the APRA had massacred a group of army officers and the military had struck back, arresting or executing anyone they could identify as communist.

The liberal tone of Bustamante's presidency had the army on edge again. Unions were making demands. Inflation was spiraling. Grim-faced men in uniform began to be seen outside the presidential palace, on street corners, chasing "left-wing hooligans" down streets. As Mother returned from the United States with Vicki, George, and her violin in tow, she noted the graffiti on the road from the airport: *Hay un bobo en el palacio!* the red letters screamed. An idiot has broken into the palace! Who was it? The president himself.

By October 1948, the military had seen enough. General Manuel Odría stomped into Lima's Plaza de Armas and announced an end to the socialist foolishness. No one so much as blinked an eye. Coups d'état were not new in Peru. Since the turn of the century, the country had seen more military coups, in fact, than democratic elections. General Odría sent Bustamante packing, moved himself into the presidential palace, and announced that he would give Peru a proper election. But seven years later, when I was standing on an empty crate, declaiming mythology to Antonio, the general was still there. The communists and anarchists had fled to the hills, or out of Peru. Their leader, Víctor Raúl Haya de la Torre, had taken asylum in the Colombian embassy in Lima, and the general's soldiers were clomping up and down with submachine guns to make sure that he stayed inside.

The fever did not abate. The early 1950s were boom years for red dreams: Fidel Castro and Che Guevara were weaving guerrilla visions in Latin American jungles, and the Peruvian left was champing at the prospect of overturning a grim and oppressive cycle. There was a long tradition of exploitation in Peru. It had begun under the Inca with the *mita*, a system in which peasants were made to contribute years of labor to the state. They were told their work would bring glory to the empire of the sun. When the Spaniards conquered Peru, they adopted the same practice,

forcing the peasants into their own version of the *mita*, this time
for the glory of the crown. Things had not progressed much in
the one hundred twenty years of the Republic. The villagers in
the countryside now were being lured to work for new masters
on the sugar and cotton plantations; they did not volunteer their
most productive years for free, as their ancestors had done before them, but they accepted pittances: a few *soles*, a thatched
roof over their heads, a ration of meat and a little rice. Antonio
and his peers were part of that cycle: boys who had grown up
watching their fathers rise from their mothers' beds at midnight
and trudge out to a mine or a field or a factory, to push cane
through a *trapiche* until dawn. When their turn came, boys
would take up that trek with their fathers, a hard route traced by
every generation in the grinding Peruvian wheel of fortune.

The eloquent Haya de la Torre, born into one of the *buenas fa-
milias* of Trujillo, was convinced he could reverse the treadmill.
While George and I were running from house to fence, keeping
an eye on the *bruja* and the *loco*, Haya de la Torre was doing
business out of the Colombian embassy compound, preaching
revolution to men like Antonio. He railed against the gradual
handover of land to "rapacious" American companies like W. R.
Grace—particularly in his home province of La Libertad—the
very corner of Peru where my father was raising American
smokestacks.

The sugar and paper haciendas of W. R. Grace were prime
targets for the anticapitalist forces of Haya de la Torre's APRA.
The company, which had grown rich in Peru as an exporter
of bird dung, was now a major trader between North and South
America. It owned Grace Line, the first steamship company
to operate between the Americas, which dominated all shipping
back and forth over the equator, and Panagra, the premier
air carrier of the Americas. The Grace family had gone from
guano to paper, from tin to railroads, and from a modest start in a

ship chandler's shop to ownership of an airline and a shipping fleet.

Grace was like any other major U.S. venture in Peru. In some ways, it brought improvements. It provided steady work in an unstable time. It delivered expertise. It built towns, set up schools, established clinics. But Grace was not in the country to do charity work. It was there to do business. Peruvian hands were cheap and Peruvian resources were plentiful. There was sugar, paper, copper, steel, oil to be had—in quantities unrivaled in other parts of the world. And, without too much fuss, a company—like a military general—could stride into the main square, start up an industry, and put the profits into whatever pockets it chose.

For Grace, as for any capitalist giant in Peru in the '50s, APRA socialists spelled trouble. The Apristas recruited actively among the young in the cities and then spread discontent in the countryside, persuading field-workers and factory laborers of their rights, building the union rolls, spinning visions of a great Utopia. My father's bosses in New York were well aware of the nervousness the socialists were sowing in the Peruvian hinterland. There was nothing happening in the north of Peru that was not also happening in places like Detroit and Chicago. But in Peru, the stakes were higher, the situation more explosive. The protections of the law were not always guaranteed—who knew if the police would be able to stand up against an angry strike, an anarchist incursion, a massacre, a revolution? And if the law did prevail, it might take a fascist turn, in the direction of a military state.

The powers that be at W. R. Grace, in their sleek Manhattan offices on Hanover Square, understood as well as any distant colonial power that the way to manage their holdings in Peru was to place bright locals in governing positions. My father was a prime candidate to run their empire and impose a shinier, American version of the *mita*: He was a U.S.-educated engineer with an American wife and solid Lima connections; a Peruvian with one foot in the old oligarchy and the other in a growing camp of young, future-minded pragmatists who hoped to sweep their country into a bright, new age. The gringo bosses would come and go from New York or, at most, sit for a few months in Lima offices. A few of the younger gringos would come and go from the *casa de solteros* next door. But when it came to managing day-to-day affairs on the ground where the cane was being cut, the sugar was being processed, the paper was being milled, and the rum was being drawn into vats, it was my father who was in charge.

The gringos at Grace had another advantage they had not even bargained for: my mother's little empire at home. If the Peruvian adage is true—that all politics is decided in the kitchen—it was being proven under our own roof in Cartavio. All the intelligence W. R. Grace needed to maintain a grip on its factories was coming from our *mayordomo*, Flavio. It was Flavio who revealed to my mother how much of a hold the APRA had on the people of Cartavio, and it was she who passed that information up the company ranks.

Flavio was a formal man, straight-backed, in his late thirties, a flinty *indígena* who prided himself on knowing how to run a house, serve a meal, please the most discriminating guest. But one morning, when Papi was away in Lima, Mother found him crouched behind the radio in the *comedor*, trembling in the corner, sweat drenching his face and hair.

"Flavio! *Qué te pasa?*"

"I had to come tell you, *señora*." His voice was high and mewling, like a child's.

"What?" and she swung open the kitchen door, looking for Claudia. "Claudia? Antonio? Where is everyone?"

"No one is here, *señora*. Just me. Claudia is in Chancay with my mother. I told my nephew to stay away as well. The others are in the village." He whispered the words, knitting his fingers in front of his mouth. She drew close to listen.

"Why are you there on the floor, Flavio? Why are you so afraid? What's happened to you?"

"I don't want them to see me through the windows, *señora*. If they find out I'm here . . ."

"What are you talking about, *hijito*? Who are *they*?"

"The *obreros, señora*." The workers. "And the union people."

Flavio spun out the story for my mother, describing the men who had come from Trujillo to meet with the workers while the people in the big houses slept. The hacienda's *obreros* were not being paid enough, they'd been told. The *norte-americanos* were sucking them dry. Rich Peruvians like my father were helping them do it. There was much grumbling— *mucha queja*—in the air. And danger. Soon there would be a strike.

"They've forbidden you to come to our houses?" my mother said. "Why?"

"Because the organizers are strong, *señora*," Flavio rasped. "They call this a revolution. They say that those who are not one hundred percent on their side are the enemy. I am not one hundred percent, *señora*. I care about you and the *señor*. I didn't want you to wake up this morning to an empty house without an explanation. Especially with the *Ingeniero* in Lima. But the truth is that they could kill me for this."

"Go, Flavio," Mother said. "You've done enough. Don't put yourself in any more danger. The children and I will be fine."

He went, scooting out the back door on all fours, pushing himself through a hole in the garden wall and then running head-down into the cane field behind. But he came back that night and every night after that to feed Mother new information.

When Papi returned from Lima, Mother told him everything. He knew just what to do.

"Fiesta," he said. *"Pan y circo."* The people would be made an offering.

He organized a *pachamanca* in Cartavio's main square and invited the entire hacienda—every worker, every vendor, every *loco*, every wife and child. He ordered up *valses criollos, música serrana, selva* drums: every kind of dancing from Andean to Amazon. He brought in a feast: goats and ducks and potfuls of savory dishes. And Cartavio rum. Lots of it. As much as a town could guzzle.

Late one Sunday afternoon, the tables were set up on the square by the central market, the band struck its first chord, and the aroma of roasted flesh began to wind through the streets. At first, the only ones there were the engineers and their wives, sipping, stepping about, glancing nervously over their shoulders. But house by house, the workers and their families began to file out. In their best shirts, with lavender oil matting their hair. *"Hola, amigo. Qué tal? Cómo te va?"* First a little plateful of *cabrito*. Then a little taste of the *carapulcra*. A *traguito* of rum. Before long the square was full. With sugarfire warming its veins, Cartavio began to dance.

There were, some *ingenieros* admitted later, people there they'd never seen before, skulking around the edges like hyenas around a kill. But the music, the food, and the rum were working for W. R. Grace that night. *Ay, ay, ay ay! Canta y no llores!* Papi was making the rounds, slapping backs with one hand, wielding drinks in the other. Before long, Cartavio was full of belly-bouncing laughter, a roaring, squealing bacchanalia. When Mother looked out into the bobbing mass, she saw Flavio, drunk as a skunk, hopping through the night on one foot.

For a while labor relations were better. A party glow buzzed over Cartavio like a sputtering neon halo. But it didn't last long.

When the strike did come, it was fast and fierce. Because of Flavio's intelligence reports, however, the company gringos knew about it and were prepared. They called for the Peruvian government to step in and keep the peace. Cartavio's Peruvian managers, many of them confirmed anticommunists—some of them sons and daughters of the forty-family oligarchy that ruled Peru—found themselves in the nervous custody of the police and the military. Papi was put under house arrest.

He wasn't there for long. The police *teniente* in charge, Pepe Canales, turned out to be a former student from Papi's engineering classes at Lima's police academy. The moment he saw him, he gave him a hearty *abrazo*. Then, when an army colonel was sent in with troops, he turned out to be a pal from the Club Regatas—a drinking buddy from the monkey-and-anteater days. Papi was told he could do whatever he pleased.

The head engineers walked into the abandoned factories, started up the machines, and kept the production lines going, doing the labor of a hundred peons.

But the climate changed when Papi went into Trujillo to report on the strike to the prefect of the province of La Libertad. Police *teniente* Canales paid a visit to my mother. He was trembling, jittery as a macaque as he marched up to us in the garden and left the gate wagging behind. Flavio had already told Mother the most recent news: The morning before, the *teniente* had risen from his comfortable bed, pulled on his brass-buttoned uniform, had a good breakfast, and headed out for his car. There, he found a slashed tire and a note slipped under his windshield wiper. The note told him to take a good look at the rubber. Unless the policeman left Cartavio, the next slash would be in his throat.

"*Buenas tardes, señora,*" he said as he approached us. His hands were jammed deep in his pockets, jangling their contents with the impatience of a crap-game croupier. I could see through the gate to his uniformed men outside.

"Everything all right?" he said. "How are you and the children?"

"Fine, Lieutenant," my mother said dryly. "We're fine."

"Don Jorge is not here, is that right?"

"No. He's in Trujillo."

"And the servants are holed up in the village, I suppose?"

"Yes. No one has come," my mother lied.

"Ah, *ya*," he said, and dropped his eyes to where we sat in front of her, our hands idle in our laps. We stared at his uniform, the shiny medals, the raised lettering on his shirt pocket.

"And look who's here!" he said with false jollity, bending down toward George so that we could see beads of perspiration spring onto his brow. "*Mi compadre! Mi amigo!* Cartavio's shortest police officer! You want to come with me, Georgie? You want to do the rounds with my men? Ride in my car? It would make your father so proud, no?"

Mother's mouth dropped open.

George jumped to his feet, eyes shining with the vision of himself behind the steering wheel of the lieutenant's car.

"Sure you do!" the *teniente* almost screeched. "*Claro que sí!*"

The men out front stopped talking to one another. They froze in rapt attention. A hand slipped around the tall spike of the gate.

My mother stood slowly, her face suddenly notched with concern. George read the anxiety in her eyes. Just as slowly, he moved back from the big man, stepping from relish to dread.

"Come on!" the *teniente* called, in a voice that was higher than his own. "What are you waiting for? Let's go grab the wheel!" Canales lunged forward and grabbed George's arm, and his men at the gate shifted like cogs in a gearbox. Mother seized George's other arm. I scuttled back on the grass, propelling myself by the heels of my boots. My brother's eyes were pinched, and I could feel myself ready to cry.

"No," Mother said firmly. "No. He's not going anywhere. He has other things to do. The boy stays with me."

"Hyeh, hyeh!" the police chief barked. "Stay here? When he can come on rounds with the *guardia civil*? Those 'other things' can wait, *señora*. You will come with your father's old student. *No es cierto*, Georgie?" Isn't that right?

The man pulled on George. My mother pulled back. She had concluded by then that this was no lighthearted invitation. The lieutenant had not come to share pleasantries and ask George on an impromptu outing. All this—the late-afternoon visit, the men at the gate, the car in the road—was part of a careful plan. They were here because the son of Don Jorge, a little half-gringo, would make a good buffer, a portable human shield. With the child of the *jefe* in his arms, the policeman could be sure the rebels would leave him alone. It was suddenly apparent to Mother that he was prepared to kidnap her son for that assurance, if necessary.

They tugged at him like that, the man babbling his baby talk, the woman clutching her child, until she threw two adamant arms around George and, in so doing, pinned herself to the policeman's chest. George began to cry. So did I. Then the wind changed, the men at the gate called out to their chief, and he retreated hastily, tripping backward along the walk like a marionette dancing offstage.

Out in the street, a car door slammed shut. Mother took us indoors, shaking.

I mark that day as the threshold of a new awareness. Until that moment, I had always feared ghosts. I had been afraid of the night, of dark forces, of the dead, black light. It had never occurred to me to fear mortal men. But I could see from the grimness of my mother's eyes, from the way she clasped George to her chest, that ordinary humans were just as terrifying—that we had survived a struggle as deadly as any bout with El Aya Uma. That a policeman who professed to be a friend of my father might steal my brother away as smartly as "The Thirsty One" could rip a head off a neck.

This lesson in the way the world worked was more troubling for another reason. I had been shown *leyendas* to live by, been given an instrument to deflect evil; Antonio had taught me how to call up *historias*, turn a *qosqo* against the night, or against a curse, or even against a root that was growing under my house. But something told me that I could not have sucked the black light out of *Teniente* Canales, spit it out into a stone. If he had not decided to let go of my brother, if he had not been called away—for whatever reason—some terrible thing might have befallen us. For all my father's bright swagger—for all our big house and lush garden and eager servants—there would have been nothing we could do.

When Vicki came downstairs from her room, her curly hair tousled and her eyes weary from reading the book tucked under her arm, she found the three of us sitting on the sofa, silently staring ahead. She rubbed her eyes with her fists, yawned, slumped into a chair, and opened her book again. We sat for hours, it seemed, like that: my mother stroking George's hair, George looking through the window, I glancing down at the place in my cotton dress where I figured my umbilical to be.

When Papi came home, he said Canales would never have hurt us. "Of course not! My old student from the police academy? My friend? Never!" But I heard him double-bolt the doors, move chairs under the knobs, just in case. The next day, Flavio told Mother that the note under the *teniente*'s windshield had turned out to be an empty threat. When the sun had appeared that morning, Canales got up with his throat intact.

Within a few days the strikers relented. Politics had promised them a workers' paradise but had left their bellies growling. They missed the rations of meat—a kilo a day—their rice and beans; and however inadequate their cinder-block housing was, they wanted Grace to bring back the water, turn the electricity on again. And so our little world went back to normal. The laborers returned to the factories, the engineers to their desks, Flavio and Claudia to our kitchen, Antonio to our garden, and the APRA slipped off to hungrier enclaves. Leaving a vague uneasiness behind.

When Peru finally elected a socialist president in 1985, thirty-one years later, the country would be a different place. Haya de la Torre would be dead, Papi would be raising factories on other shores, police lieutenant Canales would be living on a fat pension, and the godchildren of the Apristas, fierce communist guerrillas calling themselves The Shining Path, would slash through the mountains, leaving thirty thousand corpses in their wake.

Peru would be one of the world's last strongholds of communism. It would have more to fear than its ghosts.

IT WAS, IN every sense, the age of politics. Mother began to worry about her children's place in the world. How far could we possibly get along in it without the right education? She was firmly against shipping us to private schools in faraway Trujillo or Lima. The farthest she would send Vicki was to the nuns at a nearby convent, but the only things the girl seemed to be studying there were stories even more terrifying than the ones the *indígenas* had told us: tales about purgatory and damnation. Finally, it was decided that Vicki should have a tutor and that her tutor should come to the house.

Her teacher was Miss Paula Roy, an American missionary whose spindly body and fried hair were remarkably like the image of Ichabod Crane I had seen in one of Vicki's books. Miss Roy was just the kind of teacher my eight-year-old sister liked. Tough, exacting, yet surprisingly willing to spend long hours yammering about the most girly aspects of some obscure English novel.

Miss Roy was capable of surprising even me. "This is for you," she said the day George turned six. She handed me a small, painted dog standing precariously on stilts. Out of his mouth, in a jaunty display of canine camaraderie, hung a sloppy pink tongue.

"Here," Miss Roy said, bending over ceremoniously and peering at me over her glasses. "Let me pin it on you."

I wore it that afternoon and every other from then on, until the day one of the American *solteros* pointed at my chest and shouted, "Goofy! That's Goofy you've got there, honey!"

"Gufi," I repeated. An English word I didn't know. I hunted down Vicki and asked her what it meant. She rolled her eyes, set down her book, and swung around to face me.

"Why do you want to know?"

"Because one of the *solteros* called this gufi," I said, pointing to my dog.

Vicki's eyes widened. She let out a loud guffaw and thumped her pillow with a fist. "Oh, that's good! That's really good!" she squawked. Then she was up and flinging herself onto her bed, flailing her legs and laughing wildly. Finally, she turned to look at me again, red-faced and panting.

"That's what that dog is really called?"

I nodded yes.

"Goofy means *stupid*, you twirp. *Es-tú-pi-da*."

Vicki was clearly leagues ahead of George and me as far as learning was concerned. She always would be. But the day came when Mother dressed us up in sober clothes, put us in the company Chevrolet with our jolly chauffeur, Don Pepe, and sent my brother and me off to the new Escuela Primaria, a school that had just been built to my father's orders, off Cartavio's main square. The school was meant to serve every child of every race, from every walk of life in that complex socioeconomic gridwork we called a hacienda. It was meant precisely to ease the political divide between the workers and the bosses.

"When you walk in," Papi said that morning as he surveyed us with warm approval, "look at the lettering over the door. My design." He poked his solar plexus and crinkled up his brown eyes with such good humor that I was convinced his connection with that place was a good omen.

I was wrong.

We were put in a large classroom with what seemed to be children of mixed ages. They were all from the cinder-block houses. There was no Billy or Carlitos or Margarita. Our neighborhood friends had been sent off to the nuns or sent away to Trujillo. There was nobody here we knew.

"*Mocosos,*" a big boy said as George and I sat down. Snotnoses.

"*Mataperro,*" George shot back at him. Thug.

We'd never been in a room with so many children. The teacher was a plain young woman with bright lipstick and a sheath-tight skirt. She introduced herself as "*Señorita,*" made us each stand and say our names, and told us that she would brook nonsense from no one. "*Somos una clase de i-guales,*" she said. We're a class of eeee-quals. But try as *Señorita* might with her ruler and her chalkboard and her stentorian announcements, I couldn't help but gape at the rich spectacle about me. It seemed anything but equal to me.

There was a girl in front with hair so perfectly curled that it seemed to spring from her head like a doll's: straight out the hole, down the back, and coiled tight at the ends. Her dress was butter yellow, crisscrossed with blue lines. A white belt burst into a perfect bow in the back. Her shoes were smudged with dust. But they were topped with the most heartbreakingly beautiful lace socks I had ever seen: woven with ribbons as blue as the sky-kissed lines of her dress. Just at the point where the sock met her brown skin, the white lace shot out and over, like a frill under a duchess's chin.

I looked down at myself. Plain blouse, round collar, breakfast stain. Skirt swelling at the belly. Not a pretty sight.

Señorita's bullhorn voice was coming at us over our desks. "WHO knows how to write their name?" The doll's hand shot up, as did everybody else's in the room, including mine.

A round boy in the corner was stuffing chunks of *dulce de camote* into his mouth in full view of the teacher and then holding a pencil to his lips, as if that could hide the machinery of his chewing. The candy was making his black hair stand on end, and making my mouth water.

"WHO knows how to write the colors—*azul, rojo, verde?*" Fewer children raised their hands, but when I looked around and saw George punch the air, I put my hand up, too, and waved extravagantly.

On the other side of the class a gaunt girl leaned forward, her left arm stiff against her waist. One of her legs was shackled in metal, and two black straps girded the ankle and knee. I strained over my desk to see her foot, but a sharp *thwack* of the ruler against the chalkboard brought me up straight. *Señorita* had her eyes on me.

"Yes?" she said. "Yes?"

I looked at my hands.

"Not paying attention is rude. *Sí?* Staring is rude. *Sí?*" She said this, although she was plainly staring at me. "Do you suppose this is a circus, *Señorita Arana?*" she went on. "Or do you suppose this is a school?" Her bright lips stopped here and puckered.

"*Es una escuela,*" I said, with a voice as tiny as an Andean flute. Two dozen faces were trained on me.

"Good," she said. "You may be the chief engineer's daughter, but you have no privileges in my classroom, you understand?" she added, and gave me a parting glower. "Now, class. How many of you can add?"

Far fewer hands sought the air, but seeing George's there, I floated mine up, too. The bully between us snorted.

"Aha," the *señorita* said, surveying us. "I see. And now, the final question, the *big* question, the one that will tell me if I have a future Pythagoras in here: Who among you can *multiply?*"

Here, as she uttered the magnificent word—*mul-ti-pli-car*—she flung out her hands like a priest at a mass benediction. Her head was back, her white teeth bared, a feverish expectation in her eyes.

My arm shot up. I could not have stopped it if I had tried. Multiply! My hand was banner high, triumphant. When I looked around, it was the only one there.

The boy beside me exploded into raucous laughter.

"Now, Guillermo," said the teacher. "Now, now. How do you know our young friend here doesn't know her multiplication tables?" She was bouncing her ruler against her palm. *"Cómo lo sabes, ah?"*

Her red mouth spread into a smile, and she pulled her green sweater over her wide hips like a duck ready to waddle into water. "Come here, *gorda*. Come up here and show Guillermo your bright little engineer's brain."

I pushed myself out of my chair and looked over at George. His lips were frozen in a perfect O, his eyebrows suspended in the air. Staggering forward, I followed the *señorita* to the chalkboard, like a rogue to the gallows. She picked up a piece of chalk, rested it against her chin for a moment, then scratched two numbers onto the blackboard with a flourish of her elbow: 4, and then 5. Last, she punched an X between them with such fury that my knees began to give.

"Here," she said, and thrust the chalk toward my paunch. *"Tómala."* Take it.

I stood there paralyzed, the chalk poised between my fingers like a bloated caterpillar, fat and white and venomous.

"You ready, my little *ingeniera*?" she said.

I shook my head no. A tittering came from the class.

"What, you can't remember your multiplication tables, *princesa*?"

I shook my cretin head again. The snickers grew louder.

"Or maybe you never knew?" The red mouth broke into an ominous leer, an army of teeth perched behind.

I lowered my chin into my chest as my classmates slapped their desks and chortled with glee.

"She's a liar!" roared Guillermo. "A fat, ugly liar!"

It was too much for George. He stood up and threw a mean punch into Guillermo's abdomen. It folded my critic in half.

But Guillermo came up like a barracuda, grabbed George by the hair, and pulled him down, chairs and desks falling over in a clatter. The boys slugged and huffed, twisting every which way on the floor. The lame girl winced. The candy eater gawked. The doll face pressed her fingers to her temples. Finally, *Señorita*'s long green arm yanked George out by the collar, and her big voice bellowed, "Enough! *Ya! Basta!*"

"Guillermo! You sit down," she said. "The rest of you, too. And *you*," she snarled at George, "I'll show *you* what happens to troublemakers. Everyone take note! *Fíjense* what happens to this uppity boy!"

She trotted George—still dangling from her hand—over to the closet, opened the door, and thrust him in. She turned the lock with a click and whirled around. "Go to your seat, *chica*," she snapped, waving disdainfully at my chair.

I sat down and silently vowed not to move, not to open my mouth, not to bring any more attention to myself. To be as small as I could be.

The *señorita* was having us copy words into our notebooks, booming them out syllabically and then printing them on the board. I hunched into that work with intensity, laboring to copy the shapes she was forming.

But through the sounds of scribbling and coughing and shifting in chairs, I thought I heard something else. I listened closely. It was a muffled whimper, and it was coming from the closet.

All of a sudden, a wave of despair washed over me. George was in there weeping, and I was out here thinking of nothing more than my wretched self. My belly started to jump: up and down, bounce, bounce. Suddenly the skin on my face was spreading out, pulling tight. I threw back my head, gulping down air. What happened next, I cannot say, except that a sound like my father's factory whistle came out of the deepest pit of my gut, long and piercing and full of alarm.

There was a sharp pull at my elbow. As I sniffled and blinked, I could see that the teacher was pushing me toward the left side of the room. She opened the closet, shoved me in, and slammed the door behind me. *Click.*

"*Cállense!*" she shouted. Quiet! "And the rest of you take note! These children get no special treatment here. If it happens to them, it can happen to you! *Fíjense bien!*"

The air inside was black and damp. Though the classroom smelled of paint and cement, the closet smelled old, as if a thousand years of muck and llama grease had accumulated there.

"Georgie?" I whispered, my chest still heaving with aftersobs.

"I'm here," came his reply, thin and frightened.

I groped my way toward him and crouched down on the floor, letting my eyes get accustomed to the dark. A shaft of light from under the door illuminated our feet.

"Look," he said. "Look there."

I followed the gray of his profile to a place on the highest shelf, over our heads, over the boxes and books. There in the shadows, gleaming white, was a human skull.

That was how we became our mother's pupils. We did not go

back to *Señorita's* classroom. From then on, whether at the dining room table, in the garden, on car trips, or on the rocky shores of the Pacific, we were beneficiaries of Mother's perpetual tutelage. School became an all-day, year-round affair. To make it official, our notebooks—Vicki's included—began shuttlecocking back and forth from the Calvert School, a private, nondenominational institution in Baltimore that made its curriculum and materials available not only to the three of us in our Peruvian hacienda but to children in "the farthest outposts of civilization." The Calvert system boasted that it had been known to be delivered by dogsled, camel, even parachute. Every month, a box with the Calvert logo—a boy's silhouette—would arrive on a truck from the port of Callao, and we would open it with relish, removing each neat blue notebook, each spiral-bound textbook, each colored pencil with awe. Sometimes four months would elapse between our completing the work and an "evaluator" from that school passing final judgment on it, but every day it was Mother who sat us down, got out her teacher's manual, and drilled or tested us. Arithmetic, world history, English grammar, botany. If we visited a Chimu ruin, we'd go home and read up on Egypt and Greece. If we ran into the house with beetles as big as my shoes, she'd have us pinpoint the species, draw the insects into our notebooks, and guess where they figured in the food chain. Sitting at the piano would lead to a lesson about a Massenet tone poem. Scooping the dirt with a cup had its logical progression to fractions and math. If we begged for stories, we got them, from Roman to Norse. There was nothing so complicated that we couldn't be made to understand it. There was nothing so simple that it couldn't be wrapped in grand themes.

Mother was no academic. But her dedication to our cognitive welfare was nothing short of fanatical. She ordered books from the Calvert catalogs and devoured their contents. She looked things up in a fever. She presented them with flair. Not until much later did I realize that the last-ditch aspect of my education was one of the most political lessons I'd ever been given. I had not been brown enough to be welcome in *Señorita*'s schoolhouse. Mother would not surrender us to a gentrified boarding school. If I couldn't have a democratic experience, I would be subtracted from a Peruvian context altogether. Mine would be an American indoctrination, in a language I hardly used outside. In the process, I'd learn to see the world through a foreign scrim, feel apart. I'd begin to become the creature of a place I'd never smelled or seen—the product of a cloud-built school, where rootlessness was at the heart of the curriculum, isolation at the edge of the page.

IF HISTORIES ARE right, Peru has always been a racial powder keg. The Inca lorded it over the Moche, and, when Spain stumbled into Peru, the Spanish lorded it over the Inca. To be an *indio* under the conquistadors was to be subhuman. An Indian could be made to work—even be made to *pay*—for the misfortune of being born brown: The indigenous were taxed by the crown, made to pay *tributos* "for the Queen's protection," and the church's job was to keep meticulous records on who exactly was indigenous. It was crucial to know exactly how Indian a newborn was, or how mixed—*mestizo*. One's racial coordinates had economic relevance and, as such, had to be carefully set down. If you were born Spanish, you were exempt from having to pay taxes at all.

In my search to find out what I could about my great-grandfather Pedro Pablo Arana, the haughty politician who, like Napoleon, crowed that he had no ancestors, I spent days in the mountain city of Ayacucho—cradle of Peruvian communism—searching through church records to find proof that he had been born there, as my family had always claimed. I found no trace of him—the Ayacucho story had been a decoy—but I did learn something about the history of Peruvian racism. It was a closely guarded institution, maintained scrupulously by Catholic priests. A very accommodating *padre* spent days with me in Ayacucho's cathedral, taking one volume after another from the shelf lovingly, dusting it off, setting it down. Every birth in that mountain stronghold, dating back to the 1600s, is scrupulously recorded: *Miguel Angel Barada nació el 17 de setiembre 1822,* and then after that, in flowery script: *Español.* Or this one: *Mercedes Elena Burgos—Mestiza,* by which one could generally conclude the child was illegitimate. Or: *Jesús Cristo Yupanqui— Indio.*

It could seem, to the uninitiated, like an entry in a hospital log: race noted as biological fact. But other books tell the rest of the story. The *indios* and the *mestizos,* unless they could pass themselves off as white, were made to pay for having been born darker. The records on this are just as complete: *Miguel Angel Barada,* the one with the Spanish blood, becomes a landowner in Huancavelica. *Mercedes Elena Burgos,* the *mestiza,* makes a last payment, her *tributo* to the government, on her deathbed: 74 *soles.* The priest giving last rites marks it down. *Jesús Cristo Yupanqui,* the *indio,* owes the governor 1,320 *soles.* If the dark didn't pay, they were enslaved by the state. If their children looked more sturdy than they did, they were taken off in their place.

Subtract the Spanish crown, take the taxes away, outlaw the slavery, and there are still citizens of the Republic who measure by color. Peru today is a salmagundi of races, infused over the centuries by slave shipments of Asians, Africans, and Caribbeans, but the specter of racism haunts it. Who are the forty families who continue to make up the moneyed oligarchy? Spanish-blooded whites. Who are the seventy percent of the national population who live in extreme poverty? The indigenous.

It was part of one's political education.

I had, at a tender stage of my life, some experience in the huts of the poor. One day, my *ama* pushed me toward a *chacra* on the outskirts of Cartavio, on our way home from a quick trip to the *bodega china*. "Psst! Marisita!" she said. "Don't tell your mother and father. I want a little blessing from my sister. We won't be long, I promise!" I found myself stepping over a threshold of sticks onto the dirt floor of a one-room shack. It was fusty, humid, dark, and as my eyes adjusted, I could see that the walls were made of mud. Bits of straw jutted from them. I sat on the edge of the sagging cot with a hand-hewn cross above it and blinked at the scene around me. Two girls with long, tangled hair came out of the dark; they were giggling, their hands in front of their mouths. The older one wore a cotton shift with stains along the belly; the young one had nothing on at all. They studied me awhile and then approached me carefully, holding their hands out to touch my face. I marveled at their chatter. It was the first I'd heard Quechua, a language I didn't understand. They patted my knees after that, smoothed my dress, pinched my cheeks, gave me a strip of wet sugarcane from a bucket in the corner. When I thanked them they laughed merrily, and then they squatted like stones, watching me suck on the cool, sweet stem.

On another occasion, I tagged along after my friend Margarita and her mother, the Lattos' cook, following the two all the way home before the mother discovered me stepping into their *chacra* behind them. The woman clapped her hands in dismay when she saw me, grabbed me by the wrist, and ran me home.

"Mother, can Margarita come to my birthday party? I like her very, very much."

"Well, darling, yes. Of course, she can come. But if she comes, none of the mothers of the other little girls will allow them to attend."

"Why not?"

"Just because, Mareezie. That's how it is."

"I don't want the other girls, Mother. I want *her*."

"That's fine, dear. You'll get fewer presents, of course."

"I don't care."

"And Claudia won't make a big cake."

"I hate big cakes."

"And the two of you can sit in the kitchen."

"I love sitting in there."

"As you wish, Mareezie."

Looking back at that exact point in my childhood, it's clear to me that I may have known that I was divided, but I didn't know there were more classifications than two. I had believed Peru to be seamless, that Antonio was a man like any other in my family, that the starkest difference I would ever encounter was between my father and my mother. As birthdays progressed, I saw that Peru has its sediments, too, and that its lines are drawn in color. "I'm *indio* with a little bit *sambo*," someone will say on the telephone, if you're planning to meet him somewhere for the first time, so that you'll be sure to recognize him. Or a Peruvian will call a friend with distinctly Asian features *Chino*. "*Oye, Chino! Ven p'acá!*" We call each other *morenita, cafecita, cholita*: there's a name for every shade of Peruvian skin. I'm reminded of my pre-political innocence now when I go to Latino conferences in this country, when an application asks me if I'm Hispanic, when I see the children of Spanish-blooded oligarchs line up alongside migrant workers to get a piece of affirmative action, as if all of us from south of the border are alike. "You know where I'm coming from, *chacha*," says my *chicana* friend to me, "because you're a person of color." *Oye*, isn't one *hermana* like any other?

Happy birthday, my dear.

⁓

MY MOST PROFOUND political education—the one that taught me about the limitations of my own power—awaited me in my grandfather's house in Lima. It began when Juan Díaz, my father's errand boy, pedaled up one day, propped his bicycle against the front fence, leaned in, and sang out for Antonio to let him pass.

"What's inside, *Señor* Juan?" George and I panted after him, pointing to the fat envelope under his arm.

"Your tickets to the United States," he said importantly, and strode down the garden path.

"United States?" George and I looked at each other. "Who's going there?"

Everyone, as it turned out. But me.

It was time for my father to meet my mother's family. My parents had been married for eight years now, had three children, and my American grandparents were inviting them to come. The plan was for our little family—minus me—to visit them in Wyoming, drop Vicki and George off, then Mother and Papi could go on the honeymoon they'd never had. To bring me, an active four-year-old, into the itinerary would be more than they could handle. "She's too much," I heard my father say. "Too much," my mother agreed.

On the appointed day, I was taken from my sunny garden—from Flavio, from Antonio, from Claudia, from the *loco,* from all the living dead of Cartavio—and deposited, with a brown leather suitcase and a blue toy telephone, in the cathedral chill of my grandparents' salon.

"Anytime you want to speak to us, just pick up this phone," said my father, pulling my hands from around my mother's knees and placing them on the plaything. "Don't worry if you don't hear *us.* The important thing is that your mother and I will be able to hear *you* and everything you want us to know." With that meager assurance, my parents took my sister and brother and headed for the door.

On his way out, Papi kissed my grandmother and whispered

loudly in her ear. "She's not been to church," I heard him say with a nod in my direction. "She's not even been baptized. Why don't you see if you can't do it while we're away. Maybe you can teach her some manners, too." Then they were gone.

So, *that* was it. This was where I was to be civilized. This was where I would be hosed down, pounded out, ironed flat, until I became the tidy little prig they could take on grand tours to paradise. Baptism? I hunched my shoulders and squinted around. We'd see about that.

In the three months I was in that house, my father's lively younger brothers were seldom present. Tío Pedro, the handsome one, was in the navy, off on sea adventures. Tío Víctor, an architecture student at the university, was coming and going from Tingo Maria, cutting a road through the jungle. Tía Rosa, the pretty, almond-eyed sister, had just been married to a dashing, mustachioed German.

I was put in the daytime care of twenty-four-year-old Tía Chaba, the one with the face of Cleopatra, the wit of Cantinflas, and the brain of the Biblioteca Nacional. I was put in the bed of my Tía Eloísa, whose nature was sweet and whose skin was as matte and white as a geisha's.

Tía Chaba was as entertaining as she was beautiful. She told jokes, did tricks, had strong ideas about art and literature, and liked a lively argument. She had a wild laugh, a way of making me pay attention to her by screwing her face into a terrifying mask, like a high-haired harridan in a Peking opera. Her brain was a slick machine, and she liked people to know it. When she wasn't explaining the world to some visitor in the *sala*, she was reading a book a day, recording each one in her notebook, with critical notes on the side.

Tía Eloísa, a few years older, was pretty, too, but in a quieter way. She was a measured lady, with elaborate rituals. When she let me into her bed at night, she folded the blanket back carefully, so that I would sleep on it, not on the sheet; she didn't want our bodies to touch. Her eyes, which were the color of bright jade, were like tiny jewels, slanted slightly at the corners, making her look Japanese. Her movements were gentle, deliberate, and she turned her neck slowly, as if her face were Venetian glass. Her voice came from somewhere deep in her chest, and it was surprisingly masculine; one word of hers could shush me to a whisper. "So that your grandfather can read," she'd say, or "write" or "study" or any number of occupations that required me to keep my noise levels low. I was told that Tía Eloísa had stopped going to school when she was seven, because she had refused to come out from under her bed. There were no truancy laws to make a girl go. But she had been taught diligently by her aunts, given strict orders to copy out the classics, memorize poetry, do lessons from textbooks. She was well-read, curious, and could give her little sister Chaba—who had torn through parochial schools and outsmarted every nun—a good run at the dinner table. But she was shy with men, reclusive, happiest within the walls of her father's house.

Abuelita was a thoroughly social Limeña. She loved a good party, liked to dress up in her velvets and satins and wend her way across the capital to a socialite's wedding or tea with her cousins, the Ponces. Uninclined to do this alone—and married, as she was, to my grandfather, a virtual hermit and the antithesis of the bon vivants she was raising her children to be—Abuelita would go in the company of her daughters. They would clack down the stairs and out the front door in their high heels, with French silk whispering around them, veil-hung toques above their well-carmined smiles, leaving me in a trail of perfume.

Had I been a different, better child—had I been Vicki, for instance—I might have learned something from this clever and urbane household. Had I been George, I would have charmed my way into the little pots of sweet *manjar blanco* that sat on my grandmother's shelves. But I was small-minded and vain, more interested in Napoleonic wars of independence than in any genteel opportunities this place had to offer. With good reason, the house came to view me as harshly as I viewed it.

"Write my full name," I commanded Eloísa, snitching fine parchment from my grandfather's desk. She scrolled out all the contours of my magnificent appellation—Marie Elverine Arana Campbell—with a curlicued flourish beneath.

"What's that?" I said, thwacking the last word with a spoon.

"That," said Eloísa, "is your mother's maiden name. Campbell. The name of your grandfather in North America. Someday you will learn to write it—as all Spanish ladies do—after the name of your father."

"Mmm," I mumbled distractedly, and went off to practice saying Campbell out loud.

"Mother," I whispered into the blue telephone that night so that no one in the house would hear, "are you listening? I learned how to say your name."

One day, Tía Chaba was called on by an art student she had met through friends. The young man was shown into the drawing room and received by my beaming grandmother, as was the custom. Hearing his voice, I clambered down the narrow stairs to have a good look at his face. What I saw delighted me: a wide open forehead with eyes as clear as amber.

"Aha," the guest said, and I pranced up to kiss him, as I had been taught to do. It was love at first sight, a tumbling, rushing love, warmed by the red in his hair and the lavender scent of his neck. I reached up and wormed my way into his lap.

Tía Chaba ceased to exist. I could hear her gab on, as if she were chewing the hem of a distant curtain. I was happy to sit in her suitor's arms, still as a heap of stone.

"I'm not a Peruvian," I said finally, in as large a voice as I could muster.

"What's that?" he said, rewarding me with his face. My aunt's chatter came to a sudden stop.

"I said: I am not a Peruvian."

"Marisi," my grandmother said sternly, "what nonsense is that? What have you been taught up there in Cartavio? Of course you are a Peruvian. You're as Peruvian as can be. Haven't I always said that of all my three grandchildren, you're the one with the Cisneros face?"

"I'm not like them," I whispered coyly, and shrugged toward my bewildered grandmother and aunt. "I'm not." Then, with a twisted little smile I was sure would punt me leagues ahead of Tía Chaba in his heart, I added, "I'm an American. *Un yanqui.* My name is Campbell."

"I see," he said, and raised his eyebrows. "How *very* interesting."

I took that cue to scramble out of his lap and snatch my blue machine from behind my aunt's chair. "Here is my telephone to the United States. Watch." I spoke into the mouthpiece, switching to English for grander effect. "Hello, Georgie? Hello, hello! How are you? Don't forget to bring me some . . . cream cheese!" It was the nectar my mother thirsted for: the Philadelphia kind.

"Ah," the painter said tenderly. "How cosmopolitan you are."

"Marisi," my tía said in a sprightly voice, her black eyes as tipped as a cat's, "why don't you tell Diego what American city you're from, now that he knows you're a *yanqui?*"

I opened my mouth and stalled, trying to spin cities out of my brain. I couldn't think of one.

"*Qué graciosa, la Marisi,*" my grandmother sang out. How cute she is. It was the signal that my show had come to a crashing finish. I was about to be sent from the room. I lost all decorum and begged the man to take me home with him.

The women laughed in high little cachinnations, the kind with a razor's edge.

"Well, why don't you at the very least walk me to the gate?" the amber-eyed man said, concluding that his visit was over, too. We walked down the steps together. But there, the most remarkable thing happened. The gate swung open and Don Pepe's gray Chevrolet shot past, whizzing down Calle San Martin so quickly that I barely caught a glimpse of my mother's gold head as it sped out of view.

I made a dash for it. The painter lunged after me, and we both clattered down the street like city hounds after spoor. But he soon overtook me, lugged me back to the black iron gate, and handed me to my aunt. Perspiration was running down his face. "Here is Miss Campbell," he said ceremoniously in English, wheezing and swabbing himself with a handkerchief rank with turpentine. "She thought she saw her mother." Then, parenthetically, in Spanish, "As sad a *gordita* as I've ever known."

That was the day my war began.

"Being a *yanqui* does not make you better," Tía Chaba sniffed, once she'd gotten over the scare of losing me to the streets. "The *norteamericanos* have nothing over us."

"A motley race," my abuelito added in English, dipping his toast into his tea.

The days that followed were punctuated by remonstrance and retaliation. I stomped upstairs, took out my grandmother's pinking shears, and lopped off one side of my hair. There was a flurry of dismay when I leaned over the banister and presented my edited conk, but nothing like the breast-beating admissions and apologies I thought I so richly deserved.

"You know, her mother has never taken her to church, never taught her her prayers," I heard my grandmother say to my aunts one morning, as I lurked unseen on the stairwell. "Can you believe it? What kind of mother is *that*?"

I couldn't hear my aunts' responses, but my grandmother's voice was high-pitched, loud, and I could hear every word. "The woman is so willful. Doesn't she realize she has an obligation to teach a child? If children don't have proper religious educations, how can they hope to be anything other than monkeys in Manú? Have you taken a good look at that girl? Is that how gringo children are? Wild?"

That afternoon, my Tía Eloísa draped a black lace mantilla over my shorn hair and drew me into the household chapel on the second floor. It was a tiny niche with a carved altar, a towering plaster image of the Virgin Mary, and a small crucifix. A wood Jesus draped languidly from the cross. Two beautifully carved candles with miniature illustrations of flying angels stood unlit on each side. "I want you to repeat after me," my tía said in a husky whisper, pulling me down on my knees. *"Ave Maria, madre de Dios—"*

"Mother of God?" I said. "Where is she? I didn't know God had a mother," I said.

"She was at the foot of the cross when Jesus Christ died," my aunt went on, "kneeling before him, the way we're kneeling right now. Let's pray to her, Marisi. She listens to children. She'll listen to you."

"Did she listen to him?" I pointed up at the dead Christ.

"Of course she did, Marisita."

"Well, it didn't do him any good." My aunt's little eyes widened, and then her neck swiveled so that her powdered face turned up and shone white with light from the ceiling. She crossed herself, stood, and left.

I decided to stage a hunger strike. Folding my arms across my chest at the lunch table, I refused every dish that was set before me: *papa a la huancaína, sopa con albahaca y fideos, arroz verde con pollo, delicia de chirimoya.* All my favorites trooped by and lined up one by one, untouched. The grown-ups carried on, nodding and munching and savoring the delights with little sighs of pleasure.

"You're not hungry, Marisi?" my grandmother said, dispatching a glimmering morsel of sweet *chirimoya*. "How very unusual."

"Why don't you go off and play, Marisita?" said Tío Víctor, just back from Peru's interior and unaware of my state of siege.

"She will sit there until she finishes," said Tía Chaba, and flashed me a gimlet eye.

The conversation droned on, analyzing everything from El Presidente's war against the communists to the Chinese *chifa* with the best wontons. One by one, the adults dabbed their chins with ecru linen, excused themselves, and trotted off to siesta. Finally, there were only three of us around the table—Abuelito, Chaba, and I. Camped before me: a regiment of porcelain.

"Malraux's *Espoir* is far superior to anything Camus has written," Tía Chaba was saying, citing endless twists and turns that congealed in the air and floated past in dry wisps. "More alive, more potent, more *true,* don't you think?" She was trying to engage my grandfather, who was chewing thoughtfully and studying his plate.

"We don't disagree, *mi hija,*" he replied finally, "but I'm clearly willing to give *L'Homme révolté* more credit than you are." He smoothed the damask under his hands.

He looked from her to me to her again. "It seems you've lost your audience, Chabela. No use wasting yourself, no?" He smiled sweetly. And then, with all aplomb, he rose, tipped his head toward me—"*Con tu permiso, Marisi*"—and tottered off upstairs.

"Eat," Chaba said, and was gone.

What followed then can only be described as a pitched battle, complete with scrawking chair legs and heavy grunting. I left the room. Chaba wrestled me back in my chair. Tío Víctor called me to come sit in his lap. Chaba wrestled me back in my chair. I screeched, threw myself on the floor, and threatened to call the police. Chaba wrestled me back in my chair. I ran to the kitchen and pleaded with the maids. Chaba ran to her room, brought out her belts, wrestled me back in my chair, and strapped me in. When the family gathered for high tea, I was still there, fast asleep, my face in the rice.

"What on earth is going on?" my grandmother thundered.

"She was playing passenger on a plane," Chaba crowed, taking the stairs like a dancer. Abuelita shook her head, called out to the maid who hovered at the kitchen door with her apron twisted into her fingers, and told her to set me free.

In truth, Tía Chaba was the most exciting woman I knew: big-eyed, boisterous, smart. She could see the future and do magic. "I'm a wicked witch!" she'd screech. "Don't you cross me!" and then she'd tickle me with her long, red fingernails until I could hardly breathe. Being the youngest in her family, and the most resilient, she had been assigned as the baby-sitter. It was my parents who had gone off and abandoned me. My predicament was not her fault. But because she had consented to be my jailer, she would be made to pay.

I took to her things with the scissors. I locked myself up in her room. I called her a *bruja* when she ran after me with a hot curling iron, trying to impose order on my hair. I gasped and clutched at my chest when she walked through the door. There were flank attacks and aerial salvos, hit-and-run and pincers. There were strafes and blasts and fusillades, with battle raids and booty.

Finally one morning, as I was watching my Tía Eloísa carefully wrap her long-nailed toes in cellophane before she slipped on her sheer silk stockings, she turned and asked me, "Why are you so cruel to your Tía Chaba, Marisi?" and it dawned on me that I'd lost the war.

I let them take me off and baptize me after that, realizing that somewhere along the way I'd been labeled a problem, worse than the bad-mannered pagan my father had left behind. The one thing I did not want was a brisk court-martial on his return.

They taught me my prayers, trussed me up in a white wool suit tailored by my grandmother's own hand, took me to La Parroquia—a stone leviathan in the heart of Miraflores— splashed me with holy water, and pledged me to Jesus and Rome.

When my father and mother came to the gate to collect me days later, I was clean, beatific, and curly. The essence of tidy prig.

7

EARTH

Pachamama

THERE IS A story the guides in Machu Picchu like to tell, about a carefree traveler who took a stone from the trail to Inti Punku—the sacred gate of the sun—and carried it back to her home in Bremen. Or Salt Lake City or Lyon; the homeland varies, depending on who is listening. In any case, the woman descended the Andes, returned to her comfortable home on *zo-und-zo-platz*, parked the stone on her coffee table, and watched her life turn into a nightmare.

Her husband died in freak circumstances: He was sweeping their second-floor balcony, when suddenly the whole structure— German-made! perfectly constructed!—collapsed into the street, crushing his skull. Her daughter was bitten in the face by a mangy dog, behind their house, in the alley. The police claimed that they hadn't seen an attack that ferocious in years. When the woman began to get dizzy spells, falling to her knees in her own living room, her head brought eye-level with the stone, she understood why a curse had befallen her.

She wrapped up the little gray rock, addressed it to the tour office in Cusco, and mailed it to the Peruvian guide who had taken her up the trail to Machu Picchu. For the week he had it, the stone played havoc with the guide's life: His wife ran off with another man. His eyelids began to quiver. He couldn't sleep. When he placed the stone on someone else's desk one night, that person went home sick the next day.

The guide took the rock back up to Machu Picchu and handed it to a shaman, explaining the damage the thing had done, warning the wise man to be careful since the curse might fall on him now. The shaman turned the granite in his palm and nodded. He knew what the problem was. It was an *ariska salkkarumi*, he said, an unhealed stone from a bad man's grave. It had absorbed too much evil. It simply needed to be prayed over, blessed, and returned to the earth, where it would be purified in the bosom of Pachamama. And so it was. The rock was reunited with its mother, the shaman lived on to do good works, the guide flourished, and the German tourist learned something about the real order of things.

The crushing power of Pachamama. Earth mother. I had heard about her from Antonio: She was the substance from which all things were made, from which all life arose, to which all would return. He'd hold rocks aloft in the garden. "You see this one, Marisi?" he'd say. Then he'd talk about its relative density, color, weight. He'd tell me what was in it: life's dust, desiccated flowers, excrement, crushed butterflies, stillborn babies, winged monsters, flesh of snakes, bones of men, fallen monuments, fused together in Pachamama, waiting for regeneration, whenever the *apus* willed. Stones had energy and we, as earth's creatures, could call forth their ancient, cumulative power, if we were wise enough.

I figured my father was on excellent terms with Pachamama. How could he not be—a man who moved the earth, raised factories, turned cane into so many permutations? He was surely smiled on by the *apus*. Engineers as a whole were beloved in Peru. *Doctor Arana*, the workers and townspeople called him, *El Doctor Ingeniero*, with a reverence they reserved for priests. A status was accorded engineers that far outweighed any status accorded physicians or lawyers. Engineers pushed aside Pachamama, raised things up from her, the way the Inca had raised temples at Sacsayhuaman. They were rock movers, stone fitters, empire builders, with rare knowledge and intricate minds. They were respected, admired in Peru—so much so that the Republic had made presidents of them.

In any case, when I, the engineer's daughter, returned from the balconies of Lima to the well-turned soil of our garden, I was glad to be coming home. On the long trip from the capital to Cartavio, we seemed to be shucking modernity. The massive concrete and wood facades were replaced by single-family dwellings, the city was replaced by smaller and smaller towns, until there was hardly a town at all, just the spine of Pachamama. Then Cartavio sprang toward us, in all its full flower.

Antonio seemed happy to see me. I was a Christian now and told him so, brandishing the prayer cards that my grandmother had given me, with the Virgin and Santa Rosa in richly draped gowns. He nodded happily and told me that he, too, prayed to the Virgin. "She's part of it, yes. A big part of it." He took out his own prayer card: It was a greasy slip of paper, worn and yellowed by use, with a picture of Jesus' face, eyes cast heavenward and red heart in evidence, rays blazing from his chest. "Everything fits together, Marisi," he said, as I followed him back to the garden. "Because everything springs from the stuff beneath our feet, these rocks. The Virgin and the Christ are from Pachamama just as you and I are from Pachamama, just as that tree over there is, and that smokestack above the tree is. They all have a place on this earth." He held out a handful of dirt, and grinned.

I had much more to learn from Antonio, and I turned to those lessons eagerly. For every recitation I gave him about Abuelita's house and the wondrous events that had transpired in it, I was traded a lecture about centers of energy. Apart from my *qosqo*, the most powerful seat of my soul, there were the *chaki* in my feet, the *sonqo* in my heart, and the *nosko* just at the point where my forehead meets my hair. If I could concentrate all my being into these sites, Antonio said, I could use them to fend off evil or to sense things a human couldn't ordinarily sense. I might conjure a message from Pachamama herself, rising up through the bowels of the earth, passing up my *chaki* to my *qosqo* to my *sonqo* to my *nosko*, at which point a flash of comprehension would tell me what I needed to know. "Someday, when all the people of this world gain wisdom," Antonio told me, "the Pachakutekk will come."

"The Pachakutekk?" I asked him.

"Yes, Marisi, that is when the world will turn. If we are good enough, kind enough, the world will have the right sort of Pachakutekk. Evil will fly to the stars and we will live on Pachamama in peace." Until that point, Antonio added, the earth would rumble and turn, but not in a happy way.

The earth rumbled and turned not long after, and, as he had said, not in a happy way. I was sitting at the piano with my mother one evening, when she announced quite suddenly that she wanted to send Antonio away.

"He has a good head, that boy," she said. "I want to get him out of this nowhere place. Give him some *mundo*. Send him to school."

My heart plunged. Send Antonio to school? Away from Cartavio? What would I do without him to talk to about *brujas* and Pachamama and the power of my *qosqo*? I felt a wave of black light advance toward me, recede, then advance again with a terrible energy.

I put my feet squarely on the floor and concentrated every cell of me. Come into me now, Pachamama, help me. Up the *chaki* to the *qosqo* to the *sonqo* to the *nosko*. Suddenly the front door whirled open and my father stood there, framed in the doorway as the trees swayed behind him in the dark.

"We're leaving Cartavio," he thundered. "Tomorrow we pack."

So it was I who left Antonio, not the other way around. It was a strange kind of Pachakutekk, but the world was definitely turning. W. R. Grace had decided to send my father to more ambitious climes: Paramonga, where the Americans were not only spinning out sugar and paper, they were racing into the plastics age.

Flavio, Claudia, and Antonio busily helped us pack. There was hardly time to say sad good-byes, for my father's replacement was on his way to take over the house. On the morning that we boarded Don Pepe's Chevrolet to leave, I found Antonio squatting by the front gate, waiting to see me. He was wearing a clean white shirt, and his straight, black hair was brushed back against his head. When he stood, I shot into his arms. He pressed me to him and then drew away, handed me a round, black pebble, and said he would never forget the things I had taught him. "Take this bit of earth, this little piece of Pachamama," he said. "Send your worries into it. And when you speak, *gordita*, I promise it will speak to me." I turned it in my hand, its shape as sleek and cunning as the blue telephone my father had tricked me with in Lima. "Yes," I said. *Sí*.

⁓

THE ROAD FROM Cartavio to Paramonga led through Chan Chan, the thousand-year-old metropolis of the Chimu kings, a labyrinthine mud remnant of an empire that had once stretched between the Andes and the sea, along seven hundred miles of

Peruvian coast. The Chimu were a powerful, rigidly class-conscious people who cherished their engineers, abused their peons, butchered their thieves, fashioned canals, and loved jewelry. When the Inca armies swept into Chan Chan in 1470 and carried off its bespangled king, Minchancaman, the Inca inherited a vast repository of Chimu knowledge, from complex hydraulics to the forging of gold. But the Incas would not remain victors for long. When the Spanish conquest of Peru began in earnest half a century later, the mighty Incas were reduced to servants, and the mighty city of Chan Chan was abandoned to the desert wind. Now, from the roads, it was barely discernible, a long hump in the yellow sand.

We drove past the iron-girded mansions of the city of Trujillo, with their elaborate white *portales* and carved mahogany balconies. It was an ancient city, founded in 1534 by the pig-farmer conquistador Francisco Pizarro to honor the Trujillo of his birth, a town in Spain's Extremadura. By the 1800s, when the elegant liberator José de San Martín had made it the capital of the province of La Libertad, many of Peru's richest families had settled there. It was also there—in the 1930s—that the first stirrings of Peruvian socialism were felt as Peru's poor wandered wide-eyed down Trujillo's avenues, lined with resplendent homes. The revolutionary spirit of Trujillo was now stalking all Peru.

We continued south on the Pan American Highway, that dust-blown ribbon of asphalt that someday would connect Alaska to Chile and memorialize the trip primitive man had made thirty thousand years before. As we sped south of Trujillo, south of the Moche Valley, south of the Huaca del Sol y de la Luna, the land grew bleak and harsh, a terrain as implausible as it was alluring, as pocked as the face of the moon. The cordillera of the Andes raced by on our left, coal black and sinister. To our right, wind-combed bosoms of sand shivered their way to the sea.

Drop four people into Peru, the saying goes, in four different places, and though they may touch down a few hundred miles apart, they will think themselves in four corners of the world. The country is not large—never more than five hundred miles across at any point, and twelve hundred miles deep—tucked into the west coast of South America, where the breast of the continent swells. It is only three times larger than California. Yet, for all its compactness, Peru is a model of earthly diversities: icy Andean peaks, dense Amazon jungle, relentlessly chapped deserts, and a coast that glistens under the rough surf of the Pacific.

The five of us stared out at that coast as it spooled by our windows; we babbled randomly, not searching one another's eyes. It strikes me only now, as I think back on it, how little I had been told about my family's trip to the United States. It had happened only a few months before, but after George's boots and hat had been displayed, his holsters and toy guns—after I'd been handed a candy or two and a recording of Gilbert and Sullivan's *HMS Pinafore*—I pursued no further information. I don't remember asking about my American grandparents, who remained, until the moment I set eyes on them, inexplicable mysteries, cataloged under the wrong name. I cannot say whether or not it was a willful refusal to explore their experiences; perhaps it was because I was resentful, or hopelessly ignorant, or because I was content to be the kind of Peruvian who doesn't think beyond what she sees, *chica mesquina*, provincial to the core. Or perhaps it was because I worried that in some way the gearwork had shifted, that my parents had come home new, and that changes were bound to be for the worse. Or perhaps the rest of my family *was* talking about that faraway fantasyland; I just didn't want to hear it. All I remember is my father and Georgie chatting aimlessly in the wide front seat next to Don Pepe, while Mother, Vicki, and I chatted aimlessly in the rear—*hombres en frente, mujeres atrás,* Peruvian style. I don't recall hearing a word about their travels.

George and I had hoped Don Pepe would catch up with our cousin Salvadorcito, a twenty-year-old naval cadet on leave who had captained the truck that carried our things from Cartavio that morning. He was the only son of Tío Salvador, our quixotic uncle, who, a few years earlier, had deposited the anteater and monkey with my father in Lima. Perhaps only to us, Cito seemed more adventurous than his eccentric father. The last we had seen of him, he had looked adventurous indeed—sitting astride Mother's piano, bouncing down the road with his skinny elbows flapping like a *gallinazo*'s, one hand pointing to the horizon.

But Cito was nowhere to be seen on that vacant highway. Our loud game of "I Spy" collapsed into a long, contemplative gaze out the window. Sand. A whorl of dust. A pile of stones. Four poles and a sagging roof of straw. A cross thrust into a mound. Vicki read. Mother slept. Papi yammered about politics with Don Pepe. George looked out at Peru with a twitch tugging his face—one more thing he had brought back from America, apart from his cowboy gear. Six hours later we flew past a field of marigolds. It was as bold a signal of our approach as we could have wished for, but we continued to stare at the orange expanse like astronauts caught in a warp. *"Veinte minutos más!"* cried our driver, and then, quite suddenly, Paramonga filled our heads with a burst of astringent perfume.

We passed from flowers into fields of ripe sugarcane, each thick stalk raising a white-plumed banner of welcome. On the side of the road, where the blacktop sliced into the dirt, big-skirted *cholas* trudged with their children, trailing puffs of yellow dust from their heels and turning to peer at us from fossil-hard faces. A high-walled ancient *fortaleza,* once home to the Chimu, whirred past us on the left and then we saw the large white board with the crisp green lettering: HACIENDA PARAMONGA.

It was different—very different—from Cartavio. In Cartavio, Grace had built an elaborate town, with a central plaza that held a mayoral mansion; a local government office; a looming, colonial church; a police headquarters; and the *señorita*'s school. The workers' cinder-block housing had been built around that square, like spokes off a giant wheel. To one side of the plaza had been the market, where farmers could sell their meat and produce. The chief engineers' houses, where we lived, had been a paradise well apart from the hubbub, behind a high wall. In Cartavio, the roads had been improvised, the cane cut away, the dust tamped down, and surfaces slicked with molasses, so that a raw sweetness filled the air.

In Paramonga, there was no huge plaza. The streets were paved. Down the sinuous, concrete road that led from the highway, we passed the homes of the skilled workers—long cement structures, daubed over with many colors, punctuated by multiple doors. The factories dominated the hacienda, sitting squarely in the middle of it, as if here in Paramonga, Grace was past all pretense of civic-mindedness. This was industry—massive and frontal—positioned in the heart of a community where someone in a less evolved age might imagine a plaza should be. There was a busy market to one side; from its brightly painted stands, jaundiced chickens dangled from hooks, plucked clean, eyes buzzing with flies. A guest house for visiting gringos sat on the other side: It was a tall, Swiss-style chalet with brown wood fretwork and a pointed Tyrolean roof. Behind that was the engineering office, an imposing two-floor tropical command post perched on stilts, wrapped in windows, hung with lattices, and set off by a long staircase that scrolled out importantly, as if it were the approach to a sacred site. There was a melon-colored movie house, a tiny park with six benches, Wong's corner dry-goods store, and then a hillside of thatch-roof shacks. Behind all of that, in a compound that opened onto the sea, were the chief engineers' houses: a boulevard of stucco structures, each more opulent than the last. The one on the corner, the one that faced the palm-ringed Club

de Bowling, the one with a white arch leaping over the door—
the best one—was ours.

WITHIN A DAY, Cito had commandeered all the furniture into
place and was spread-eagled on a club chair poolside, throwing
back *pisco sours*. I could see his pale forehead and lanky figure
from my bedroom window. It was the lookout on Cito that gave
me an indication of how different a vantage Paramonga would
offer me. This was no inward-looking house like the one I had
come from; no tall walls shielded us from the boulevard. There
was a stern-looking fence between us and the outside world, that
was all. I surveyed our dominion from my new post and then
turned back to my room. All my belongings were in their place,
put away, save one. I took out the black pebble Antonio had
given me the morning before, polished it with the hem of my
skirt, and placed it carefully on my dresser.

The following day, George and I took stock of our neighborhood: The *soltero* house where the bachelors stayed was next
door. The Pinedas, a mild-mannered couple with a *loco* son,
lived two houses down—we could see the gigantic boy through
their window, being spoon-fed by an Indian girl. There were five
boys our age in the neighborhood, all available for afternoon fun.
A number of ladies in multilayered, many-colored skirts hawked
bread and fruit in the mornings. No vines grew under us. Our
house sat squarely on Pachamama, tight against rocks and earth.
From the second-floor windows we could monitor the sweet-
smelling factory on the other side of the compound walls. Just
beyond the tangle of iron, the black smokestacks, and the flat
trucks with their mountains of cane, we could see a gargantuan
molasses pit: a still, black lake where the fragrant residue of
cooked sugar lay, thick as quicksand. But our perch was urbane
as well as strategic: If we stood out under our archway, in front of

the door that was shaped like an Inca *tumi*, we could see all the activity at El Club.

One morning, as we stood there, we saw the birdlike woman who tended the gardens around the club pool come running out to the street where a *huachimán* stood guard. She was panting, hunching her shoulders like a nervous crow, clutching her big black skirt in her hands. She shouted something to him that we couldn't hear and pointed a clay-reddened finger back through the club entrance. She seemed to be imploring him to go back through the portal with her.

We heard later that they had found a dog floating in the pool that morning, its neck twisted clear around as if it were a chicken being readied for dinner. Word raced through the service ranks up and down the boulevard that it was Tommy, the *loco* boy, who had escaped from his house the night before, attacked a village dog, wrung its neck, and flung it into the Bowling's placid waters to float there with its eyes popped out like limpid gooseberries. "Oh, that's so silly," Mother said, when we told her what we'd heard, but all day long we saw servants gathering on street corners, whispering to one another and casting accusatory glances at the unfortunate boy's house. Never mind that the door was locked: He had flown out a window. *Locos* could do that. Never mind that the dog was too heavy to wrestle and throw: The boy had acquired superhuman powers in the light of a full moon. The boulevard's grapevine was atremble with gossip, and the *señoras* in fancy houses all hurried out to lend the servants an ear.

Nothing was ever resolved about that ill-fated dog. Rumors raged through the hacienda for one day and night, and then they evaporated like tiny bubbles, leaving a different sheen in the air. If nothing else, the incident proved we had embarked on new terrain in Paramonga. Cartavio, our old home, had been a place where we only learned about the world when it strode into our garden. In Paramonga, fences were permeable, real life close by. We were part of a thrumming world.

Although Paramonga offered a new, more-social life than Cartavio's, I could see that there would be no Antonio in it. The gardens in front and back were tight little clusters of flower beds. There was no earth to turn, no animal pens, no servants' quarters apart from a single whitewashed apartment out back where, we were told, a surly old cook once had lived. Our *amas* and cook had been hired for the house by the company, and they came and went from the hillside shacks; I hardly knew their names.

There were some marked improvements, however. During our first week, Papi brought home a German shepherd and told us it was to make up for the friends we had left behind. We called him Sigurd, like the Nibelung hero of Mother's stories, and we thought him by far the best gift we'd ever had.

He arrived full-grown, in a crate on the back of a mud-caked pickup. It took three men to lift him and carry him into our garden. The crate was smaller than the dog, and he hunched inside, growling through wooden slats, slavering at the hapless *indios* who struggled under the angry cargo. We stood on the balcony when they released him, and he sprang from the box like a mythical creature, suspended in air for what seemed an eternity before he touched ground and sent his deliverers squealing to the gate. He bounded along the fence for a full hour, barking furiously, spittle flying, until he finally sank to the grass, exhausted, his long pink tongue hanging out in what looked to be a truce.

When George and I came down to meet him with kitchen scraps, it was as if he knew we belonged to him. He trotted up, nuzzled our legs with his big blond head, licked our damp faces, and ate from our hands. He took his commands in Spanish: *Piso*, we'd say, and he'd fall to the floor, limp as a rug. *Puerta*, and he'd shoot to the gate with his eyes on fire. He was gentle with those in our company, fierce with the unintroduced. The cook told us that he had been raised by a German who lived in the far-off hills. The man had been a Nazi, they said—a word we'd heard often in stupefyingly wearisome dinner conversations—and now he'd gone native, living in a shack with a *chola*, raising dogs to be killers.

It seemed an unlikely story to me. It was true Sigurd was a colossus, but he was full of love. When he sat on his haunches, I could draw up all seven years of me and meet his snout with my chin. When I put my hand on his shoulders and looked him in the eye, he would cock his head and place a soft paw on my foot. He would allow George to lasso, even mount him, and then he'd turn circles, flashing my brother a tender grin. He was attentive to the point of obsession, following us around from morning until bedtime, pushing his wet nose into our crotches, wagging a long, fringed tail. It wasn't until later that I realized the dog didn't exist to entertain us. Sigurd had been my father's way of shoring up our fence, raising a wall against those nervous times.

As George and I grew closer, forging a lifelong collusion, Vicki seemed to float off to far corners of consciousness, like Abuelito in his towered world. She was, to us, an adult, even though she was barely eleven. Her hair had gone from gold to black. She had turned into a serious girl with a serious air and a low tolerance for fools. We could make her wince just by giggling. Hearing us approach, she would recede: into the next room, out to the balcony, up to her bedroom. She was happiest when reading or painting, pursuits that busied her days. Now that she no longer had Billy, the sun-faced Scot of Cartavio, the only company she wanted seemed to be Mother's. We'd find her hunched over a table by the piano, drawing detailed tableaus of all the Olympic gods, as Mother played "Barcarolle" beside her. Or we'd find her out on the porch, belly-down on a lounge chair, twirling her black hair over a Brontë novel, with Mother in the next chair, deep into a teacher's manual. Vicki was slow to move, quick to bristle. Her features would shrink, her neck grow short when something was said that irritated her. When the Club de Bowling's *señoras* addressed her, I could see her neck virtually disappear: Oye, *Vicki!* Chica! *When are you going to lose that baby fat, learn to mambo, get yourself a good-looking* novio? *Better start soon,* hija. *You'll be an old lady quick as you can say Hac Roboso!*

To me they said equally confounding words: Oye, *Marisi! You fat-faced little monkey! Climb up on the diving board like you did yesterday,* beba. *Come on, give us a flying jump. You're a jungle Arana, no? Like the* cauchero—*the rubber man—no? Go ask your papi to tell you about him.* Then they'd cackle into their drinks.

I shrugged my shoulders. El Bowling's *señoras* were brightly painted, strident, and silly, but they were harmless as toucans; they didn't bother me at all.

They bothered Mother. She had announced to the *señoras* that she would not be available for coffee klatches or *chicha* lunches. She was not to be disturbed during the day. From early morning to late afternoon she would be teaching her children. We saw the ladies lift their brows when she said that one day, at poolside. As we moved away, they watched us silently, slurping purple *chicha* from their straws. When I glanced back from the gate, they were already leaning into one another with commentary.

My mother didn't seem to care. She hardly socialized any-more, hardly sought adult company, hardly played her violin. From the moment my father headed for the factory's command post to the hour the cook bustled about preparing dinner, we were the center of her universe. If she was still playing the piano, it was because it allowed her to pull one of us down on the stool beside her to teach us a thing or two. Otherwise there were sums to be done, essays to compose. We wrote in our neatly lined notebooks stamped *Calvert School, Baltimore,* and imagined cool-eyed gringos in that distant port city parting the blue covers, contemplating our brilliance, pressing their heads in awe.

Come four o'clock, George and I were released for garden maneuvers with our ragtag neighborhood platoon. Five boys helped us build a tepee one day, although the concept was alien to everyone but George, who had actually seen one in *Norteamerica*. The rest of us played along, pretending we knew who the Indians were, but understanding that if they were fighting cowboys with blades clenched in their teeth, they were nothing like the mild-eyed Peruvian *indígenas* we knew. Nothing.

George stood on the sidelines shouting orders and waving his pistols as the rest of us wielded bamboo poles and sheets, tying the top off with chicken-coop wire. We worked feverishly, glancing down the boulevard from time to time, scaring ourselves with the possibility that the big *loco* boy might stagger our way any moment and strangle us with his beefy hands. Tommy never did make an appearance that day, except long after nightfall, when I looked out my window and caught a glimpse of his doughy face over a bib, and the girl patiently shoveling food into it.

One of our neighborhood friends, Carlos Ruiz, was rod-straight, doe-eyed, with a lick of brown hair shooting up from his crown. He was the son of one of the machine specialists and liked to talk about his father's expertise. According to Carlos, all the factories, all the output of Paramonga, depended on his old man. He was a handsome boy, tidy and scrubbed, with lemon skin and a chiseled nose. "*Listo,*" he said as he stepped away from the tepee to survey our handiwork. Ready. He tucked his shirt into his shorts and grinned.

Carlos's *ama* peeked through the gate, where she stood with the other *muchachas*, chewing stalks of warm sugarcane and talking of love. "Carlos," she pleaded in a voice that issued, high and reedy, from her nose, "*no te ensucies!*" Don't get dirty. "Your mother will yell!"

"*Vamos*," said Carlos, ignoring her and nodding toward our lop-sided tent. "Let's go in."

"No, no," said George. "Not like that, *tonto*. You can't just go in. This is a club and I'm the president. We have to have rules." Then he turned on his feet slowly, thinking what those might be.

"I know," he said finally. "Rule number one: You have to learn the handshake." He made it up right there and then—grab the right with the right, slide up, clasp the elbow, swipe arm against arm, one side then the other, intertwine fingers, and shake. We all did it after that. Again and again, messing up hopelessly, laughing, then starting over, until it was neat and rote.

"Rule number two!" said George. "In order to be accepted into the club, everyone has to go into that tepee with my sister. One at a time. And once you're inside, you have to kiss her."

"Yechh," said Carlos, his chest caving with the thought. "Will you go first?"

"Not me!" said George. "I told you, I'm president. I'm already *in* the club."

"Okay. Me!" said Manuel, a buck-toothed boy with droopy eyes.

"George," I protested. "I—"

"And, Marisi, if you don't like him, you have the power to say no."

My protestation hung in the air. The power to say no? To say who gets in? All of a sudden, the kisses seemed trivial, no more than sealing wax on a queen's table.

I was so quick to trot along behind George, I never stopped to wonder at the fact that I was the only girl there. It is clear to me now, sitting as I am forty years later, looking out over the rooftops of Washington, seeing other people's daughters scoot by with their skinny little arms around boys, how different I was from my counterparts in the hacienda. The girls of Paramonga—at least the ones of a certain class—were in their houses, in starched dresses, teetering on their mothers' high heels, kissing their dolls. They were acquiring the manners my abuelita expected of me: learning to contain myself when others were too boisterous, to be pleasantly outgoing when others were too shy. They lived monitored girlhoods, in aesthetically pleasing places, with carefully selected playmates, and someday they would pass into chaperoned young womanhood, during which their virtues would be guarded like family jewels.

Peruvian girls were not running about, pounding stakes into earth, tying a tepee down. They were securing respectability, studying the polarities between *señor* and *señora*, grooming their lives accordingly, making themselves scarce. Now that I recall, the only ones who came around unannounced were daughters of servants, dirty girls who would shuffle up with their eyes cast down, offering themselves wordlessly to our games.

It didn't occur to me that I was anything but a boy's equal. I was my mother's daughter, ready to pit myself against boys if I had to, ready to grin at them openly, as I'd seen my mother grin at the *solteros*, facing them squarely when they strode down the streets, tipping their hats her way.

But there was a dichotomy at work, and it would take a long time for me to understand it. As much as I was a gringa, chasing through that neighborhood in the wake of my big brother, I was also studiously acquiring a Peruvian femininity. It came in subtle ways: During one of Tía Chaba's visits, when she stepped into the garden, leaned over, and hissed in my ear—"Marisi, cross your legs, *hijita;* you're showing the world your very soul." Or, "Don't sit there with your mouth hanging open like a lizard; close it until you have something interesting to say." Or hearing an engineer's wife gossip at my father's table—"*Oy, por Dios*, Jorge, have you seen that *criatura* the Martinez girl has turned into?

She walks like an *hombre*, waves her hands about like a *chola*, props her fists on her hips, and spits out ear-singeing *groserías*." So that by the time I was grown, I knew there were two women I could be—the Latina or the gringa—and that at every juncture I would need to choose one. I picked my way through life, deciding to try one identity and then the other. I transformed myself into an all-American in high school; became Peruvian again in college. I was a good Latina in my first marriage, going to the altar with the first man who ever touched me, hanging my future on his, never reaching for him in bed. And then I was a good gringa in my second, throwing out all the rule books and following my heart. But all that came later, after Paramonga. Long after I discovered a thing or two about boys.

It was in George's club that I learned boys were clannish. They loved the company of other boys. Backslaps and fellowship. The code of the gang. For these things they were willing to undergo any humiliation, suffer any outrage. To be *in*. But if it was true for them, it was also true for me. I longed to be part of a team, to wield a little power. Were kisses the price of admission? *Caramba!* They could kiss me all day long. My hair was too long, my dresses too girly, God hadn't bothered to fit me with a hose, but that hadn't seemed to stop me so far. Kisses? Sure. I could do that. I'd get by. I'd belong.

"Okay," I said to Manuel briskly. "Follow me."

The buck-toothed boy came through the flap of the tent meekly and watched as I tramped to the center and sat on the grass, cross-legged.

"Now what?" he asked, his skewed eyes focusing.

"Sit here and let me see if I like you," I said, and motioned to the space before me.

He sat down and I studied his face. "Look," he whispered nervously, and put a hand in his pocket. "I have something I can give you." He pulled out a *caramelo* in red wrapping and offered it to me. His face was mottled with expectation.

"What flavor?" I asked.

"Strawberry."

Candy. I hadn't anticipated bribes. My power was beginning to seem infinite. I could hear the giggles and guffaws outside.

"Fine," I said, and put out my hand. He dropped the warm cube in. "You tell anyone about this and you're gone," I said. "*Ciao.*"

"And the kiss?" he said. *El beso?*

I put out one foot. "On my shoe."

He obliged.

"Okay. You're in."

He scrambled to his feet and burst outside with a whoop.

Three more filed in, one at a time. I extracted a variety of treasures from them: a green marble, a Coca-Cola top from the *loco* boy's garden, a fifty-*centavo* piece. The kisses were minor obligations: my elbow, my wrist, a hand, and with each, the promise to never tell.

The last was Carlos. He came in, peering up through his lashes.

"You want to be in this club?" I said, narrowing my eyes as he sat.

"*Sí.*"

"*Bueno.* You have to do two things. First, the kiss. And then you give me something."

"Give you what?"

"What do you have in your pockets?"

"Oh." He checked. There was nothing there.

I looked him up and down, taking my time to think. Outside, the boys were crawling up, trying to eavesdrop. I could hear George wrestle them back.

What could I get the boy to give me? And then I thought of Antonio.

"I know," I said. "Tell me something. A story. But it has to be true, it has to be secret, and it better be quick."

He frowned, smoothing his cowlick. "Okay," he said.

"Un beso primero," I said, and pushed my lips out for a kiss.

He didn't hesitate. He sucked air, leaned in, pecked me on the mouth, and sat back down.

"And now, *el secreto*," he said calmly, folding his manicured hands together in his lap while I caught my breath and wiped his kiss onto my forearm. "It's something I heard my mother say to my father. And it has something to do with you. She said your mother is weird. *Rara.* She talks funny, doesn't fit. She should get on a boat and go back to wherever she came from. She doesn't belong in Peru."

I could feel heat rise through my chest, fly up my neck, and lodge in the back of my throat. A boy staggered through the flap, fell, and rolled in at us, red-faced and cackling, but I hardly registered him at all. Carlos stood, brushed himself off, and walked out of the tent. "She said yes," he announced to the others, assuming consent when I'd sat there with my mouth hanging open like a reptile.

Doesn't belong in Peru? What did that mean exactly? Did she fit any less than anyone else in that makeshift hacienda? There was a carnival of misfits here: Tommy the *loco*, the long-legged *solteros*, and—*por el amor de Dios*—how about Wong?

Step inside a corner bodega anywhere in Peru and you were likely to see a Chinese face behind the counter. Step inside Paramonga's shabby little *bodega china* and there would be Wong, his colossal head trailing a goatee to his abacus the way a genie trails a wisp to its lamp.

"Qué quiele? Tulón?" You want a *turrón*? And a long, bony finger would point to the tall glass jar with its colored chunks of nougat. "One *sol* buys five!"

"How about *flan*?" we'd call out, just to tease him. Just to ask him for something we knew he didn't have.

"*Mo lo!*" he'd bark back in Cantonese. "All gone."

Wong, we had been told, was from the village of Huarmey. His parents had been coolies from Shanghai. Slavery had been outlawed for almost a century in South America, but a new "Chinese law" was in place when his family was lured to Peru. The sugar and guano moguls paid one pound sterling for Wong's father, half that for his mother. The two made the nine-thousand-mile voyage to Callao in the hold of a ship with four hundred others like them. By the time they stepped into the cane fields five months later, they knew they should never have come. Wong's father had to be shackled to keep him from trying to make a run for the sea. His mother took an overdose of opium and lay down by the sugar shoots to die.

Old Wong grew up, married, had sons. But he stayed in Paramonga, peddling his dried food and sweets, clinging to the cane field as tightly as a locust husk—as shriveled as the shrimp and *tau-err-tong* that filled the barrels of his shop.

"*Mo lo!*" the Peruvian children would mimic as he hobbled home in the dark. All gone.

Doesn't fit. Like who? Like the Dane who lived next door in the lemon-yellow *casa de solteros*? He had come years before, bright-faced and handsome, bragging of pink-assed women. At first he was one of the ordinary ones, shuttling out to the factory in the morning and sucking on rum at night. Until one fine day when he began to drool, drop things, and spin through the rooms with his hands on his head. They took him to a hospital after that. "Nerves," they whispered, "something to do with his spine." Then they brought him back to the house beside us, and he was all fixed, shiny as a new steel tool.

But one afternoon George and I looked up from our cowboy wars and saw the gringo flinging tables and chairs through his second-floor window, wriggling wildly, pausing only to hang his head out over the sill and gurgle at the pile below. When they edged upstairs to grab him, they said the man had gone crazy. When they took him off and opened his head, they found a fistful of worms inside.

We Peruvians have a name for that. *Taki Onqoy*: a plague of worms that fills a body with an irresistible urge to wiggle. The mountain Indians had been known to invoke the *Taki Onqoy* against the Spaniards for all the agonies they had brought to Peru. The Spaniards danced and writhed until they flung themselves into the rivers—a useful thing to have happen to foreigners, a curse to slam them back where they belonged.

Back where she came from. All these years later, I am still drawn up tight by that phrase, with a fury I can hardly contain. Who was to say that Carlos Ruiz's mother with her roots tracing back to Segovia belonged in Peru? Or the king's conquistador, Francisco Pizarro, for that matter, an illegitimate pig farmer from the Spanish fringe—did he have a birthright to the land of the Inca? If *Señora* Ruiz and Pizarro had pioneer birthrights, as my Peruvian family claimed to have, did they have one any more than my gringa mother?

Before that moment in the tepee with Carlos Ruiz, I did not know that my mother was an outcast in my father's country. I knew that she was different, that she and my grandmother were at odds with each other, that she seemed awkward in Peruvian settings, that people giggled at the way she spoke. It wasn't that she was reviled in any way for how she looked, for the color of her skin. Not at all. Light complexions were admired in Peru, and her alabaster skin seemed an asset: a credit to my father. He had married a *blanca* and in so doing whitened future generations of Aranas. It was good to be pale. What I learned from Carlos Ruiz that afternoon was that the problem with us was not about skin. It was not about language. It was not about money. It was about being American. It was about seeing my mother, despite all evidence to the contrary, as a cartoon *yanqui*: the big-boned, clumsy, loud-mouthed, bragging, dim-brained, swaggering kind.

MY ANGER EVENTUALLY subsided, but it never quite went away. There was much to signal the growing antipathy against Americans in Peru. I could stand at my window and watch it. The way the guard at the club across the way picked his teeth when he stared at the *solteros*; the way the guest-house servants laughed into their hands when a visiting New Yorker pulled away; the way the *señoras* fell silent and swiveled their heads as my mother walked past. I didn't realize it then, but I know it now: My world shrank a few sizes when Carlos Ruiz confided his secret. I pulled back, became a distant satellite to the boys' club, and began to wish George would spend all his time alone with me, digging into the loam of Pachamama—contemplating the wonders of dirt—as Antonio had taught me to do.

Papi must have seen that I needed to be aired out and pushed into the open of Paramonga, because he announced one day that he had arranged for *Señor* González, the hacienda's horse trainer, to bring us his tamest mares, teach me and George basic equestrian skills, and take us out three mornings a week for a good look at the topography we lived in: the cane fields, the rocky shoreline, and the arid stretches that circled the hacienda. George and I would emerge from the house after our morning lessons and find the gentle creatures waiting for us by the gate, fanning their tails in wide arcs. *Señor* González would be perched on the fence, his face lean and hard as a saddlebag, his eyes framed by a fretwork of lines.

If the weather was good and the horses were willing, *Señor* González would let us ride to the *fortaleza*, the pre-Colombian adobe fortress on the other side of the Pan American Highway, about three miles from our house. It had been raised in the early 1400s by the Chimu, the most powerful people to rule Peru before the Inca. As wide as a city block, the *fortaleza* was an enigmatic hulk, built to house Chimu eminences and the warriors they had conscripted to defend against Inca invasions.

I loved that tiered leviathan. I loved the way it hoisted itself out of a jaundiced earth, smelling of urine and gloom. I loved to run its dusty maze—room after room of pocked floors and walls. Life was good when George and I could jump off our *yeguas*, pat them on the nose, hand *Señor* González the reins, and scamper up that sunbaked scarp.

The purpose of the *fortaleza*, as far as we could tell, had shifted from stronghold to cemetery. Burial vaults yawned at us as we clambered through the labyrinth, yielding up skulls and femurs that had been tossed there by fellow thieves. Our servants had told us how robbers had ransacked those graves in years gone by. Some called themselves scholars, others were fortune hunters, still more were just thugs, angling for easy money. They had come from far and wide, slinking in through the night, plunging picks into Pachamama, pulling out Chimu bones, killing one another in the process, but they emerged from that place with wonders: Capes made of hummingbird wings. Gold nose hoops. Towering headdresses. Earrings with gems the size of our fists. "They're either sitting in a museum or adorning some rich man's table in San Francisco," Papi commented. They were long gone, in other words. But we didn't believe him. We searched anxiously for *fuegos fatuos*, will-o'-the-wisps that Antonio had told me would waft out of the soil if treasure were buried below. When we didn't see them, George and I would thrust our hands in anyway for the simple joy of rooting around that dirt. But the only thing we ever unearthed was bone. We'd study it, keep it if it interested us, fling it aside impatiently. Veterans of the dig.

"What do you think you're doing?" said *Señor* González, as he puffed up after us one day. A look of disgust twisted his face when he saw us handling the remains. "What in God's name—"

"I need these," I said, yanking the teeth out of a dusty skull. "For my collection."

"I have more than you do!" sang George, jangling his pockets.

"*Que Dios los perdone*," said the saddle-faced *señor*. "And may the *apus* be looking the other way."

"The *apus*?"

"The spirits of these mountains. They won't like that you're heckling the dead. Hurry it up and let's go. I don't need any more bad luck than I already have." He swung into the sun and headed back down, hitching his shoulders as if a chill air had suddenly swept the *fortaleza*, rubbing his sleeves.

We found a dead rodent as we clinked and rattled our way down that day. George picked it up and thrust it in his pocket along with the teeth. "For Doctor Birdseye," he said. "Maybe he'll give us a good price."

Birdseye was a *norteamericano* scientist who had come to Paramonga to advise the paper engineers on new ways to cook down bagasse, the woody pulp of processed sugarcane. Paramonga was on the verge of being one of Grace's greatest successes, marking a company shift from merchant to innovator. Whole warehouses of sugarcane byproducts were whirling from the engines, from toilet paper to corrugated boxes to gin. The engineers already knew what to make with the residue: polyvinyl chloride, one of the plastics of the modern age. Paramonga had become the sort of showcase presidents visit, and Birdseye was one of its stars.

He was a naturalist, a botanist, a biochemist, a pioneer of cryogenics, and "an all-round genius," according to my papi. But more important, as far as we were concerned, he was a pushover for us.

He was small, spry, and wizened, with shocks of white hair sprouting from either side of his head. When he caught sight of us, his eyes would grow bright, almost numinous, and he'd wave us forward to hear his thoughts about some natural wonder. On his first day in the little house beside the Bowling Club, Birdseye had announced that any and all children were welcome in his home. "Especially welcome," he added with a twinkle in his eye and a shiver of his wild mane, "if they bring me good business."

Business meant animals of any kind, dead or alive. Insects, small mammals, snakes, lizards, birds—it didn't matter—he would buy them from us for a few *centavos* and add them to his working lab. His lab, he told us, might be working on anything, so it was best to haul it all in. He never knew when inspiration would come. On an expedition to Alaska, studying the habits of bears, he had thought of a way to quick-freeze fresh vegetables. Years later, when we saw his colorful Birds Eye bricks lining the frozen-food aisles of U.S. grocery stores, we realized that the work he was doing out in the field, including Peru, had ended up making him a very rich man. But at the time, he seemed little more than a madcap Merlin with pint-size associates. And a can full of cash on his desk.

When we got home, we left our horses with *Señor* González and traipsed down the street toward prosperity and the Birdseye house. It was a one-floor structure with a towering casuarina tree flaunting its bright yellow flowers by the front door. No gate, no fence. Every time we saw that door we marveled at the fact that we were approaching it immediately from the street. Until we'd laid eyes on Birdseye's house, the only portals we saw so directly were the doors of indigent shacks. The place was open, permeable, accessible from any side. In the back, where the sweet-natured Mrs. Birdseye spent most of her days, there was a flower and orchid garden. Peacocks wandered through, unfurling their tails and flouncing about like Inca conquerors. Parrots chattered in the trees. Birds, animals, people like us, could drift onto Birdseye property freely. An aura of welcome surrounded the place.

The manservant who answered the door received us warmly and led us to Dr. Birdseye's massive garden table—a green slab of wood cluttered with sticks, instruments, glass, and a large tin can. The doctor was perched on a high chair behind.

He was gray in every aspect except for his eyes, which were sharp blue and glistening. Through the glass of his spectacles they seemed large and material as planets. There was a slight hunch in his spine from bending over tables too much, peering into a gallery of lenses he kept in a box on a shelf. As we approached, I saw that he was in his threadbare white lab coat, buttoned right up to his chin.

"My assistants!" he called out when he saw us, flinging his small arms wide.

George produced our rat, brandishing him by one foot.

"But that's not a legitimate rat, dear Watson!" the doctor said, taking the scraggly creature between two fingers. "It's a *cuy*, don't you know? A guinea pig. You Peruvians have them for dinner! Haven't you seen one toasted and floating in a nice peanut sauce? A few hours sooner and you might have made a good *criollo* meal with this little fellow. As it is, he'll make a better tidbit for me. What'll it be, my dear Watsons? Twenty?"

We nodded happily. Twenty *centavos*. A candy at Wong's. Birdseye scrabbled noisily in his tin can, pulled out a coin, and slapped it on the table. "There."

We reached for the money, passed it to each other, and studied it closely before George tucked it into his pants. Birdseye smiled and pulled a foot-long stick of wood from a pile on the table. He was clearly in the middle of building something.

"We're not just Peruvians," George said then, standing there with his chin pushed out, two hands thrust in his pockets. "We're Americans like you."

"Yes, you are, but better," Birdseye shot back.

"Better?"

"Well, sure, son. You two are hybrids. You know what that means? Half-breeds, half and half. In scientific terms, you're better specimens for that."

"Half and half is better?" I squeaked.

"You bet it is," said Birdseye. "In the natural world, you bet. Take botany. You want to make a strong plant? Get two weak ones. Cross 'em. You'll get a hardier species every time."

I looked at George quizzically, trying to imagine my brother as a plant. How could he, as big and strong as he was, possibly be any stronger than Mother or Papi? But Birdseye continued, working as he talked, whittling the stick to the size of others that splayed out from the incomprehensible edifice on his table. "And then, of course, Peruvians are half half. Half Spanish, half Indian. A little Chinese. A little Arab. Americans are half this, half that, too. Down, down, down, five million years through the generations. It's the cross-fertilization that improves things. Haven't you heard about mules? They're stronger, can take more weight, do more work. They're hybrids. Half donkey, half horse. You're a couple of mules, you two. Stronger than plain old Americans. Stronger than Peruvians. Mixing! See those flowers over there?" He pointed to a pot of roses, standing amid an army of labeled plants. "The hybrids are the proud and straight ones. See what I mean? Like you! Mix it up, mix it up! That's what makes us more advanced. It's a scientific fact. And you can tell anyone I said so."

He went back to his whittling, but when he looked up, he saw us staring at him, still in thrall to his words, little minds reeling at the thought of our superiority. Laughing, he put down his knife. "You're good listeners, you two," he said. "Almost as good as Tommy."

George and I sneaked looks at each other. Tommy?

Birdseye peered at us over his wire-rimmed glasses, and I pointed a tentative finger in the direction of the house across the street. "That Tommy?"

"Yes. That Tommy," said the old man unequivocally.

"The *loco*?" sputtered George.

There was a long silence, and then Birdseye took off his glasses and placed them carefully on the table in front of him. "Martha?" he called. "Martha, are you there?"

"Yes, dear." A white head bobbed up in the greenery behind, and Mrs. Birdseye wiped her forehead with the back of her hand. She drew herself to her feet and set her spade down carefully. "I'm here." She came toward us, clapping her hands and dusting them off.

"These fine children, Martha, seem to think that Tommy Pineda across the street is a *loco*."

"Oh, no, no, little ones." The sweet lady came at us, bending over so that we could see the gold flecks in her eyes. "Tommy's not a *loco*. He's *slow*. That's very different. It's something that happens to children sometimes, a sickness. He was born that way. He has a little trouble eating and a lot of trouble talking, and maybe he makes loud, funny noises. But, well! He's a big boy, seventeen, after all. And he brings Dr. Birdseye the most interesting things—beetles and bird feathers. You see, everything in this world has a sound explanation, a good reason. You mustn't believe everything you hear. He's not crazy. Oh, no. And I tell you this with all the confidence in the world: He wouldn't hurt a flea."

"How about a dog?" George asked.

"Nor a dog. No."

"They found a dog floating in the Bowling's pool," George ventured. "There was no blood in him. Wong said he was dry as salt shrimp."

"It certainly was no fault of Tommy's," Mrs. Birdseye said.

"Our *ama* says he flies through the night looking for love," I said.

Mrs. Birdseye seemed physically drawn up by that remark, and then, just as suddenly, her shoulders relaxed. "Well, yes, he very well might," she said. "And wouldn't you if you were locked up in that big house all day? I don't know why the Pinedas feel they have to do that to him. It must be a...well, I just know there's a reason why. But there's nothing wrong with that, children—flying through the night looking for love. Poor boy, with all his troubles during the day. Can you think of anything more right for him than love? My word! Nothing wrong with that at all."

That night I took the antique gray teeth from my pockets and lined them up on my dresser, next to my prayer card of the Virgin and my shiny black stone. I had a lot to atone for. I had ransacked a tomb, wished a plague of worms on *Señora* Ruiz's brain, mistaken a sick boy for a *loco*. Surely the jaws of hell would creak open and thresh me under. Surely the *apus* would call a curse on my head.

I stroked Sigurd's wheat-colored brow for a while, then sat on my bed and thought about Antonio. We had never spoken much about the Virgin or about the power of the *apus*, but Antonio had always made a point to teach me about my fundamental link to Pachamama—that I was a product of natural forces, that I was another version of earth, that I could prevail against evil if I would only learn how. Was it really possible to open up your belly and take in the world? The bad with the good? Could I bring it all in—the ghosts, the demons, the dead, the *loco*, the vine, the *bruja*—breathe them in, and then let them ride off on a beam of black light, into the heart of my stone?

Could I fix Tommy Pineda? He might not be a *loco*, but Mrs.

Birdseye had conceded that he was very capable of making nocturnal flights through Paramonga. Never mind that he was looking for love; the very thought of that thick-necked boy, drooling and lurching through the night air, was terrifying—proof that there were strange forces at work in the world. But was it possible to bring Tommy in through my *qosqo*, pluck him clean of any negative force, any tiny germ of malevolent intent against our bright-eyed Sigurd, and shoot his sickness deep into my pebble?

I pulled up my shirt, bared my *qosqo*, and turned so that it faced the stone, unobstructed. Assured that my alignment was perfect, I closed my eyes and thought of that poor benighted boy down the road.

Open up, I willed myself. Bring on the storm. Let the *bruja's* vine in. Let me be as still as the earth, as steady as Pachamama.

Nothing. There was a gentle rustle of wind through the casuarinas on the boulevard. Not a voice was heard in the house, no sound save the clickety-clack of knives and forks in the kitchen. I couldn't tell whether my parents' dinner was just beginning or ending. There was an eerie quiet through my window, as if the Bowling across the way had been emptied of all revelers, as if the *casa de solteros* had bolted its doors. Sigurd let out a long sigh, smacked his chops, and shifted his body. He stretched his legs, pointed his toes. Eventually, his eyelids fluttered shut. I sat like that for what seemed a long time, barely breathing, holding on to my shirt, pushing my belly toward the stone, trying to rid my mind of everything but the image of Tommy Pineda's monumental head.

I have no recollection of how much time passed before I felt the bed jiggle under me. My eyes flew open. The room was trembling. The teeth, the Virgin, and the stone were dancing on the dresser, ticking across the top like a company of infantrymen. Sigurd sat up wide-eyed, then yelped and fled, skeetering down the corridor and banging down the stairs.

The furniture was hopping across the room now, and I could hear glass crash to the floor. My father's voice boomed through the house. *"Terremoto!"* he yelled. Earthquake.

Mother flew in the door and grabbed me, her robe flapping like wings on a bat. Then the night went black. Somehow, we made it down the stairs and under the front arch, where my father stood, legs apart, his hands gripping the plaster above him. Vicki and George huddled beneath. We stayed there until the shaking stopped. Out in the garden, the servants were sprawled facedown in the grass.

"Ya," said Papi finally. *"Ya terminó."* It was over.

We could hear running from the boulevard out into the street. "Anyone hurt?" yelled a *soltero*, hiking himself over the wall and squinting through the dark.

I started to cry. "It was me!" I squawked to George. "I did it! I made it shake. It was all my fault!"

He looked at me as if I had lost my mind.

No one else listened to me. Neighbors rushed down the boulevard, assessing the damage. Papi went to the factory. A *soltero* checked on my mother. The servants lit candles and clasped us to their chests.

When I was carried back to my room, my things were as I had left them. Except that the little black stone was on the floor.

There is a part of me that still believes I caused that earthquake. Maybe that is why of all the quakes I lived through in my first six years of life (almost two dozen, according to seismological records, some of them far more violent), this is the only one I can recall. I try to muster a memory of the others—the screeching, the running for clear ground, the tinkle of glass. But all I can summon are the hours between dark and dawn of that one night. After I was deposited on my bed, I sat there stiffly, monitoring my navel, cupping my hand over its little void. A number of adoring faces approached to soothe me, but I couldn't bring myself to close my eyes. The *amas* brought me linden tea. My mother put a cool rag on my fevered skull. At midnight I fell into a deep sleep. All night and all the next day I remained in bed.

On the second morning, *Señor* González rode up to tell us that he had found Sigurd in the molasses pit, belly up and floating.

THE EARTH WAS always moving in those days. Pachamama was temperamental, moody, shifting her weight heavily beneath us, tossing from side to side. My mother and father were pricked with that same petulance, contemplative and sullen since our move from Cartavio. Since—for that matter—their return from the United States.

I did not identify these things at the time, of course, but that frame of mind is easy enough to locate and retrieve now that I find it cataloged in the same drawer with a lifetime of other vague dissatisfactions. A tight-lipped foreboding moved through our house and, were it not for earthquakes and molasses-coated carcasses and the providential distraction of childish games and of scrabbling in ancient graves, we might have turned to it, pointed, and remarked.

I cannot tell you what actually happened, what incidents signaled the widening gap between my mother and father. Even now, after much reflection, not one specific event rises to mind. I knew it by the way they moved. Or didn't. The hand that no longer slipped around her waist. The way he propelled himself away from the dinner table. The tic in her brow when he said he hoped his mother would come visit the children. The flare of his nostrils when she drew old letters from the bed table and left the room. The melancholy way she played Palmgren on the piano. The rush of bubbles when he poured himself another rum and Coke. The click of her shoes coming back from a party alone. The sight of his men carrying him home by the elbows after a night of drinking. The angle of Tía Chaba's glance when she came for a weekend visit. It was as if all Pachamama's convulsions had joggled them loose.

Shaky days. The earth beneath us was putting on a show, wriggling our toes. *"Por fin!"* Tía Chaba told us our Spanish forebears had cried when they set boots on Peru. At last! *"Terra firma!"* Little did they know we descendants would spend the rest of our days quivering on our legs. "Stand your ground!" Mother taught us the gringos had said at Lexington. It was a phrase that sounded very silly to our ears. "The firm ground of result," she quoted the sainted Churchill, whose name she had given her son. And George Winston and I fell to giggling.

We knew, if no one else was admitting it, that there was nothing firm about Pachamama. I remember being struck by the way northerners look up at the sky when they're told disaster is coming, but of course it makes perfect sense: It's from air and water that their dangers come. In Peru, we look at the ground. We are worried earthlings, fitfully tied, creeping about on volatile real estate. We fret about impetuous floors. We shuffle when we dance. We keep an eye down when we do it. There is no Peruvian exempt from geologic upheaval: not the rich, the poor, the beautiful, the ugly. There is a bond of the abused in us, a certain fatalism that accrues to children who are shaken by the earth.

In those years of tectonic uncertainty, we talked constantly about earthquakes. The rumble of a passing truck would set us to grabbing our chairs, cocking our ears, making ready to scamper away. Some of Paramonga's residents were so practiced in the subtleties of geologic motion that I could see them from my window—the bread vendor, the street sweeper—staring down at their feet, shouting *"Temblores! Temblores!"* when the rest of us couldn't feel a thing. George and I would sidle around the garden, feigning a palsy, screaming that we could feel a

terrrrrremoto, and then we'd fall to the ground, laughing maniacally, rubbing our faces in dirt.

Papi motioned us to him one evening when he overheard us
talking about such things and told us about a quake that had
rocked Lima when he was a young man of twenty. Not with the
bebecita tremors of our own experience, but with a jactitation
that could rip cities asunder. He had been standing on a high
floor in a federal building in downtown Lima, waiting to get his
driver's license. Frustrated and anxious to get back to work or
school—for those were hectic days—he stepped from side to
side in the long line, eyeing the government goon at the counter,
muttering curses under his breath.

All of a sudden, the floor began to undulate. He braced himself against a post and took a good look around him, trying to get
a sense of what was going on. Where two walls joined, he saw a
corner of the room open, each wall shrugging in an opposite direction, leaving a gap in between. As plaster dust drifted past, he
looked outside to a patch of blue sky. Below it, suspended, was
the church of San Francisco with its bells swinging frantically in
its towers. He said that the walls of the building stood cleaved
like that for what seemed an eternity to him, the din of bells in
his ears and the image of the church etched hotly on his brain.
Then the walls closed shut just as neatly as they had opened,
and the building seemed none the worse for wear. The bureau-
crats slid the government desks back to where they had been,
they straightened the president's portrait on the wall, and before
he knew it some hatchet-faced functionary was pointing at him
and yelling, "Next!"

In the world of the Inca there are tidy explanations for these
things, as tidy as the lectures my cravated grandfather would issue on torque, or as tidy as the earthquake quotient my father
would diligently build into his structures no matter where they
happened to be. According to the Inca, the earth is made up of

energy bubbles—one *apu*'s domain is here, another's there—and
it is only natural that the earth should react violently when energy
bubbles cross. Two force fields meet and you have confrontation.
Simple as that. But the ability to take that phenomenon to a
higher level—to go from shaking to awareness, from confrontation to enlightenment—is a goal we terrestrials seldom reach.

The crossing of my parents' force fields was now entering
a volatile stage. They had been drawn together at first by a fierce
and inexplicable magnetism; they had fallen in love, married,
had children; and now they were rolling back in their separate
energy bubbles, startled by the ways they had changed.
My mother was no longer free, untrammeled, able to pull an-
chor, move off, and reinvent herself, as was her American
way. She was in a small place, with small-minded people and
unfamiliar traditions, who found her independence bizarre. As
for my father, he was in limbo—living in the country of his ancestors, speaking his language with his children, continuing
to act as if he were fully Peruvian, but his house was an alien territory.

Not only was each of them now breathing a different, altered
air, they were also uncomfortable among people they'd once
thought they knew. How could my father confide in his Peruvian
compadres? They couldn't possibly understand what it was like to
be the husband of a gringa, to not be puffed up and coddled the
way a Latina learns to baby a man. My mother's American
friends could hardly suggest how incomprehensible they thought
Peruvians were. Nor, for that matter, did she feel she could confide in them about how increasingly difficult she was finding
Peru. There were stop-and-start conversations. Awkward moments. A feeling of irreconcilability filled the air.

Perhaps that is why the subject of another mixed marriage began to interest our household. The romance between Ralph
Cunningham and Carmen, the laundress's daughter, became the

topic of intense conversation between my mother and father. It, too, was a flash fire between two opposite fields of energy. My parents found they could talk about Ralph and Carmen and in the process say a great deal about their own feelings. They could do it without being accusatory or hurtful. It was something akin to the manner in which timorous Chinese women once talked to their doctors: by pointing to taboo body parts on ivory dolls and saying where the poor things hurt. My parents would talk about the Cunninghams in endless and heated exchanges. We knew because we listened at the doors.

Ralph Cunningham, it seems, was an Englishman from Dover, a *soltero* whose solid frame, thick eyeglasses, and stubborn ways belied a hunger in his heart. He had come to the hacienda as a large mule comes to water, in the simple trajectory of a man coming to work. He did not realize he was looking for love.

But love found him. In the form of Carmen, a tiny, brash woman standing in the *solteros'* doorway with black hair down her back and one hip dangling midair like an itchy question mark.

Her mother was Mrs. Gilfillen's laundress, a hardworking *indí- gena* from one of the villages that dotted the nearby wilderness. Even when engineer Gilfillen had been alive, his wife had taken an interest in her employee, as loyal and pleasant a human being as the Scotswoman had ever known. But when Mr. Gilfillen died, his widow took that interest a good notch higher, investing a missionary's zeal in the welfare of the laundress and bringing her daughter into her home to teach her the manners of an Edinburgh miss.

Carmen learned to speak, read, and write good English. She learned how to set a proper table, serve a square city meal, hold forth in polite conversation, and cite a line or two of Robert Louis Stevenson as ably as any silk-gloved debutante. In the mornings, the young girl would leave her mother in the back with her washboard and come in the house to sit at Mrs. Gilfillen's table. She started at twelve and was schooled till sixteen. But her hips filled out, and her walk took on a market-day waggle. When she learned to squeeze her breasts up between her elbows—a lesson Mrs. Gilfillen did not teach her—and when she colored in her mouth, she began turning heads. That was when the *señoras* started to squawk, and that was when Carmen found herself spinning through our airtight hacienda toward the door of the *solteros*.

At first it was a jolly Dutchman who took the luscious bait, flashing his blues in her direction with an irresistible wink. One after another, they all began to play, batting her around the *casa de solteros* like cats with a soft new toy. Mrs. Gilfillen never knew about Carmen's visits to the *solteros*, or, perhaps, being a perfectly proper Edinburgh lady, she chose not to know. But when walnut-skinned Carmen landed—full-mouthed and ripe—on a chair beside Ralph one night, he blinked and gawked and asked her to marry him.

The news shook the hacienda when Mrs. Gilfillen announced it. "I am so ple-e-eased," she sang to the ladies at the club, "that Carmen has accepted Ralph Cunningham's proposal. What a lovely couple they will make." Lovely couple? The wives looked around at one another. A poker-stiff Brit from a cottage in Dover and the hot-bottomed spawn of the splay-footed washerwoman? As opposite energy bubbles as ever there were. Yet, for all the malicious prattle, no one could deny there was electricity there. But a biracial marriage was a current no one wanted to touch.

Pueblo chico, infierno grande, the old adage has it. Small town, big hell. When Ralph Cunningham announced the happy day, the Club de Bowling women stared at the walls. The *solteros* got out the good gin and begged him to reconsider. When he asked Papi to be his best man, Papi gave a long lecture on *como se hace,* the things you can and cannot do in Peru. When vows were exchanged in church, a crowd of revelers was there only because the good Scottish widow had insisted on it. And when the new Mrs. Cunningham arrived at the club in her citrus-green sundress, ready for *chicha* and gossip, she found herself at an empty table, watching the smokestack pump black into the sky.

The *como se hace* of the Cunningham situation was the theme on which my parents' bedroom conversations focused. You can't turn your back on a lifetime, they agreed—and much to our surprise, since even at our tender ages we knew it was exactly what they'd done. You won't fool anyone; blood will tell. Did those two lovebirds really know what they were getting into? Why didn't Ralph save himself a lot of heartache, my father lamented, and find himself a nice Englishwoman? And so my mother was made to understand what was in his own heart. Why didn't Carmen get out of this hellhole, my mother countered, and head for a city where people were more enlightened? And so my father was made to understand how she yearned to be free of small-minded Peru.

The upshot was that my mother quickly befriended Carmen Cunningham. At company parties, at the Bowling, I would stand at my window and watch her make a beeline for the hacienda's pariah. The two would sit and talk for hours—blond hair grazing black—finding comforts in their otherness. At a distance, the club's *señoras* could be seen shaking their heads in bafflement. This one was too *extranjera*, that one too *indígena*. What could the two possibly have to say to each other?

The following month, Papi got word he would be transferred to Lima. I took down my relics—my prayer card, my teeth, and my stone—packed them in a box, and, before I knew it, all our possessions were boxed, wrapped, and carried out onto a truck. Lima's splendors beckoned: our tíos and tías, the urban bustle, the grandness of it all. After many years of home learning with Mother, we were to attend one of Lima's best private schools.

On the evening before our departure, we were dressed up and taken to a *despedida* for my father at El Bowling. We were scrubbed and cinched and slicked and told to mind what we said. Vicki pulled her hair into a curly cataract and tucked a book under her arm, just in case. Papi wore a white guayabera, his cheeks flushed with accomplishment. Mother wore a dress of bronze satin, swept up in bright folds at her waist. They moved through the party, cutting their own paths.

A live band was playing *música criolla* out on the club lawn: "José Antonio" and "La Flor de la Canela." George and I shot down the walk, between the pool and the tennis courts, and headed for our favorite waiter at the bar. Three knocks on the window and he looked up and gave us the nod. A moment later we were strolling the grounds like grandees, with cold bottles of orange Crush in our fists. We looked for our boys and fed on skewered beef heart: succulent *anticuchos* on bamboo spears, arrayed on terra-cotta slabs.

"Come on," said George, finding Carlos Ruiz's face in the distance. By the pool I caught a glimpse of Mother in animated palaver with Mrs. Cunningham.

We did our boys' club handshake with Carlos: grab the right with the right, slide up to clasp the elbow, swipe arm against arm, one side then the other, and intertwine fingers and shake. Carlos snuffled loudly and drew a dead lizard from his pocket. It was squashed flat, translucent at the throat, gray with dirt. "I think I have business for *Señor* Birdseye," he said, gloating proudly. "*Ay, pues! Sí!*" we shrieked, and looked around for the old man. "Tell you what," George said. "Let's fan out and look for him. Whoever finds him comes back to tell the other two."

"Right," I said, and took off for the thatch-roofed dining room.

No sooner did I step into the candlelight than I saw Mrs. Birdseye's white hair. She turned and met my gaze with a twinkle of recognition and a forefinger in the air. She was standing with someone—I couldn't see who—and now she reached down, took the man's hand, swiveled around, and marched toward me with him in her wake.

It was Tommy Pineda. I drew myself up and considered running away. But Mrs. Birdseye's mouth was moving at me, and as she pushed through the party with Tommy in her grip, she shook a finger at me mischievously.

"There you are! There you are!" she puffed. Behind her, the huge boy was plodding toward me, his heavy feet turned in, his guayabera loose and yellowed. I recall thinking that his head was as squirmy as a rum-drunk turkey's just before the cook swings it from a pole—upside down—to drown it in its drool.

"Here, here. Look who I have here," she said. She took a deep breath and looked from me to him.

I had never seen the Pineda boy this close. He was thick and pale, with black hair cropped short and dimples like navels. His forehead was flat as slate, his eyes creased like Wong's. When he focused on me and grinned, bubbles danced from the corners of his mouth.

"Tommy, this is the little Arana girl I was telling you about. She and her brother live down the street. The ones with the dog that died." *El perro que murió.* "You remember, dear?"

"*Perrr,*" he said, and grunted, his large head bouncing vigorously.

"*Muy triste,*" she said. So sad.

"*Trisss,*" he repeated, his spit misting my face and neck.

"I told Tommy what happened to your dog," said Mrs. Birdseye. "That earthquake—it seems so long ago now—and the terrible way he died. I hope, little one, that when you get where you're going, your mama lets you have another." Her curls were shimmering in the candlelight. The giant's eyes shone black as stones. It struck me how impossible it would have been for this docile colossus to kill a dog, suck it dry, float it out in the country-club pool to be screeched at by servants.

He then reached a ham hand in his pocket, pulled out a fist, and held it in front of me, fingers curled tight.

I was fascinated. I stretched one finger out to touch it. He smiled and opened it up like a flower.

I know now that what I saw there meant I was leaving Pachamama. It was a tiny seashell, as pink and as perfect as a freshly cooked shrimp.

"*Adiós*," he said, working his mouth with his tongue. "*A-Diósss.*"

And then he took me by the wrist and turned his gift into my palm.

8

SKY

El Mundo Arriba

THE SHELL WAS more than a good-bye gift. It was an omen. Not only would I say good-bye to Paramonga, I would say good-bye to my closest link to Pachamama, to the ground beneath our feet. We skimmed south along the dunes, down the Pan American Highway, eyes riveted on the sea. The Pacific was grizzled and unruly, spitting with indignation. I clutched Tommy's shell, fiddled with Antonio's stone, imagined my future as a city girl. But by the time we arrived at Abuelita and Abuelito's house in Miraflores, eight hours later, it was clear that Lima was not our final destination. Not for a while at least. A telegram sat on their mantel, and when we entered, my grandmother shooed the children into the *comedor*, seated my mother in the *sala*, and slipped the bright yellow paper into her hands.

The notice was terse but said all Mother needed to know: Grandma Lo was dying. She wasn't likely to last through spring. By the time Mother raised her eyes from that missive, she had made a decision: She would travel to her mother's bedside, take us with her, stay through midsummer if necessary, until Grandma Lo died. The Grace Company routinely granted Papi three months of vacation for every three years of work. That arrangement had allowed my family to go to America three years before, when I had been deposited in Abuelita's house. My father was due another three months of vacation now, and Mother proposed we spend it in Rawlins, Wyoming. "I've lived years with your mother and father," she said to Papi curtly, "and not always in the most pleasant of circumstances. Now you can make an effort to spend a few months with mine."

"Wyoming?" Abuelita asked as we kissed her good-bye that evening. She was trussed in a wine-dark suit, her shoes so tight that the skin of her feet plumped over the leather like dough on the rise. "*Adónde se van?*" rasped my grandfather from the top of the stair, blinking as if he'd just strayed into the light. Where are they going? "*Parece que se van a* Wyoming, Victor," my grandmother called up to him—*Woy-yo-meen*—and she might as well have said "the Yakutskaya tundra," for all that the name summoned to her mind.

To Abuelita, my mother's family was a blank no one had bothered to fill. She had not been told—even though my parents had made a trip there a few years before—exactly where my mother's family lived. Mother and Papi had taken Vicki and George on a long tour through Miami, Chicago, Denver, Wyoming, California, Washington . . . and the family was somewhere up there. The few facts Abuelita knew had been printed on wedding announcements disseminated eleven years before: *Mr. and Mrs. James B. Campbell of Seattle announce the marriage* . . .

"*Woy-yo-meen,*" my father repeated for his father. "*Nos vamos a* Wyoming, Papa. I'm leaving the address here on your radio console. We'll be back by July."

By sunset of the next day we were over a pearly ocean and I was hoping fervently that we'd see the likes of Paul Bunyan,

Davy Crockett, Pocahontas, George Washington, and Betsy Ross along the way. But the truth of exactly who it was we were going to see would be refined further as we touched down in Miami, boarded a train to Denver, and sped north in a Greyhound bus. Somewhere in that rush of American countryside, I asked Vicki, "Will we see Davy Crockett?"

"No, silly girl. He died at the Alamo."

"And so where do the Campbells live?" I asked then.

"Not Campbell," Vicki said matter-of-factly. "Their last name is Clapp. And you'd better not make that mistake in front of *them*." She nodded toward our parents across the aisle.

"*Oye*," I said, turning to George. "Tell me about Wyoming."

He shrugged. "I don't remember much. There's just Grandpa Doc. He's huge."

"A cowboy, no?" I asked, prodding him. "With a gun?"

George squinted at me, his lip in a vigorous tic. He said something back to me, but I was no longer listening. I sat and stared into the whir of green. I'd never seen so many trees before: at least not like this, with wide trunks and round, verdant pompadours. Backs of houses flew by; laundry flapped in gardens. Streets gleamed with shops. There were no ramshackle stands, no hawkers, no one pushing a cart, touting wares. There were front doors, which, like the Birdseyes', you could walk right up to and knock. There were dogs lazing by. There were stretches of farmland, heaps of rusted-out cars.

Where were the rivers sparkling with gold dust? Where were the gem-lined streets? Where was the money growing on trees? Where were Moby Dick, Sitting Bull, Honest Abe? I was looking at a place unrecognizable from my mother's *historias*. The only Americans, as far as I could see, were hurtling by behind glass, over black rubber, down a long asphalt snake.

Our train was a Union Pacific Pullman, a long gray bullet on a string of long gray bullets just like it. It was tidy and comfortable, with ample seats and chummy passengers.

"Where you from, honey?" a towering woman asked me, shoving her head in my face when she heard me chatter in Spanish. I didn't understand a word of what she said.

Mother reached across the aisle to fend for me. "She was born in South America. This is her first trip to the States."

"Well, I'll be," the woman said, taking me in, head to toe. "She's a little foreigner."

"No, ma'am," Mother said with a tight little smile. "She's one hundred percent American citizen."

"Unh-huh," the woman said, and shambled down the aisle.

"You're an American," Mother lectured me gravely, "through and through. Don't let anyone ever tell you anything different." She looked through the window and sighed, stroking my hair. In time, she began reciting a verse or two, in her funny macaronic way: "Breathes there a man with soul so dead, who bumpdy-bumpdy-bumpdy said, 'This is my own my native land!'"

I could see why she loved her native land. It was clean, polished. Even the garbage was tidy. The stops along the way in it were linoleum oases, fitted with candy counters, milk-shake vendors, hot-dog grills, and wide arcades. Tallahassee, Birmingham, Memphis, St. Louis, Topeka, Denver. I wanted to swing through those train stations like a monkey through rain forest, but George held me back, skittering after Mother and Papi, fretting that I'd get us lost or that we'd miss the next train. He was preoccupied and surly since we'd left Paramonga. His words were herky-jerky, full of worry. His face was leaping with tics.

In the St. Louis station, Vicki and I took off in search of a bathroom and came to a stop before two doors marked *Ladies*. One said *Colored*. The other said *Whites*. We puzzled over the words, wondering what they meant, but Mother came by, grabbed our hands, and pulled us through the second door.

"Why does that other one say *Colored*, Mother?" Vicki asked.

"Because only the colored are supposed to go through it," she replied.

"Colored?" my sister asked, revealing a rare lack of enlightenment.

"Yes. Haven't you noticed in the station, darling? Or on the train? The black people?"

"With black hair, you mean?" Vicki said.

"No, dear," Mother answered on her way into a cubicle, latching the door behind her. "Not black hair. Black *skin*. You have black hair, but you're white. Your skin is white. So is mine."

I listened and looked down at my dark-olive knees dangling over the snowy commode. They were green. They were yellow. They were brown. They were colored. Never in a million years could they be called white. But when Vicki and I emerged from the bathroom and looked around the station, we saw what was meant. There were Americans of a deeper hue. Not ocher like me, not hazelnut like Antonio, but chocolate. We had boarded the trains with them, peered into their faces when they leaned over to chat, bought candy from them at counters. It had not occurred to us that we wouldn't be allowed to go through the same doors.

I had not yet turned seven, but I knew what race meant. There were Peruvians who measured color with what seemed the precision of laboratory calipers, but I had never suspected that any of it would pose a danger to me. I had balked at not being permitted to invite an *india* to my birthday; I had pressed my ear against bedroom doors to hear the scandal of the laundress's daughter, I had been humiliated by a schoolteacher who didn't think I was sufficiently brown. But race in Peru was a subtler issue than in the United States. *Indios* came down from the mountains, in from the jungle, went to convent schools, mixed with *mestizos*, and then their *mestizo* children mixed with the *blancos*, mixed with the *chinos*, mixed with the *sambos*, moved to the cities, mixed it up more. I cannot claim, at such a young age, to have understood any of it really, but I'd seen Peru in shades, felt it. Here in March of 1956, in the St. Louis train station, however, where black and white was spelled so boldly—where colors were carved on doors with directives—I do believe that for the first time I feared a little for myself.

⁓

AFTER FIVE DAYS on the rails, we arrived in Denver and boarded a bus for Rawlins. "We're almost there," Papi told us; half a day to go. The view from my window flattened into long stretches of prairie with barbed-wire fences winding like Möbius strips, to the horizon and back again. I tried to count telephone poles, the only promise that life awaited us somewhere up the road, but by the time I got to 157, my eyes surrendered to the landscape itself. There were sprays of tall grass, forlorn and yellow, whipped by a furious wind. Pale tufts of sagebrush and greasewood squatted along the highway. Every once in a long while, I'd see an oil rig, or a cattle shed, or an abandoned shack with its roof blown off and a trail of sun-bleached wood tumbling after. These looked like Peru to me—dunes, ramshackle *chacras*, dusty remnants of life—and so I found myself dozing off, unmoved by the sights that reeled past. A leaping jackrabbit, the quick duck of a prairie dog, wings aflap in the vaulting blue sky would bring me scrambling back to the window. Until quite suddenly, in the distance, I saw a mountain flex up—white-haired and mighty—under a salmon sun.

"There, children, there," said Mother, pointing to the peak. "Your grandparents are down the road now, just up ahead." She drew out a tube of lipstick and slicked her mouth.

We passed Walcott Junction: a combination of filling station, general store, and "café lounge." A sign flew over it all, perched so high that it summoned a clientele for miles. MOJO GAS, it said. A solitary word pulsed in a window—*Pabst.*

So much was familiar. So much was not. The earth, the bareness of it, could have been Pachamama. But there was a different life to it, something else there I couldn't make out. It wasn't the prairie that was drawing my eye. In Peru, ground was all I had looked at: the mountains, the deserts, the rocky shore. My orientation had always been down.

In this place I found myself looking up, scanning sky. A canvas arched over Wyoming, a vast brilliant dome that made my head rise, drew my eyes up. If Pachamama were alive in that dust, you would hardly have noticed her. There were hardly trees anymore in this part of America, no branches for spirits to wave from. Not one gurgling stream to satisfy a ghost. No vines. Were the *pishtacos* that stalked Peru not here in these flatlands at all?

Fifteen miles past Walcott, a ganglion of metal loomed out of the plain. As we drew nearer, we saw the full immensity of the thing, a steel-pipe cathedral against a darkening sky. SINCLAIR OIL, the billboard said. And then a boulevard of houses trailed past, under a brume of smoke. Gringo machines. If their *maquinaria* were here, so were their *pishtacos.*

I started from my seat, convinced this was our destination, but Papi looked over at me and shook his head. The factory and the hacienda were a mirage. A familiar door in an unfamiliar world.

When the bus lurched into Rawlins, we might as well have lurched onto the moon. The town was unlike anything I had ever seen. Gray buildings, massive and squat, sprawled against a hillside. Trucks lined the streets. There were offices, shops, hotels, but no one came and went from them. A stillness reigned. I could see lights winking in windows and doors, illuminating the signs: BOOTS, LIVE MUSIC, WESTERN BAR, RIFLES, BAIT, SHERIFF, FEED, MEATS, SPIRITS, THE FERRIS HOTEL, and then, down the road with a well-lit driveway in front, WYOMING STATE PENITEN-

SKY 1 7 7

TIARY. On the other side of a bright white train station, a profusion of little houses—clapboard, metal, brick—spilled over the hill and down to a two-lane highway. Tidy patches of green lay in front. The bus made its way to Main Street, lumbered around corners, screeched and then rumbled forward again, until it pulled to a stop.

The driver barked out the destination—"Rawwwlins!"—yanked back the door, and a night wind sliced in. I pulled my alpaca sweater around me, ran in front of the rest, and hopped two steps down to the pavement in front of the Come On In! lounge. In its window, a row of dust-caked bottles lined the sill, and through the glass pane, over the bar, I could see a giant moose face. The head was outlandish under the antlers, its dull eyes dazed, as if the animal had needed a drink and walked through the wall to get it.

"Hullo there!" a voice said, and I spun around to see a tall, broad-shouldered man coming toward us in the twilight. He was wearing a bone-white hat: guttered on top, dipped at the brim. Around his neck hung a string tie with a quartz stone as blue and translucent as the eyes he trained on us. Blue as the blue of my mother's. "Hullo there, Takey," he said, using her baby name, and she flew into his arms.

Grandpa Doc seemed big as an Inca fort, larger than any gringo *soltero* I had ever known. He whopped Papi on the shoulder, welcomed back Vicki and George, and then swooped me up, past all six feet of him, so that I could take a close look at his face. His chin was square as a shovel, his cheeks ruddy. His head gave off the irresistible scent of whiskey and tobacco. His breath was sweet as molasses. I instantly liked the man.

He helped Papi organize our luggage and then walked us down Cedar Street to the Ferguson Building, a mausoleum of red brick and white stone, where he insisted on installing us in an apartment of our own.

The Ferguson was where he and Grandma Lo lived during the week. The building took up a whole city block and housed a dry-goods store and grocery downstairs, apartments and offices above. We clattered up the metal stairs to the second floor, marched through the cavernous hallway, and passed brass plaques that proclaimed a spectrum of pursuits from large-elk taxidermy to the appraisal of rare stones. Eventually we reached a door marked *Number Six, James Bayard Clapp, Dental Surgeon,* and Grandpa Doc ushered us into the rooms we would call home for the next four days.

It had been only three years since Mother had seen her mother, but clearly Grandma Lo's health had slipped away in that time. Mother was tense, nervous, pacing the floor as my grandfather told her what she would see. Lo hadn't eaten in weeks, he said. Was in constant and excruciating pain. She floated in and out of consciousness. Was dying for sure. Grandma Lo had had the care of two of Mother's three sisters, he said—women whose names I wasn't sure I'd ever heard before—but they had gone now, back to their families: down the road, or somewhere in Nebraska.

Grandma Lo, it turned out, was in the next room. Mother hurried in alone and the rest of us prepared for a long vigil. George and I slumped on the floor, too tired to talk. Vicki, who had come to know Grandpa Doc on her last trip, nestled into his lap and took his large hand. Papi settled down with a *National Geographic.* At first our silence was punctuated only by the grim cadence of a clock. But before long, we heard Mother's moans—muffled and desolate, as if something were wringing her heart. Papi stood sharply and went out into the corridor for a smoke.

One by one, we were waved in to see Grandma Lo. When I first met her, she was lying on her side, facing the wall, her soft white hair matted against the back of her head. I could hear wheezing, as light and regular as an ailing child's.

"Mother?" my mother whispered, and my grandmother's mottled fingers fluttered up like flags in wind—up and then down again—but her wrist never left her hip.

"I have my littlest here," Mother said gently, wiping her eyes with a handkerchief. "You've never met her." She nudged me. "Go on up, Mareezie, give her a kiss. Let her see your face."

I came up to the narrow bed, and my grandmother's head rotated slightly so that her face shone with light from the ceiling. Her profile was waxy and yellow, her forehead grooved with pain. She opened her eyes and I could see how pale they were, how preternaturally blue. Then, quickly, she squeezed them shut. "Pretty little thing," she said, although I was sure she hadn't seen me. "Such a sweet face."

"Go on," my mother urged me, and I leaned down and pressed my lips against her cheek. She was cold as a gila, even though an electric coil heater hummed and sputtered at the foot of the bed.

I had heard of death, felt human bones in my hands, picked teeth out of skulls. I'd watched Flavio drown drunken turkeys upside down for our dinners. I had seen people wail and screech in funeral processions down the narrow streets of Paramonga. But I had never felt such proximity to death.

I waited there, one hand on the chenille bedspread, my nostrils twitching like a rabbit's against the acrid smell, but my grandmother did not move, and so neither did I. Mother was like granite behind me. Perhaps it was fear, perhaps it was the way of this strange, inscrutable land, but I did not see her reach out to touch her mother.

Grandma Lo's night table was filled with an assortment of things I longed to inspect. There was a black Bible with her mother-in-law's name—*L. E. Clapp*—stamped with gold into the leather; a white linen handkerchief with an embroidered, pink ballerina; a slender flask with a cascade of lilies down its side; a row of brown vials; a hypodermic needle; three rectangular bottles with cork stoppers and scribbled labels; a wooden ring; a spool of lime thread.

I took in these details as I listened to my grandmother's labored breathing. From time to time a shudder rippled through her as if some unseen creature were darting down the tunnels of her body. When, eventually, we backed out of her room, my mother's face was swollen with sorrow.

I realize now how little I felt for Grandma Lo. She was not the vibrant, commanding figure of my abuelita, the sort of presence I would have expected from a woman of her generation. I studied the photographs of her in those apartments, looking for some sign of my other grandmother's brio, but all I saw was a mild sweetness unlike anything I had encountered before. Even in photographs taken in younger, healthier times, Grandma Lo was an unassuming woman. She used little makeup, dressed modestly in starched white medical vestments, did not dye her hair. She was only three years older than Abuelita and had a prettier face, but there was no vanity to her. As if she didn't want undue attention from the world.

"Stomach cancer," my grandfather said plainly when we joined him in his office waiting room. We had heard Mother say those words before. A hat and sheepskin jacket hunched on the coat stand behind him, confirming the grimness of his message.

Hungry for distractions, George and I began exploring Doc's bookshelves and cabinets. Dentures grinned back at us. Miniature curios had been fashioned from dental enamel: a shiny white bear with his claws in the air, an Indian in full headdress. As we marveled at these, Grandpa Doc explained to my parents how my grandmother's illness had advanced.

For the more than ten years since they had come to Rawlins, she had been his nurse, secretary, and accountant. He had performed the surgery; she had passed him the tools. He had thrown the X-ray switch; she had held the film. He had built the practice; she had kept the books. But in recent years, he said, he would chance upon her in a corner, overcome with pain, or doubled over behind a door, so that a patient wouldn't see.

I hardly knew who Lolelia Brooks Clapp was, but I could see that my grandfather loved her. Her dying was breaking his heart. He was a man of few words, but as he talked, and as George, Vicki, and I gathered at his feet to listen, a hazy picture of their life emerged. She had given him four daughters. She had been the compliant partner, tolerant of his caprices before he'd settled down to doctoring: his land deals, rodeo-impresario days, bridge-building businesses. She had been a lover of books, had persuaded him to stretch out on the waiting-room sofa between appointments to listen to her read Coleridge, Whitman, Kipling. She had played the piano to his violin. She had lounged in his canoe as he fished in Lake Seminoe, crooning sweet verses about happiness to come. But what had come, in the end, was punishing—pain, shrinkage, a flickering in the world.

He told Mother that he had driven her out to a hospital in Denver. He had flown in specialists from the East. He had devoured every medical journal he could find. Now, steeled against the inevitable, all he could do was sit in his own waiting room, marking time.

His life did have distractions, as we came to learn. Grandpa Doc was raising two teenage grandsons in the Ferguson Building—Huey and Nub—sons of two of his other daughters, my Aunt Erma and Aunt Helena. He was also minding an ancient mother, Lucinda Ellen Clapp, who, we'd soon see for ourselves, was deaf as a billiard ball, and wild; and he was building a house out on his ranch, thirty miles away, at the foot of Elk Mountain—a neat wood box on a level sprawl of sage. Anything to take his mind off what was happening in the other room.

Now there was us.

"You hungry, Takey?" Grandpa Doc finally said to my mother.

She looked at Papi. He was arched over the desk, studying a map now, running one hand through his curly, black hair. "Well, maybe the children are," she said softly. "How about you, Daddy? How about Mother?"

"Aw, hell. She won't eat much," my grandfather said, and then he reached around and spat a black gob of tobacco juice into a brass spittoon.

George and I glanced at each other and grinned. Vicki's eyebrows shot up like two birds.

"Well, go downstairs to the store and charge up anything you like," he said. "Tell 'em to put it on Doc Clapp's account."

"All right, Dad. Tomorrow Jorge and I will start looking for our own place to stay." She walked over to her father and put a light hand on his shoulder. He looked up at her with a wistful smile. They did no more than that, and yet I felt a bond between them. A language they understood. They didn't need to fill the air with chatter, these gringos, unburden their hearts, peck each other noisily on the cheek. They could sit stonily by, staring down at their hands, and communicate. They could tend a dying mother without touching her. As we said good night to him, I vowed to learn how to do all of that someday. But first, I'd learn how to spit.

AS THE HOURS unfolded on that first day in Rawlins, Mother made a point to tell us about the Clapps. It was clear we were disoriented, out of our element, and her teaching nature returned in the form of quick lectures on family history. She began by describing the great-grandmother I had yet to meet, Grandpa Doc's mother, Lucinda Ellen Adams-Hatter Clapp.

Great-Grandma Clapp claimed to be a descendant of John Quincy Adams. The rest of the family accepted that lineage without argument; her mother, Matilda Adams, had said it was so. She had married young and come west with James A. Clapp, my great-grandfather. James A. Clapp had descended from one of five Clapp brothers who had set sail from England six years before the American Revolution. Two of those five original brothers had sought prosperity in Canada. Two eventually built names for themselves in Boston. The Boston Clapps produced lawyers and bankers, one newspaper editor, one famous etymologist, one generous patron of Amherst College—pillars of New England society. But the fifth of those English brothers went west to preach God's word. That was the Clapp of my line.

In 1880, James A. Clapp, who had studied law, and his wife, Lucinda Ellen, established a merchandise business in Hollenberg, Kansas, which included a bank, a law firm, a U.S. Post Office, and a dry-goods store. Within twenty years, they had amassed a fortune. When my great-grandfather died and left his wife everything, she proved a gritty businesswoman. By 1908, she had sent one son to medical school, another to law school, married off their daughter, and made each of their children the gift of a farm.

But Great-Grandfather Clapp's death was not her first challenge. Great-Grandma Clapp had known her share of disasters. She had survived a Civil War. She had seen insect plagues descend in black clouds and chew landscapes bare. She had seen Indian braves whack their way through white settlements to avenge the death of Sitting Bull. After her husband's death she outwitted two World Wars by having had sons and great-grandsons who were too old or too young to fight. She survived the Great Depression because her store was stocked and debtors paid her with real estate. Acres and acres of it. She owned so much land that it almost didn't matter whether she lost a little to the government now and then. "I know all the crooks and turns of the mercantile business," she crowed to newspaper reporters, but the worldwide financial disaster would change everything. The Clapps became land rich, suspicious of banks. They began carrying their money in satchels, twenty-five thousand dollars at a time. They owned chunks of Kansas, chunks of Wyoming. When two of Great-Grandma Clapp's three children died of leukemia, her only living son, my Grandpa Doc, inherited the wealth. Grandpa Doc had grown up with plenty of money. His instinct, unlike his fore-fathers', was to spend it. But another of his instincts, right down the family line, was to head west. Ever west. When his four daughters were grown, he took Grandma Lo, left Kansas, and followed that impulse. When my mother became a widow and her Uncle Elver proposed to pay her way through a music conservatory, it never dawned on her that her father might have made the proposal. She did not ask him; he did not offer. Grandpa Doc took his money satchels to Wyoming. He dusted off his medical degree and hung it on a wall.

On our second day in Rawlins, Papi took me into Room 7, one of the apartments in the Ferguson Building, to meet Great-Grandma Clapp. She was a dried-out little husk of a woman in a black taffeta bonnet, a calico dress, and a circus magician's black cape. Her long white hair was gathered into a jelly roll at the back of her head. Her jaw was set in a flat grim line. I bowed and kissed her leathery cheek as my father had instructed me to do and then perched on the edge of a hard wood sofa while her two steely eyes took me in. She was stringy, puckered, thatched with a frizzled brow. *She's a big help to your Grandma Lo,* my father was saying—in a booming voice so that she could hear—but I could see that the woman was a big help to no one. She seemed unreliable, cracked.

We sat there awhile before she got bored and began shuffling her newspapers. She bought two or three a day and went at them with two pairs of glasses—mounted on each other over her nose—and an enlarging glass to boot. "So long as I live in this world," she squeaked triumphantly at my father, "I want to know what's going on." Papi glanced at me and winked. Clearly, he had reached some level of comfort with her on his last visit. "Just how old are you now, Grandma *Viejecita*?" he shouted in her ear. She squinted and stuck out three fingers in response. She preferred to reckon her age toward a date rather than from one. She was three years from a century. Ninety-seven. She had been born in the age of the musket and would die in the age of the nuclear bomb.

I had no equivalent in my Peruvian life for Great-Grandma Clapp. I had met elderly aunts in Lima—lively, bustling round women with silky soft faces and bosoms redolent with perfume. I knew about femininity, had heard my abuelita say that fine shoes and conversation could carry a woman far. But this wizened little ancestor was like no woman I had ever known: I had no way to gauge her. In her boots, she stood little taller than I did, swaggered as if she were a man. She was beyond my powers to compute.

It wasn't much later that I found that Room 8, next door to Great-Grandma Clapp, was where my cousins lived. Huey was Aunt Erma's son—a tall, gangly eighteen-year-old with radiant eyes. Nub was Aunt Helena's boy—sixteen, unruly, brooding, and beautiful. They were students at Rawlins High School and temporary wards of our grandfather, who had volunteered to break them in.

When we saw the boys, they seemed different as a pair of wild broncos, on the far side of tame. In Huey's case, he was there because Aunt Erma, my mother's oldest sister, was a teacher out on the range, in a log-cabin schoolhouse, improving the minds of a rich rancher's children. We saw Erma only on weekends, mincing up the metal stairs of the Ferguson Building with books under one arm, a pencil jutting from her hair.

Nub was there because his mother was "plumb out of her gourd," living in an asylum, having her skull rocked with electric shocks, and because his father was nowhere to be found. He was a bad-boy virtuoso, a genius for testing the law. He had started small: joy rides in the wee hours of morning. A little gas from a neighbor's truck. But soon enough he was heading down Route 30 in swiped cars, siphoning out filling stations, drag-assing home in the back of the sheriff's car. He was reckless, raw-boned, irresistible.

Grandpa Doc felt a keen responsibility for those living under his roof—or the roof of the Ferguson, anyway. He told us a story that summed up what he was having to shoulder. One warm spring day when he was working on a Comanche, he found Nub on the waiting-room sofa, a freckle-faced girl at his side. "You two there long?" said Doc.

"Nope," said Nub, flashing a rakish grin.

Grandpa Doc proceeded to work on the Indian, slipping out from time to time to shoot tobacco juice into the spittoon and eye the two on the couch. He could hear Great-Grandma Clapp clanking up and down the metal stairs, knocking on doors, visiting with the uranium prospectors down the hall. "How's business, folks?" she barked. "You found some good rocks today?" But she was too deaf to hear their answers, and so she continued to career through the corridor like a bat with bad sonar, bumping against the walls.

Doc was excavating his patient's jaw when he realized that the conversation in the waiting room had grown muffled; there were unmistakable sounds of clothes rustling, heavy breathing. Doc weighed his choices. Should he stop midsurgery and let his patient bleed? He wavered there, one foot on his chair pedal, his scalpel midair. Until the solution came a-knocking.

The sheriff was at the door. Next to him, ashen, diminutive, crowlike in her floor-length black cape, was Doc's mother. Nub rose. Grandpa Doc stepped forward. The Comanche's eyes rolled up in alarm.

"Ho, Doc," the sheriff said, shifting cud to the other side of his smile. "Doggone if she ain't done it again. I found her streaking through town like a banshee, screeching to everyone, asking if they seen her daddy." He nodded toward Nub. "You keep your kin reined in now, hear, Doc? Two generations of your folk are working me up one side and down the other! I'm gittin' a little raggedy."

As little as I could relate to my dying grandmother and her wacky mother-in-law, I found myself drawn to my pretty-boy cousin. I was crazy for Nub. In a time when the world seemed to have more moving parts than an Andean earthquake, he struck me as someone I could rely on. He had a will of his own and a wry, wicked humor. I began seeking him out the way I'd sought out Antonio: On the roof of the Ferguson Building, where he went to smoke. Down in the grassy alley between the dry-goods store and the sheriff's office where I'd find him chewing on a weed. Like Antonio, he welcomed me, grinning wide, patting whatever ledge he was perched on, signaling me to put my little rump by his side. Whereas Antonio's lessons had been about laws of nature, rules of energy, the consequence of *historias*, Nub's school was something else: Laws were for breaking. Rules were for chumps. History counted for nothing. Mornings were for shuffling the deck.

More than anything, Nub taught me how to throw my head back and take in the sky. He'd lean against a wall or stretch out on a patch of green, blowing circles of cigarette smoke at our sheltering firmament. Sometimes he'd pass me a butt end and let me try puffing my own. More often, I'd put my elbows behind my head and watch his perfect rings rise, curling high into the crisp spring air.

From time to time I'd scramble into his lap, place my hands on his shoulders, and hoist myself up so that I could look down into his eyes. They were a crystalline blue. Just as Antonio's eyes had been the color of a rich brown loam, Nub's eyes were alive with clear hyaline. Looking into them buoyed me up, made me feel light, dizzy, high.

I know now that to Nub I was just a silly child with amusing eccentricities. But from time to time, when I'd lie beside him as he looked into the blue serene, something would move him to pour out his heart. I'd stare into that vastness listening to his voice, the warm twang of it, and hear about his world. He would talk about his mother, my Aunt Helena, who had been institutionalized for some years now but was forever escaping from the asylum, found heading down some highway, scampering off in her nightgown. Or about his father, who was somewhere in Nebraska or Kansas or Colorado, on an endless rye binge. Or about the incomprehensibility of being made to sit on a hard wooden chair in Rawlins High School to acquire the kind of learning he'd never use. "I jist wanna git," he'd say to me. "Jist wanna make myself scarce. Like Uncle Jabez."

"Uncle Jabez?" I asked him. "Who's Jabez?"

"One of your uncles, Mareezie. But I doubt you'll ever meet him. He's out in the mountains. Far away."

Jabez wasn't my uncle, as it turned out. He was my second cousin. I learned a good bit about him in those conversations with Nub, but as spring wore on and the years went by, Jabez's story emerged like a full-fledged *historia*.

Even as Nub and I lay there, Jabez Clapp was whiling away time in a cave on an Indian reservation, somewhere in the cliffs of Arizona, under the same cosmic void. He was my mother's cousin, the son of Grandpa Doc's brother, a fugitive from the military. Gone AWOL in '29.

As Nub related it, Jabez's father—Grandpa Doc's brother— had died young of leukemia, and little Jabez had been raised by his mother, a Southern belle more intent on teaching him pretty verses than the hard rigors of life. Jabez was a dreamer, inclined to stargazing and poetry, reduced to openmouthed wonder by the smallest manifestations of things. A lacewing over the nettle. An ant hauling grass across rock. The prospect of a long, shiftless afternoon. Somewhere along the way, someone made the disastrous decision that the U.S. Army could make a man out of him, be the father he'd never had.

One night as he wandered away from his barracks, he went farther than he meant to go. "Imagine it, Mareezie," Nub said. "He took a gander around. No one was there! That's when he decided to do it. He lit out. Skedaddled!" Down the asphalt he went, across the plain, over the horizon, past the rocky crags into a hole on the side of a mountain. Apparently, he fed on wild berries, roasted roots over a fire, grew a beard down to his knees. The Indians said they saw him drifting through their hills, his face forever turned up. Looks At Stars, they called him. They figured much of his spirit had already departed, gone off to the Great Beyond. So they left him out there to his thoughts, and they taught their children and their children's children to do the same. For thirty years, no hunting posse, no military police could find him.

But long after those lazy afternoons with Nub, long after we were back in Lima, long after history had passed Jabez by—long, long after his military cohort had marched into Nazi camps or dropped death on the Pacific, after Stalin had purged millions in the name of the proletariat, after Mao descended into Beijing with red dreams and promises—Mother got word of what had happened to Jabez. It was 1959, and a group of government workers had come onto that Arizona reservation to canvass the terrain. One blizzardy morning, they looked about for shelter and saw the great stone at the mouth of Jabez's cave. They moved it aside. They huddled in. And there, to their surprise, they found themselves surrounded by strip after strip of bark etched with poetry. There were necklaces of bloodstone and jade. There were three feather dream-catchers, a U.S. Army identification, a pan full of gold dust, a diary with silver initials.

Deep in the heart of that stone sanctuary, they found Jabez's bones, strung out in repose, cold as the ash of his fire.

The story of Jabez—even in its thin, original version—was the single *historia* that Nub offered me. I listened hard to that story, as I had to so many of Antonio's, puzzled over its meaning, turned it over in my mind, decided it must be important. All these years later I understand why. It has to do with my own longing for the horizon. It has to do with a part of me—a very un-Peruvian part—that wants to run. Leave. Go.

The sky can have that effect on you. Look out at the Gobi Desert and the eye hugs the ground. Stand by the sea and the urge is to wade in, gurgle under. But gaze up at sky and the soul rises, floats up, off, as helpless as a feather in warm wind. Before you know it, you're looking for roads, leaving your family, searching for something beyond the comfortable world you know. Catholics always sensed this and learned to use images of sky sparingly, in domes of churches only, under the watchful eye of God. But out West, as I was learning, a big sky was everywhere. Little wonder a spirit yearned to move on.

～

BY THE END of our first week in Rawlins, our parents had found a house with a comfortable ground-floor apartment on West Buffalo Street. It was small and furnished, less than three blocks from the Ferguson Building, between the penitentiary and the railroad track. It was a cheerful little place, a two-story structure raised high off the street, green and white, with a double-A roof and small windows. There was a kitchen that opened to a dining area, something we'd never seen before. A pullout couch in the living room, which Georgie immediately claimed. The two bedrooms, allocated to my parents and to Vicki and me, were joined by a common bathroom. The best thing about it was that there was no fence, no wall, nothing to keep us from exiting that front door and running down the street on our own. There were no servants to stop us, and Mother didn't seem to mind.

George was increasingly nervous. It was almost as if he were a mirror of our father's disorientation, our mother's jitteriness. He seemed delicately strung, too easily affected by noises, too cringing in public spaces. He preferred to play inside. Mother was consumed by Grandma Lo's illness, constantly at Grandma Lo's bedside, but George's condition did not elude her. I could see that she was watching him, and I noticed that they'd both begun to chew their nails.

The day we moved into the house, I felt a new life had started for us. Vicki was enrolled in an elementary school down the street. Papi wandered down West Buffalo to look at cars, inspect new machines, figure out Rawlins, look at the oil refinery in Sinclair. "Hey, you!" a butter-haired boy yelled at me. He was hanging off the porch next door as I trudged up the walk with my suitcase. "Jist who do yew think yew are?"

There was a five-and-ten-cent on the corner. George and I begged Papi for a dime, ran to the store, wandered through rows and rows of knickknacks and candy, and settled on a pack of Juicy Fruit gum. We crossed the street, sat in front of the school, and shoved the sweet sticks in our mouths. The children we saw through the school windows were about our age. They were pasty, nondescript, fading into their flannel clothes.

"*Extrañas a tus amigos?*" I asked George, searching his twitchy face. Do you miss your friends?

"Nah," he replied. "*Te tengo a ti, no?*" I have you, don't I?

An old man hobbled up the street and turned to look at us. He was grizzled and gaunt, with a long, beaked nose and a crumpled hat. He crossed to where we sat and stood awhile, listening to our chatter.

"What you yunguns doin' sitting there?" he said finally, drawing himself up by his bony shoulders. "You spick-a-da Spanish? You Mexican or what?"

We stared back at him, speechless.

"On the wrong side-a town, ain'tcha?" he continued. "Suppose-ta be across those tracks over there on the niggah side, ain'tcha, now?" Spittle was gathering in the corners of his mouth, and his stubbled chin was trembling.

"Cat got yer tongues?" he said. He took his hands from his pockets and wiped them against his little protuberance of a gut. Then he stamped on the grass and clapped his hands at us, but the sound was little more than a pathetic *thwap*. A bird scooted across and flitted into a tree.

"Well, go on, git!" he screamed. "Git!" His tiny eyes were burning and red. "You deaf'r sumpin? You li'l chiggers don't belong here and yew know it! Whole damn Mexico gonna come up here and take over uf we don't watch out!"

"Hey, Pop! Pop!" a large woman called out, waving her arms and waddling toward us quickly.

"This man is a *loco*," George whispered to me, his eyes aglow. "Don't move until I tell you to."

"What do you think he wants?" I said. "Our Juicy Fruit?" A *loco* was supposed to be made an offering, after all.

The old man was muttering to himself now, pawing the ground with his feet. The figure behind hurried closer. "Come away from there, Pop. Leave those kids alone," she called. The woman was wide, dough-faced. Her straw hair flapped in the wind.

"Don't it steam yew up?" the old man said to her. "They just sittin' there spick-a-da Spanish. What they doin' here anyway? They got a school over there fer these varmint."

"No, Pop. It don't steam me up. What do steam me up is yer standing out here yellin'. Come on home now. Come on home."

She led him off without a glance our way. I fingered the gum in my pocket, weighing whether I should run after him and put it in his hand. If I did, he could swallow me whole. If I didn't, his curse could prove true: Maybe I didn't have a right to be here, maybe my mother was wrong; maybe I wasn't an American after all. But George just sat there, and so did I. We drew up our knees and watched the man and his big daughter toddle down the street and disappear into a pretty little white house.

I had never paid much attention to the way I looked, but I found myself standing in front of our bathroom mirror after that, studying my short dark hair, the skin on my face and neck, stripping myself naked and watching the way I moved. I barked in Spanish at my own reflection, then mouthed the words, imagining how the motions of my face would look to people who couldn't understand what I was saying. I mimicked the boy next door. "Hey, you!" I shouted to myself, putting on his scowl, drawling the words like a native. "Jist who do yew think yew are?"

Just who had that old man thought we were? He had said we belonged on *the niggah side* of town. Was Rawlins cut in half? Was there a Whites side and a Colored side, like the doors we'd run up against in the bathrooms of St. Louis? Would Mother be taken away from us? Would Papi be forced to *go back where he belonged*?

"Your hair is black," my mother had said to Vicki. "But you're white, like me."

I, on the other hand, had suspected my skin would fool no one. There was nothing white about me. I was colored, for sure.

There is a trait I recognize now in the child I was then, a curiosity about my own physical composition, an obsession bordering on fever. Perhaps that inquisitiveness is common to children of mixed parents. You till, you dig, you paw, searching for bits, scrabbling at roots, eager to learn to which tribe you belong. Are you more like one or more like the other? Are you one way when

you're in one country, but another when you're not? You dangle
from that precipice, wondering where to drop.

It is exhausting work, that transit between worlds, that two-
way vertigo. I was half and half. Dr. Birdseye had told me so. But
I hardly thought I was better off for it. I had two heads, two
hearts. I was as unwieldy as Siamese twins on a high wire: too
awkward for equipoise, too curious about the other side.

⁓

FRIDAYS AFTER SCHOOL, Huey and Nub would head for
Rattlesnake Pass, Doc's ranch at the foot of Elk Mountain. They
were helping him build a house. Out there with them were two
of Doc's drinking pals: a beer-guzzling Mormon and a saloonkeeper from the oil-refinery town of Sinclair. Mondays, my
cousins would come back full of stories about the men's
booze binges, each tale giddier than the last. The cabin floor, it
seemed, had started out well enough—the tiles straight-edged
and orderly—but by the time the last squares were laid, the rows
were as swacked as the hands that had laid them. Grandpa Doc
didn't seem to mind. The boys were out on the prairie, out of
harm's way.

Each day in town, however, brought its grim turn, a shift in
the bearing walls. Grandma Lo was in and out of a coma; her
doctors' efforts were proving futile. She was taken one day from
her bed in the Ferguson and driven down the street to the
Mormon's house. Grandpa Doc's weekend drinker had turned
out to be married to a nurse. It was a matter of shepherding now.

Mother and Papi continued on their respective reveries—she
at her mother's bedside, he on his shop-by-shop tour of the latest
American inventions. Vicki was lost to her books. With no one to
mind us, George and I started combing Rawlins like truants on a
spree. We shoplifted candy from the five-and-dime, provoked
rumbles with the little gringos next door, snitched cigarettes

from our parents and puffed them out back. When George stole a toy truck at my instigation, Mother threatened to turn him in. She walked him, as he snorted and sniveled, all the way to the gate of The Pen. When she brought him home and thrashed him under the dining room table instead, he scrambled out with blood on his face. Soon after that we were marching down the street, our hands in Vicki's firm grasp, headed for another kind of incarceration, on the very grounds where the *loco* had cursed us: the school with the pasty-faced children. Within its walls we spent endless days, freeing our parents to squarely face the anxieties, look death directly in the eye.

Grandpa Doc, too, was tense as a buckjump rider, numbing himself with work. He took on more surgery. He had always offered it free to Indians who needed it. Now he'd book himself solid for days, spelunking in heads, yanking his way through teeth, emerging one afternoon with four of my father's molars. On weekends he was out on the ranch, working on his house, or down at The Rustic Bar. "Come with me, honey," he'd say, when Georgie scampered off after Huey and Nub, volunteering to help them pound nails. "Let's go look at them bobcats awhile." We'd jiggle down the dirt road to Saratoga, where he'd sit and sip whiskey for hours. I'd sit at the oak bar beside him—silent as a stone—watching two stuffed mountain cats claw at the carcass of a doe.

The Clapp ranch spraddled out beyond the tracks of the Union Pacific, where Rattlesnake Pass cut through to a creek. The land was grave-slab flat, running a fast course to the horizon. But due east, just where the sun rose, Sheep Hill leaned up against Elk Mountain the way a calf in high wind leans into its mother. That bigger mountain rose haughty, unknowable, thrusting its snow-covered hump into a nimbus sky.

Doc's brand—reverse Z, double quarter circle—was burned into the haunch of every cow, bull, and horse that grazed his many acres. There was a cabin, an outhouse, a shed, and, behind these, his new house, going up all white and perfect, like a jewel box sitting out on a table. Out by the corral, where the animals were kept, a weathered wood fence traced the foot of Elk Mountain.

There were only two other houses the human eye could see from Doc's land. One was an abandoned shack he had given to Clem Riley, a black ex-convict who had knocked on his cabin door one winter morning, looking for a place to stay. Ole Black Riley, my grandfather called him. The man had lived there for years, working a vegetable garden and hunting jackrabbit, until he woke up one morning and wandered away in search of a better life. "Hey, Grandpa Doc, what happened to Old Black Riley?" I asked, looking out toward that shack and feeling a certain affinity for a man who would have been consigned with me to the other side of the tracks in Rawlins proper. "Dunno, honey. Took off, I guess."

On the other side of Grandpa Doc's land, where stone cliffs ran west like a frill collar of gray, where coyotes bayed at the light of the moon, stood the second house. The Widener place: It was four miles down the Pass and barely visible from Doc's new house. Jack Widener was the cattleman who had hired Aunt Erma to teach his children. On a good day, you could make out the pillbox that was her school.

Over the rise, behind the Widener house, lived Old Joe Krozier. He was a wild man with a mysterious past—eyes as flared as roulette wheels, hair all a-kilter. "Now, he *truly* is a heavy drinker," the Mormon and the saloonkeeper would say to each other, and then they'd both bellow and guffaw until tears ran down their cheeks. Rumor had it that after Old Joe's wife had left him, he'd vowed never to own a car again. He was the only man in America—as far as I could tell—who had ever sworn off cars. There was good reason why: One hot August morning his wife had taken his last one and torn down Rattlesnake Pass in it to meet her boy lover. She had never come home again. We'd see Old Joe hunched over a slung-back mare, making his way down the ruts of Rattlesnake Pass, or ambling along the railroad tracks on his thin bowed legs, alone.

"Get up, you lazybones, and get me a stone!" Gramp sang out to George and me when we were out at the ranch, to get us out of bed and into the morning. We'd scramble out and find one quickly, about the size of a mango, and run back to the house, knowing we'd hunt that day. Doc dropped the stone into the bottom of a large pot, rattled in some beans and a ham bone, added water, and left it to cook.

Learning to shoot was the first order of business when Doc took us out to Rattlesnake Pass. "You can't live on this land and not learn how to handle a rifle," he'd tell us. "I don't care if you're knee-high to a grasshopper. There are snakes out here. Bears. Wolves. And by my sights, you two look like juicy little morsels. You need to learn about guns." At first we shot cans on the fence or potatoes set out on the brush. But soon we learned to fit the butt of a .22 into a shoulder, line up the crosshairs, finger the trigger, feel the *ping*, and see our bullets twig to their targets like *qosqos* to black light.

Doc killed deer. We killed rabbits. Doc killed antelope. We killed sage hen. Running after them through the brush as they warbled and lumbered away, eyeing us with alarm. When we were done, we would drag the carcasses onto the pickup truck for the ride back to the house. The beans would be waiting for us, fragrant and steamy, cooked evenly through by the stone. But we wouldn't be allowed to sit down to them until all the animals were clean.

Doc taught us as equals, and taught us well. We knew to shoot heads, kill quick. We knew to snap necks, be sure. He had taught us to skin our game, chuckling at us when we crept away pale and green. But it was cousin Nub who taught me how to gut a sage hen and cut fast to a butcher's fortitude. Slit the throat so it bleeds to the ground. Grab the hen by the anus and pull. Take her wings and swing 'til the guts fly. Pluck her to pink-butt tender.

"You're the only one around here who ain't flat-out bats," Nub told me one day. "Course, you're still young and all. You could go any minute." He'd stick out his tongue and roll his eyes until I screeched with delight.

"Reckon I'm takin' a big shine to you," he'd say. He'd lift me up and set me down on the long fence at the edge of Doc's land and listen to me talk a blue streak about the power of my *qosqo* and Peru's *pishtacos* and the spirits in the trees. Then he'd yelp and pound his knees with his hands. Whether it was my accent or my tales about ghosts that amused him, I never knew, but the more he'd laugh, the more I'd perform: louder, faster, scarier. Then I'd sit back and survey his face.

Nub was almost golden, openly handsome, honey hair hanging down into his eyes. He was slim-hipped, slim-chested, with eyes that flashed up hot.

"Should I tell you some more?" I asked him. "About the Danish man with the worms in his head?"

"Yip. I'd like to hear that one. You've got the damnedest stories I ever heard, tyke."

"Do you think I talk funny, Nub? You think I'm a foreigner?" I was remembering the large woman on the Pullman train, the old man who had growled at us in Rawlins, every gringo that raised his eyebrows when George and I walked into the shops, chattering.

"Naw, Cousin, sure don't. I git what you're saying fine. But tell you what. This'll prove to me that you're not." Nub mounted the fence beside me, reached into his pocket, pulled out a pouch, and grinned. "Here." He thrust it under my chin.

I looked down at the pungent brown strands in the bag. "Tobacco," I said. "I know what that is."

"Have some." I looked up at his face. He was serious. "Go on, girl, take a hit."

"Sure will," I said, "yip," and grabbed it. I pulled out a handful and shoved it in my mouth.

"Aw-raaat!" he sang out, and beamed a bright row of white.

That was how Nub introduced me to chaw and how I finally learned to spit. It took more than once—a great deal of hollering along the way—but I got so that months later, by the time I left Wyoming, I could hold my tobacco and squirt it from the side of my mouth just like him.

Hit the cowpie. *Squeet!* And Nub would hold his sides and laugh so hard I thought he'd fall off the fence and die.

"You know what you look like? You look like some pea-size cowboy on a drunk, that's what!"

"Oh, yeah? How about a llama?"

"A what?"

"A llama. Aw, Nub, c'mon, you know—the Peruvian animal I was telling you about."

"They chaw?"

"Naw, you dummy, but they spit!"

"Haw!"

"Yeehaw! Watch this. Just like a llama. *Peeew!*"

"Well, I'll be damned. More like a whale, I'd say. Out the ole blowhole. Pow!"

I reckon it was the ole blowhole that did it. In any case, something was pushing. I pulled up my shirt, aimed my belly at the stone cliffs, and howled, *"Qosqo-o-o-o!"*

Nub gawked at me as if I were mad, his eyes glittering and wide. Then he threw back his head and roared his big laughter into the sky.

WHILE THE SKY was getting our attention, it turned out there was much going on in the landscape. A strange phenomenon was under way, underfoot, in Wyoming. Nothing familiar. Nothing we understood. Nothing like shifting plates of subterranean rock. Nothing like forces that had bucked us before. Nothing like those moments in Peru, when Pachamama heaved and buildings collapsed and glass flew and we would run screaming for our lives.

No. This wasn't rambunctious or noisy. This was coal fire, silent and eerie, smoldering just below the earth's surface. Burning, with time on its hands.

We were told that the prairie could fool you. Sage and grass sitting innocently out there as if all were right in the world. Mirages. Beneath them, a quicksand inferno. One wrong step— like Persephone's encounter with Hades—and you'd drop to the hellfire below.

There were stories about trucks crossing to Hanna, between Walcott and Medicine Bow. Without warning, the earth had caved in and swallowed them up with a yawn. We imagined the drivers descending. We imagined trucks sinking and rocking, the way camels go down on their knees. We imagined men watching their cars melt, just before they were sucked into ash.

On one of those anxious evenings when worry festered behind an illusion of calm, I burned my mother's incense and prayed that no harm would come to cousin Nub. He had been known to get in cars and take off across prairies with a bottle or girl by his side. I blew on the incense and watched its red eye wink at me from under a pointy white hood.

"What are you doing, Marisi?" my father asked me. *Qué haces?*

"Thinking about Nub," I said. George was on the floor, pushing a toy truck down an imagined road.

"Come here, then; I have a job for you."

"What?" I said, and walked over to where he lay on the couch with a newspaper, the *Saratoga Sun,* splayed out on his chest.

"*Aquí.*" He bent his neck up and motioned me under it. "Sit, put my head in your lap."

I did as I was told.

"You see what this grand all-American vacation is doing to me? You see those white hairs on my head?"

I leaned in and saw them—a dozen, not more—sprouting from the V of his hairline. "Yes," I said, and smiled at the thought of him searching the mirror. An engineer with nothing to do.

"Pull them out. I'll give you five cents for each one that you show me." And greedily, I set to work.

I was like this, curled over my father's head, when Mother and Vicki came in. "They did it," said Mother, lowering herself into a chair. "They took her off to the hospital." My father patted my hands and sat up.

"Unconscious?"

"Barely breathing," Mother said. Her eyes were sunken, jaundiced.

There was a silence then, as we shouldered the weight of her news. Papi folded his newspaper into a neat square and set it carefully on his lap.

"Well, well," Mother said at last. She took a deep breath and glanced around the room. "And what's new with you two today?" She looked from George's face to mine and back again.

"Georgie has a new girlfriend," I said, and there was truth to it. A girl in George's class at school had followed him home, giggling and grinning like an imbecile.

"I do not," George said, and scowled at me.

"He does?" My mother's face brightened. She sat up in the chair as if a harness had been lifted from her.

"Oh, yes, you do," I said, standing up and facing him now, my hands on my hips like a martinet. "And she's a real princess, too. A *narigona*." One with a big honker.

"She is *not* my girlfriend," George screamed. Red was climbing his neck, red as the eye of the incense. His tic was dancing, wild.

I was exhilarated by the sight of my brother's quaking face. Perhaps it was because I was bored, perhaps because I'd had a surfeit of gloom. But I felt a perverse pleasure in goading the god I had worshiped so long. Blow the cone, make it glow. It felt good to bicker. Felt right.

"And another thing," I gloated. "She's a *potona*." A fat ass. I jumped up and waggled my tail.

"*Ya, ya*, Marisi," Papi chuckled, in spite of himself. "That's enough."

George sputtered.

"I don't know why you find it so surprising," said Mother, "that Georgie would have a new girlfriend—that is, *if* he does—"

"Do not!" he screeched.

She winked at him knowingly. "Remember when you told me how you loved Antonio, Mareezie? Do you remember that? And do you remember when you fell in love with the young man who called on Tía Chaba?"

"Now I'm in love with Nub," I confessed.

"Nub? Your cousin?" said Papi. "*Dios mío*. What next? You'll have to get a special dispensation from the Pope. Your great-great-grandparents on my side were first cousins, too, you know. That's what *they* had to do."

"Well, maybe she's not thinking of marriage just yet, honey," Mother said. "Maybe just love between friends, eh?"

"Love friends," I said, and nodded.

"Aha, I see," said my father, smiling. "Better not tell your husband about those," he added, and winked.

"Love friends, my butt," said George under his breath. "There's no such thing."

"Is so!" I barked.

"Is not!"

"Is so! Mother has one!"

And then a hush fell over the room as I gaped around like a stunned animal.

"Mother has one," I repeated, more softly this time. There was a scent of danger in the air, but I yipped my way through it. I wanted to prove to them that I knew what I was talking about.

"A love friend?" Mother said, and leaned into the room, smiling thinly, her elbows on her knees.

Fermata.

And then me again. "Yes. You have one. A love friend. In Cartavio. I saw you sitting with him on the couch. You were staring in each other's eyes. One of the *solteros*. The tall one with the yellow—"

"Enough!" yelled my father. *Presto.* He stood now, a coal fire behind his eyes. Georgie was frozen on the floor, his shoulders hunched up to his ears. Vicki got up and banged her way into another room.

"I can't imagine who you think you saw. In Cartavio or anywhere else, Mareezie," my mother said in a voice full of calm. "I can't imagine."

"It's true!" I yelled. "You were over there! He was over here! I saw you. You *know* it's true!"

Papi whirled around, slapped the newspaper down on the table, and lunged for the front door. The screen door snapped back with a loud slam, then shuddered against the frame. My mother stood and walked into the dining alcove. Her back to us, she pressed her knuckles down against the table, pushed her shoulders up into a shrug. But she didn't say a word.

He didn't come home for dinner that night. I lay in bed sick with worry that he would never come home again. That I had driven him out to a hellhole in Hanna, somewhere between Walcott and Medicine Bow. When he staggered back through the front door at about four o'clock the next morning, I heard a sharp *thwack* and then a *whoosh*, as if air were rushing out of a tire. I crept from my bed, peeked into the living room, and saw an empty bottle with a dapper little man on its side, doffing his hat, swinging his cane. It was planted on our coffee table, where an angry hand had smacked it. Beside it on the couch, laid out and pickled as a corpse, was my father.

Dawn brought one more thing. The news of Grandma Lo's death.

I'D SEEN A photograph of Abuelita's dead sister. I'd come upon it in her family albums, pasted in between portraits of my be-whiskered ancestors in their starched collars and fancy top hats. Her little sister had been laid out in white lace on her funeral bier with garlands of roses cascading about her, a cluster of lilies in her hair. In the photo, her white shoes point like a dancer's, her arms lie peacefully across her chest, her curls are combed down on her brow, her eyes stare out, wide open. My Great-Grandfather Cisneros stands behind the body, and, above his black cravat, his face is long and gaunt. His eyes seem to be sliding down his cheeks like stones in a mountain *huayco*. His oldest daughter, my grandmother, stands beside him in a veil of black lace. Her eyes are dry but haunted. Although she is seven, her little face appears even smaller than her sister's. Her sister cannot be two.

I had seen this. I had seen funeral biers of the poor go by in

Peruvian streets, the women wailing and staggering after, their heads draped in black cloth. I had seen men of society file into a church alone, their wives too delicate to see an inert body—for all the fragrant blossoms tucked in around it. But I had never seen a cadaver stretched out, serene, staring up into the ether.

Grandma Lo's body was set out for family viewing at Frank Wooten's Funeral Home, three days after it expired at the Rawlins Hospital. "I'm taking the children there," Mother said, sitting in front of her mirror, pinning a hat to her head.

"You're what?" I heard Papi say. "You can't be serious. Funerals are not for children. You're going to make them sick. Twist their minds for life."

Mother turned, her head tilted down like a bull's, one hand jabbing a long hat pin in the direction of her brain. "Jorge, I'm taking them with me. You want to talk about twisting? Let's talk about your *borrachera*. Your stinko night out on the town."

A truck rumbled down Buffalo Street, speeding its way out of Rawlins. My parents stared at each other and then Papi started again. "We're talking about the *dead* here," he said. "Where I come from you wouldn't dream of taking a child to see one. Children are too impressionable. Even grown women don't go."

"Well, where I come from you learn to look death in the eye," said my mother. "They might as well learn it right now. It's an important lesson."

The mortuary was on the outskirts of town. It was a clapboard house, dove gray and windowless, with no greenery save a struggling azalea in a clay pot by the stoop. "Clam-Hand" Wooten, the undertaker, lived on the right, behind two thick white pillars and a fusty porch. On the left, where the viewing parlor led into the embalming lab, was Grandma Lo.

She had died on the morning of Mother's Day. Clam-Hand had slid her into his refrigerator and gone off to Laramie. Three full days crawled by before we could trudge up the steps to view his rendition of my grandmother.

The Wooten parlor was set up like a schoolroom. There were four rows of wooden chairs behind a raised platform. Twenty-four chairs in all. The room's ceiling was low, its walls hung with blue wallpaper, fleur-de-lis against yellowy cream. The carpet was dingy, worried by prairie grit, thinned by the boots of the be-reaved.

Mr. Wooten's pocked face met us at the door. He was wringing his hands in dismay. His fingers were long, cool as fish when he slipped them around our wrists and into our palms. "On Mother's Day, of all things," he whispered. "Terribly sorry." A wan smile coiled across his face and was gone.

Mother pushed past him into the parlor. There were candles set out on a table and a body behind them, under glass. The lady was dressed in flowered cotton, her hands folded neatly over her still heart. A white satin sheet covered her legs. I saw no more than that at first. A quick glimpse, and then my eyes were back on my patent-leather shoes.

We were the only ones there. Grandpa Doc was nowhere to be seen. When we hurriedly whispered to Mother, asking her where he was, she simply turned and rapped one gloved fist on her left breast, over the chambers of her heart.

As we filed into the last row of chairs, the candles flickered against the warm May breeze and Clam-Hand spun around to shut the door behind us. A fat black fly buzzed in. We lowered ourselves onto the hard-edged chairs and looked out at the table in front.

"That's not Grandma Lo," said Mother in a voice that seemed somebody else's. "That's just her body. She's off with God now. I wanted you to see it for yourselves."

It was clear she was right. The woman up there was pink and smiling. Her hair was in tight little curls. On her mouth was a smear of vermillion, on her cheeks powdery circles of rose. She looked more like Mrs. Birdseye than my grandmother. She was puffed out, painted, and pert. Any minute now, she was going to roll over, prop her chin on one hand, raise the glass case with the other, eye the fly, and say in Mrs. Birdseye's earnest little voice, "Well, dear ones, everything in this world has a sound explanation. There's nothing wrong with dying. Nothing wrong with it at all!"

Where had Grandma Lo gone?

Off. Like Grandma Clapp, clanking downstairs in the Ferguson Building, flapping out Cedar Street, chasing the ghosts of her past.

Off. Like Nub's mother on her sprees from the loony bin, bolting through gardens into the night. Down, down, to the *rumdrumdrum* of the road.

Off. Like Joe Krozier's woman. Never to be seen again. Off, down some great stretch of highway, as Americans were wont to go.

⁓

THERE WAS NO more reason to stay in Wyoming now. We packed our bags and went out to the ranch one last time. Grandpa Doc was in the new house, sitting in his chair by the fire, poking at cinders with his long iron brand. His face was ragged, hanging down from his skull like hide that's been out in hard weather. A tumbler of scotch sat close by.

"You be sure to take good care of yourself, Daddy," my mother said, and he nodded, but his eyes weren't those of a man who planned to take good care of anything. They had the flat glint of lead.

That evening, I sat out on the porch with him as sunset stole over Elk Mountain. A ribbon of color slid from the clouds and spilled over the crest: shell pink, then hot methyl orange. We watched it in companionable silence. I had finally learned how. George was walking the prairie with Great-Grandma Clapp, and her skirt billowed out like the jib of some large sea creature, ready to engulf him, pull him under. In the distance someone was singing.

It was dark before someone switched on the light from inside the house and I turned and found my grandfather's eyes. They were talking at me, in the way gringo eyes do. I eye-talked him back. Then he spoke.

"See over there?" He motioned to a place in the sky behind me. I wheeled around. Two eagles were circling the pearly night.

"Yes. I see them," I said.

"There are two," he said enigmatically, and then fell silent. We watched them wind lazily, then fly off toward the cliffs.

"You know about eagles, do you?" he asked. I shook my head no.

"They fly upside down when they're courting. Go crazy, they do. Put on shows. And then when they mate, they mate for life. For *life*. If one dies, the other won't last very much longer. Not without the one he loves. Not long."

More than anything I wanted to ask him if he had been married before, like my mother. Or if he would ever marry again. He was seventy years old and, judging by Great-Grandma Clapp, was looking forward to another thirty years of life. The answer to those questions was no—he had married one woman and would die married to her only—but I never asked. I didn't dare risk annoying him the way I had annoyed my mother. I slipped my hand into his large palm and focused on the black hulk in the distance.

"Grandpa, does Elk Mountain have an *apu*?"

"What's that?"

"An *apu*. A spirit."

"Well, yes. I suppose so."

"How do you know?"

"Do you see how we all gather around it? Old Man Widener over there. Joe Krozier there. Me here. Wouldn't sit here looking up at it if something weren't drawing us, would we? That's how I see it."

"Does the *apu* ever get angry?"

"You mean like a volcano? No."

"I mean if you do something to make him mad. Like if you dig in him for bones."

"Oh, well, I reckon the Injuns think so. They tell me things like that. But I don't know. Never seen anything like that myself. And I tend to believe in what I see."

I must have looked at him with a puzzled face, for he continued, "Wish it were different, honey girl. Sure would like to believe in something otherworldly. Something that would make me one hundred percent sure I'll see your Grandma Lo again. I just don't know what to believe." He squeezed my hand, lifted his heavy frame out of the chair, swung open the screen door, and disappeared inside.

That night I overheard my parents discuss our three months out West. The house was small, the walls were thin, and I could lie in the blanket spread out on my grandfather's sofa and listen to every nuance of conversation. Vicki was doing fine, they said, but needed some distraction: something to get her mind off death, something to make her laugh. Maybe a museum, a quick visit to a historic site, a concert in some park. Marisi was a sport, no problem there; she seemed to have taken it all in stride. But George, it seemed, was suffering. Oh, he's all right, my father said. No, he was *not*, Mother insisted. He was ill. Some shock; hadn't he noticed? A *trauma* of some kind. Probably because he'd been made to look at his dead grandmother, Papi said. *No*, Mother said sharply, it started long before that. In Peru. Nonsense, my father said, but we'll make a point to see a doctor while we're here, if that will make you feel better.

The next morning, old wifeless Joe came winding up
Rattlesnake Pass on his mange-bitten, swaybacked mare. As we
downed the last of Grandpa Doc's flapjacks—lighter and sweeter
than any a servant had made us—Old Joe thrust his mug in the
door and called out, "Goin'ta Rawlins, anyone? Got room for a
big-fisted horseman with no car and a li'l ass?"

We did go to Rawlins that day. We dropped off Joe, watched
him go into the bar down the street from the Ferguson Building.
Then we boarded a train that took us to Boston. It was a big
town, hard town, with nothing to recommend it except that my
parents held hands briefly when they walked down the Fenway.
But I do recall that we saw three things there we'd never
dreamed we'd see: a television, a jukebox, and a psychiatrist.

The television was in a hotel lobby; there was a Cuban man in
it, scolding his redheaded wife. It was just the thing to make
Vicki laugh. The jukebox was in a corner soda shop; I fed a
nickel into it and our waitress stood over us and bleated every
word of the song. The mind god was in Children's Hospital; he
gave George a vial of pills and made his face go slack, smooth—
tranquil as the dunes of Pachamama, smiling and beckoning us
home.

POWER

La Conquista

PACHAMAMA WAS NOT the only one welcoming us to Lima. Tension greeted us, too. There was an arch in Abuelita's spine.

"*Y la Abuela* Clapp?" Abuelita asked me, issuing the right name like the sharp report of a gun. "Did you see her before she died?"

So. She knew about the Clapps. With that volley, it was clear to me that the skirmish between her and Mother would resume. Much later, when I was grown, Papi told me that for years letters had been delivered to Abuelita's door addressed to Mother, with *Clapp* printed neatly on the envelopes. When Mother's remarks to him indicated that the letters were from her parents, he didn't say a word, never posed a query. But then he found himself rushing to flood walls, plugging the leaks in advance.

"She changed her name to Campbell before I met her in Boston," he told them once. "Clapp has an unfortunate medical meaning in the United States. Not nice for a woman."

Not nice? Clapp, as in *cloepian*, Saxon for "name"; or *clappen*,

Middle English for "strike." To wit: The angel yclept Clapp clapped his wings, clapped a saddle on his horse, and clapped to the pearly gates. What's not nice about that?

Well and good. But a French calque got in the way in America and made life miserable for Mum. Clap, *c'est à dire, clapier,* a brothel, or more to the point, *clapoir,* a venereal sore. To wit: *Le diable, en visitant le clapier, a trouvé un clapoir dans une partie de son corps que je ne veux pas mentionner ici.* In other words, not very nice at all.

Or, to put a sharp point on it, see the 1828 edition of Webster's: *Clapdoctor: one who is skilled in healing the clap.* But if the name had been good enough for six generations of Clapps in America—a very nice oral surgeon among them—why wasn't it right for my mother? No, no. That explanation would not do. But the issue was never addressed openly.

Other questions hung in the air like malodors the family was too polite to acknowledge. "Now that you'll be living in Lima, Marisi," my abuelita asked me on our first day back, as if I were a full-grown *señorita,* "where will you be attending church?" The sheer force of the question, when I repeated it to Mother in our *pensión* on Avenida Ricardo Palma, drove her into the next room. Even my soul, it seemed, would be their battlefield. I had heard Mother complain that Abuelita had had no right to baptize me a Catholic behind her back. She had tried to do it with Vicki, Mother said, and failed; the only way George had ducked it was by having the good sense to be born in Wyoming.

When, on our second day back in Lima, Abuelita announced she would pick me up at the *pensión* and take me to mass, Mother countered by saying she had already enrolled me in the American Union Church. No one seemed a bit concerned that I would burn in hell if I shuttled between churches. I had heard a priest say so myself. But the dispute clearly wasn't about hell. It was about will.

"What do I do that makes your mother dislike me so much, Jorge?" Mother whispered one day. They had taken to pulling each other into the next room and speaking in ill-tempered voices.

"Nothing specific," he replied. "But you're a gringa, honey. Your presence offends her."

"Somos culturas distintas," my abuelita declaimed about the difference between Lima and Rawlins. We are two very different cultures. But I could see she meant hers was better.

Within a week, my parents found a place to live. We slipped into our new quarters on Avenida Angamos as if it were something familiar, but there was an otherness to it. A change. There was nothing grand about the house. Certainly it was not the sprawling colonial construction we were used to, with leaping arches out front and servants' quarters in the rear. I hadn't understood it when my parents had decided it over the kitchen table in Rawlins, but Papi was resigning from W. R. Grace to start an engineering firm in Lima. It was a dream the Arana brothers had, a bond that would honor their father. At thirty-eight, when he finally handed Grace his resignation, Papi was the oldest, most beribboned, most successful of Abuelito's three sons. For him the launching of their new engineering company, Techo Rex, was the fulfillment of an obligation. For my uncles, Víctor and Pedro, far younger men with skyscraping ambitions, it was a leap at wealth. For us children, prosperity had long been delivered— we'd tasted the good life already—and change meant something else. In real terms, we had ceased to be wards of a rich gringo company: We had less money, less prestige, less protection against the harsh winds of Peruvian politics. Less power. We were in a small house, facing the cinch of a city life, sensing an ebb to things.

Nowhere was this more evident than in the ranks of our servants. There was one where there had been six. Nora was nineteen, a shy girl with a pretty face and a thick black ponytail. She scrubbed and swept and cooked and shopped, but she barely touched our conscious lives, bustling to and fro with all the exigencies of her day.

Our home was the first floor of a stone and stucco duplex in the residential area of Miraflores. Black iron girded its windows; nothing shielded its door. Across the avenue was an open lot with little in it save dirt and the sketch of an imagined apartment tower. Down from that, the American ambassador's mansion: a Spanish colonial with graceful wide balconies. A riot of fuchsia spilled over its walls.

Our rooms were narrow, closed, dim on a sunny day. The vendors who came hawking bread and fruit were impatient urbanites with jingling pockets and places to go. The garden was minimal—a Potemkin illusion—with no room for children's games. After the scale of Paramonga or Wyoming, George and I could see that we needed to rein in, straiten the radius, think small. We had, in every material measure, stepped back. Qualms were starting to show.

"The children need school uniforms, Jorge."

"Buy them the minimum, please."

The last luxury that was left us—our mother's classroom, a luxury of the spirit if not of the purse—was traded in for the sepulchral halls of the Roosevelt School. "A real school! With English books and American teachers!" my mother beamed, but when we went to register, it seemed a vast building, full of arrogant gringos and a brain-numbing clangor of bells. *"La escuela Americana?"* my grandmother gasped when we told her. "With so many fine old Catholic schools in this city?"

We were squeezed into gray wool and starched shirts. On our first day of school, Papi motioned us to the walkway where our geraniums stood sentry, bright red and anxious.

"This is Tang," he said, pointing to a round Buddha of a man who nodded genially from inside our yellow Studebaker. "First he takes me to work, then he drives you to school. Pay close attention. This is a big city. Bad things happen."

Mother stood in the frame of our carved front door and waved. "You're going to learn so much!" she called out. But she turned back into the house as if there were something she'd just mislaid.

THE PLAYGROUND OF the Roosevelt School was swarming with hundreds of children, milling about and yammering, waiting for the bell to ring. We edged through the gate and stood in awe.

A girl about my age leaned against the wall and stared at us. She was dark-skinned, frail, her eyes bulging from her face like boiled eggs, blue-white and rubbery.

"*Primer día?*" she asked. First day? I was gawking around me, an obvious newcomer. I nodded that it was so.

"You speak English," she said, more of a fact than a question.

"Yes," I answered, ready to prove it. But she continued in Spanish, and my affirmation hung in the air like a hiss.

"Then you'll be fine," she assured me. "Don't look so worried. I'm Margarita Martinez. My English is not so good. They put me in *Señora* Arellano's class."

There were two streams for every grade at Roosevelt, Margarita explained. The main one was for English-speakers, a smaller one for those who spoke better Spanish. I would be tested for my abilities and streamed according to my tongue.

The man who would decide my fortune was vexed in the company of children. I could see it the moment he called out my name. He was frowning and fidgety, flicking his hair with his fingers and peering impatiently at his wrist. I followed his orange head into a room next to the headmaster's office.

"Do you speak English or Spanish at home, *señorita?*" he asked me in Spanish, motioning me to a chair.

"Both," I replied, and stared at his hair. There was something miraculous about the way it cocked up on top and slicked flat around the ears.

"Which do you read?"

"Both," I answered again.

"No," he said, drumming a long white hand on the tabletop. Gold fuzz sprouted on his knuckles. He was wearing a ring, ponderous as a prime minister's. "You don't understand me. There must be a difference in the level at which you speak and read your two languages." *Ee-dee-oh-muzz.* His Spanish was broad and drawling, like my mother's. He opened a green folder and looked through it, and then switched his questions to English. "What I'm asking you, missy, is which language are you more proficient in? There are no records or tests here."

"I think I'm about the same in both," I said.

"Sir," he said.

"What?"

"I think I am the same in both, *sir.*"

I repeated the phrase after him. I had never heard anyone in the United States of America talk like that. I wanted to fall on the floor and squeal, his words were striking me as so idiotic. But there was nothing amusing about the man.

"Here," he said. "Read to me from this book." He shoved a brown volume across the table, pinched two fingers, and then plucked a white shirt cuff out of his jacket sleeve.

I turned the book in my hands. *Indians of the Great Plains,* the cover announced. I opened it. "What part would you like me to read?" I asked.

"Any page," he said. "Pick one." He sat back and crossed his hands behind his head.

I flipped through, looking at pictures. Somewhere near the

middle, there was one labeled *Medicine man with a rattle,* or words to that effect. The witch doctor was peeking out of a tepee, holding an artifact. In the foreground, an Indian brave in a loinflap ran down to a river with his hair spread behind him like wings. The text was interesting enough, something like this: *After the last steaming and sweating ceremony, the Indian plunged into water during the summer, or into a snowbank in winter. Thus purified, he was ready to make an offering to the Great Spirit or seek a sign from the Great Beyond.*

I stared at the words and considered my situation. I could read this aloud and be waved into the English stream. It was clearly as simple as that. Or I could play possum, as Grandpa Doc liked to say. Put one over on the prig.

I snapped the book shut and set it down on the table. "I can't read this," I said, and looked up.

"You're not even going to try?"

I shook my head. "Too hard."

"Well, read this, then," he said, and slid another book at me. It was thin and bright as a candied wafer.

I picked it up, leafed through. Then I smoothed it flat on the table in front of me. "Jane . . . puh-plays . . . wi-i-ith the . . . ball."

"I see," he said, after some pages of this. "I thought as much. That will do." He scribbled a long commentary into my file.

I was put into *Señora* Arellano's class and, for what seemed a very long time, my parents were none the wiser. I toted my children's illustrated *Historia del Perú*, memorizing the whole litany of Inca rulers until I could recite their Quechua names with all the rattletybang of gunfire.

And Margarita Martinez paid attention to me.

❧

THERE IS A STORY they tell in Cajamarca about four sons from an honorable family that knew the value of honesty, the pleasures of hard work, and the worth of a job well done. The first son set out to build houses. The second became a general in the army. The third founded a bank. The fourth went east and made hats. Time passed, and the hatmaker fell in love with a green-eyed woman. He asked her father for her hand. But, as fate would have it, her father rejected him. It wasn't only that the commerce of straw hats wasn't grand enough. The suitor's skin wasn't fair enough, his eyes not clear enough, his language not elegant enough, and, to seal the rejection: Of all his brothers, he was told, he had the least clout.

The hatmaker wouldn't take no for an answer. He was intent on winning the green-eyed lady. First, he took stock of his situation. There was nothing he could do about his shade of skin, the brilliance of his eyes, nor the cleverness of his tongue, but he certainly could do something about his clout in the world. He swindled a mansion out of his first brother; he killed the general and took over his men; he kidnapped the banker and created an empire. And when he was done, the green-eyed woman was his.

So what is the moral of this story? The answer out of Cajamarca is: Do what you can. You can't change skin, can't fix tongues, can't brighten eyes, but power is for the taking. Steal it, lie for it, kill if you have to. You can win the girl with the interesting eyes.

Looking back, I understand what was happening—though I certainly didn't understand it at the time. Mother had made a bargain with Papi: He could take the risk of resigning from Grace and joining his brothers, he could even put us in a smaller house, but the first cut of his salary would go to the Roosevelt School, and her children would be educated as Americans. She hadn't factored in the realities of that decision. Roosevelt was where the prosperous Americans were. It was where the sons and daughters of diplomats, industrialists, bankers went to be schooled. Had I continued to be a little princess of the Grace regnancy, I might have had some currency there. As it was, we had become children of diminished circumstances—we never said so, never complained—but the knowledge that we had lost our power did not come without its consequences. My instinct was the Cajamarca instinct: Do what you can. Get it back.

I had no power among rich Americans. I could fool them, however. Trip them up. Dodge their game. I would lie for it, cheat for it, dance fast if I had to. I would get the girl with the bulgy eyes.

Although I fooled my way into a desk next to Margarita Martinez, I didn't turn out to be a particularly good friend to her. We played together when we could, but she was far too interested in dolls for my taste. Her house was down the *avenida* and around the corner from ours, much grander, with a host of servants trailing her down the street. She hadn't been able to get into the fancy Catholic girls' schools for some reason, and her father—a restaurant owner—had done what he could. He wangled her way into the Americans' school. She was timid, something of a priss on the playground, and I enjoyed lording over her far more than I should have. I made her do things my way.

I cannot say what was in my brother's or sister's heart, but an appetite definitely stirred in mine. I found myself looking around, assessing what kind of power was available to me. There did appear to be some: With Peruvian children at Roosevelt, I bragged I was really a gringa. With gringos, I crossed my eyes and retreated into Spanish. With sissies like Margarita, I played queen. I did what I could.

But there was something else, far more potent. As I settled into that Lima house, with its front door smack on the street, I began to decode a system I had never even suspected in the haciendas, for all that the hierarchy was obvious. I began to see that not only did the rich gringos wield a good share of the power in the city—this was all too apparent in their houses, their cars, their clothes, their toys—I could also see it was the fairer Peruvians, the ones with less visible Indian blood, who ruled Peru. The more Spanish blood in your veins, the more power you had. Maybe I had an advantage here; maybe I could reap the benefit. Nobody was posting signs about it or sending the less fortunate to the other side of the tracks, but the evidence was everywhere: The Indians were the servants, beasts of burden, construction workers, street hawkers, beggars. The *mestizos*— people of mixed race—were the shopkeepers, office workers, scrappy entrepreneurs. From time to time I would see a Chinese or Japanese woman behind a counter, or a tall black man in a uniform guarding the doors of a fancy hotel; the variations were relatively few. But the highest caste of all—the landowners, intelligentsia, the moneyed classes—were almost always *los blancos*, the whites. Clearly, my grandparents weren't rich. But, even though my grandfather had hightailed it upstairs and forfeited his career, the two had a respectable position in Peruvian society. They had inherited a hacienda in the mountains when Tía Carmen had died. They had a comfortable house in an attractive neighborhood of Miraflores. We also had something we could never lose: We were *gente decente*. From the good families. As my grandmother was fond of saying, *somos puros Hispanos*—we were Spaniards to the core.

I had had some exposure to the power of skin: I had been of a questionable race in my mother's country. For all our material slippage, I remained a member of the upper class in my father's country. I did not use this information immediately, but I logged it away, in the spirit of one-upmanship. It was the coin of the realm.

⁓

THROUGHOUT CHILDHOOD AND down to this day, George would always be our psychiatrist, the seismograph of the fam-

ily—his delicate emotional tissue warning us of subtle shifts in
our terrain. His little yellow pills were working so well now that
he was no longer twitching, walleyed, and fearful. The medicine
man in Boston had brought back his beautiful face. The pills
were a six-month treatment for stress, so effective that my
brother had become valor itself, running through traffic, jumping
from treetops, rappelling the neighborhood walls.

He was so boisterous that the ambassador's boy would not
play with us. His maid shook her head no at the gate. Too busy
with a tutor, she said, or at a party, or splashing about in his bath.

But there were others willing to join us in the dirt lot under
the imagined tower: Barbara, the helmet-haired Swiss, whose
toenails were scrubbed clean as shells. Roberto, Margarita's
brother, a scamp who won points by intercepting secrets Vicki
was scribbling on paper, stuffing in cans, and pulleying to her
friend upstairs. Albertito Giesecke, who refused to kiss me
because he'd given himself to God. Sandra, the Japanese-
American, whose U.S. Army father was stockpiling Swift Armour
hams in a bomb shelter he'd carved under their house. Margarita
herself, who sat on a curb and watched us carry on, her egg-ball
eyes abulge. George had had no trouble convincing her to kiss
him. I had seen them go at it in the lot, behind the retaining
wall.

"Let's play Pizarro," George said one day, coming out to the lot
with a bowl on his head. "All I need is a *lanza* and a *caballito*."
He picked up two lengths of wood. "Here," he said, and put one
between his legs: "My horse." Then he swung the other above
his head like a crazed conquistador at the apocalypse: "My
weapon."

Conquest became our game in that viceregal city. We returned
to it day after day the way a gambler staggers into a casino to finger a table's felt. Buy the chips. Win the kitty. Win a war, win a
kiss, win Peru. You want to taste my sword? *Thwap.* You die. I

draw and quarter you the way they drew and quartered Tupac Amaru. The way they strapped his limbs to four horsemen and charged. The way they pickled his penis.

I put aside *qosqos* and *apus* and energy bubbles and Antonio's black stone for a piece of *la conquista*. Perhaps it was my schoolbooks that convinced me, with their lavish praise for Pizarro and splendid woodcut illustrations of his subjugation of the Inca. Perhaps it was the city that beguiled me, with its concrete palaces and pomp. "You see this magnificence?" Papi said as he strode through the Plaza de San Martín, his arms thrown up into the air, his torso turning like Caesar before Rome. "This is our patrimony. This is your birthright. Your forefathers built Peru. Your great-grandfather lived over there in his last days, on the top floor of the Hotel Bolívar. Every day he put on spats and a waistcoat and walked to El Club Nacional for a *copita de jerez* with his friends. Our family lived in these streets. You see these lampposts on the square? I helped build them myself when I was fifteen years old and an apprentice at an artist's foundry. Your world is here. Your history is here, Marisi. You are the heart and soul of this country."

La conquista. In a day when the world was for the taking. When the Huari conquered the Moche, and the Inca conquered the Huari, and the Spaniards conquered the Inca, and the Arabs poured into Spain, and the Vandals overran Rome. What could be more exhilarating than to spring into alien land unexpected? Take it. Claim it. Put a flag on it. Until something more powerful comes along.

"I command you to stop!" Canute said to the sea. But the waves lapped the sand as they'd always done. Ah, but there's always something greater. Call it God. Call it Death. One should *take* things while one can.

Fewer than two hundred men took the Inca. They trekked from Tumbes to Cajamarca with horses, a little gunpowder, and swords. They captured an empire that ruled more than twenty million: the Tahuantisuyo, mighty domain of the Inca. How? Certainly not because they were any more clever; the Inca had reached a level of civilization that Spain itself did not know. The lords of the Andes were orderly: They fed their people, irrigated their deserts, built impregnable fortresses, ruled with an iron hand. Certainly not because that straggly regiment of 168 was powerful enough to stop a sea of natives. Had the Inca wanted to, they could have swallowed the dogfaces whole. Drunk their blood. Why didn't they? Here it is: Because they felt a magic at work, some undefinable force of destiny. Black light. Open the *qosqo:* take it in. Spain strutted through Europe, bragging about its military victory, but this was no victory. No. The truth was all there in that city, slow though I was to see it. Peru was no product of conquest. It had been forged from transcendent surrender.

Our little band ran through the neighborhood day after day after school, enacting the Spanish side of the story. I marched out to the empty lot with cardboard strapped around my knees, a tin pot on my head, a garbage cover in one hand, a strong stick in the other. I was Don Pedro the Cruel. I was Boabdil. I was El Cid, ready to die, hungry for revenge.

It was hard work, this autoindoctrination. This ad-lib curriculum in power. Often, I just scraped by. One of my lions broke out of its cage one day, surprising me and my men. I had been sleeping by the fire, sated with rum and skewered heart. The roar was faint at first, like the rumble of a distant *huayco*—rock grinding on rock—and then I woke to see the animal coming at me through the hall. He was massive, blond, padding across the tile with his shoulders churning. His head hardly moved at all.

I snatched my cloak and wrapped it tight around my arm. My guard staggered back, a fringe of straight hair flopping against her forehead. She fell into an empty vat. The clatter awoke my minister, who stood and dusted off his robes. His eyes widened when he saw the approaching cat, but he didn't spring out with his bludgeon; he slinked behind my couch like a ferret into a hole, afraid. I went forward to meet the beast, swinging my sword—Tizona—above my head. Then a most magical thing happened. The lion stopped and stared at my advance, as if my very form were mesmerizing. He snorted once, raised his magnificent brow, and sent his eyes from side to side.

I strode up, grasped him by the mane, led him back to his cage in the adjoining hall, and thrust him in. When my brother rattled in with his armor clanging about him, ready to defend me, I turned and raised two fingers to signal that I had been blessed by the shield of God. Then I slapped the fur from my hands.

We went into the desert after that, in search of the counts of Carrion. They had committed dastardly acts against me and their wives. Me, they had betrayed with talk, with oily, insidious promises they had never made good. Their wives, they had nearly killed. They had lured them out to a meadow, offering words and wine. But once there, they had kicked them, lashed them, stripped them, and left them there to die. I had heard of these cowardly deeds from my scribe, who read me the news from a scroll of blood-smudged parchment.

I rescued the wives and bound their wounds while George rode on to give the fleeing counts their due. He found them just outside Valencia, sniveling by the retaining wall, seeing the reflection of their absurd little selves in the shine of their conqueror's eyes. They threw their hands over their heads. When I galloped up in my chariot with their women huddled against my legs, they surrendered to my chains.

I died some days later, but not before I made plans. I gathered my men. Embalm me, I told them. Find Clam-Hand Wooten, bring him here in the silver bullet with the flying dogs on the sides, tell him to fix up my face, scarred now from so many battles. Then strap me to Babieca. They balked at this, thinking my horse would sense that I was dead and buck me into the dirt by the side of some *carretera*. But no, I said, Babieca is loyal, he will carry my corpse. Do all this, men, then point the horse toward the battlefield. Send him against King Cúcar, with my body on his back.

They did exactly as I said. They cleaned me and trussed me and strapped me to Babieca. And then the two of us rode out to meet the Moors. They were terrified when they saw me, clutching their breastplates at the very sight of my hair on the wind. "But she was dead!" they cried out. "They told us she was dead!" And then they scattered like crazed cockroaches. Vanquished.

"Of course you like to play those games," Abuelita crowed as she poured tea for us one evening. "You two are probably very good at them." Papi had taken me, George, and Vicki to our grandparents' house for what would become our traditional Sunday visit. Mother had excused herself and stayed home.

"It's in your blood, you know!" Abuelita continued. "Don't forget that your great-great-great-grandfather (*el bis bis bis bis!*) General Joaquin Rubin de Celis de la Lastra was the first Spaniard to fall in the Battle of Ayacucho. You might even say that the fall from his horse marked the independence of Peru!"

"And how about Pedro Pablo Arana? *El bis* of the other side!" Tía Chaba chimed in, one eye on my shrinking grandfather, her hair piled high in a twist. "He led three hundred rebels on horses! *Cataplún, cataplún!* Swooping down from the mountains to fight the corrupt military tyrants!" She rapped the table with her beautiful long red fingernails, as if they were hooves. She flashed her eyes inside exquisitely drawn lines of kohl. Vicki grinned triumphantly.

Power. It was a family thing.

⁓

AS THE ARANA brothers were making their bid for power, establishing Techo Rex offices in Lima, importing the latest American engineering equipment, plotting like Cheops to erect something monumental, every law of thermodynamics was being played out within the confines of our house. Push was coming to shove. Electricity was filling the air. Even the nervousness that once coursed through George now snaked, through some Newtonian concatenation of converted energy, across the house to creep into Mother. Her brow was perpetually dug with Trouble, her eyes gun-barrel gray. Her fingers were chewed back, raw. I no longer saw them dancing along the neck of a violin or drawing on the wand of a bow. She seemed limp, lifeless, moving through rooms as if she no longer knew where she was. Looking for cues that weren't there.

She seldom went out. Far from the gringos in the haciendas and free of the obligations of a teacher, she was afloat in an alien city, hovering above the ruckus like gossamer on the fly.

She tried to bear up by reading philosophy. The books were barometers of her mood: Nietzsche's *Thus Spake Zarathustra,* Will Durant's *The Lessons of History.* The themes were will, control, subjugation: off a broad brush, on a large scale. When we'd walk in from school we'd see her reenter in stages: the chin up, the quick blink, the realization that we were standing before her, and then our mother descending the staircase of her mind, peering down at us from some far landing of consciousness. She was there, but she was somewhere else, too, like a lynx with its nose in the wind, sensing trails that could call her away.

Something had wormed deep into Papi, too, but it was

Trouble of a different sort. He was home later and later. Out with old school friends. Out with engineers. Out with club mates. Out with old friends he met at the bar. Out.

There were endless excuses, dragged forth in the wee hours of morning. Words that slithered under doorjambs, over pillows, wedging their way into dreams. In all, there was a sense of intemperate crescendo, as when opera swings into a devil's dance. The slurred opening, the long growl, the hammering on the door, the plangent trill of my mother's voice when he staggered in under the influence, "This is what *macho* means, eh, Jorge?" Is this what Lima men do? They bickered at night, they sneered in the morning, they rolled their eyes heavenward, he lurched from the room. Our air was filled with their static.

The electricity was so pervasive, it eventually coursed into water as well. We couldn't get any. Water, the very stuff that the Chimu had handled so deftly, that the Inca had mastered after them—labyrinths of it, pulsing through desert like veins through a warm animal—water had stopped cold in Lima. It trickled reluctantly from faucets, thinning to a sullen drip, stopping altogether by late afternoon. When the family above us cooked or bathed, our supply was paralyzed, and our throats would fill with the stench of ripe commodes.

It happened in August, when the *garúa* squatted over the city the way smoke squats on peat fire. A gray haze locked itself in between Cerro San Cristóbal and the Pacific so that we could see nothing beyond our own walkway. So that a priest approaching his church would wonder if it still flew a cross. It was clear the *apus* were angry, mocking us from their perches. You say you need water, you miserable *olla podrida* of pig-farm conquistadors and faithless *serranos*? Here you are. Take it. Fog.

It seldom rained in Lima. The city hadn't seen real rainfall for years. Water hung in the air, it pounded the shore, but the kind you could use was rare. Even then, in Lima's splendid modernity.

Even then, with engineers all about. Whatever water there was, we were looking at. It sat in our faces, curled around our hair, wound its tubercular coccus into our lungs. We could not drink it, we could not clean ourselves in it, we could not boil an egg for dinner. But the worst of all worries was this: Lima was thirsty. The bodiless head was approaching. *Tac pum.*

There was a race to see how much we could collect in our buckets, save up, for all the times the spigot ran dry. Next door in Sandra's all-American house, ready as her father was for nuclear missiles or an atomic holocaust—his basement shelves creaking with pig—they were having trouble finding enough water to brush their teeth. In our house, things were worse. We had to compete with the people upstairs.

One Saturday, Vicki turned on the faucet, thrust a finger under the trickle, and found herself tingling with electricity, her crisp hair standing on end. Our water had become charged, galvanic, but only at certain times of the day; it would begin about noon, when Nora prepared the main meal of the day, and it would last through evening.

Papi puzzled over it for days, banging tubes, twirling nozzles, poking rubber cables deep into the metal. Eventually he pulled out the reason why. Someone was dangling a live wire into our tubes from the upstairs bathroom, and the someone was doing it whenever we needed water the most.

Our father stomped to our neighbor's door, with the evidence in his hand. They denied everything. But the next day, our water was back to a magnificent trickle. We took shallow baths in it, luxuriating in the warmth.

I went to bed cheered that night, feeling things had taken a turn for the better. My parents had gone to a wedding. Nora had made us flan, kissed with anise and doused in burnt sugar. I slid under my covers and watched Vicki's eyes tick rhythmically across her book pages, until a sweet sleep swallowed me in.

I was jolted awake by a loud *thwack* at the other end of the corridor. I sat up straight. Vicki was fast asleep in her bed. It was dark, but the eerie glow of the moonlit fog spilled its silver on the floor. My father's voice skipped down the corridor, over the tiles. "*Sin zapatos?*" he said. "You're going out like that? Without shoes?"

"Yes, I am," came my mother's reply. "Did you ask my opinion when you decided to get pie-eyed and leave me to wander around that idiotic party like some idiot *mujercita*...so that I had to get some stranger to take pity on me and bring me home? No. So here's some news for you, *hombre*. I can walk the streets of this city whenever I want and however I want to. Barefoot if I *feel* like it. I am going *out*."

"Go out then! *Ciao!*" and I could hear my father stumble through the room, grabbing at walls.

The front door crashed shut. Then there was a silence, pregnant and laden as the eye of a hurricane.

I slipped out of bed, tiptoed to the door, pulled it open, and leaned into the hall. It was quiet. I squinted into the light. There was a mark on the far wall where my mother had thrown her philosophy book. The volume lay sprawled on the floor. Suddenly my father turned the corner and hung there, one shoulder against the portal. He was looking at me, trying to focus.

"Myaaah!" he said, and flicked his hand up and down like a puppet with a floppy glove. "Nothing! Nothing! *Tsk tsk tsk! Imagínate!* She went out *sin zapatos!*" He pushed himself away, tottered into his bedroom, and flung himself on the bed.

I ran to the living room window and pressed my face up against the pane, searching the street for my mother. I heard her before I saw her. The *slap slap slap* of bare feet. There she was, launching into the Lima night, disappearing into the white curse with the tail of her nightgown behind her. Missile afterburn.

It was the year of the exit, the out-the-door flounce being

crucial: the climax, the pageant, the show. Papi was going for freedom. Mother was dodging despair. Our two anchors were dragging free, dancing along an ocean bottom, headed for opposite shores.

Entrances were more humble. The quiet creak of the door, the shuffling retreat to a back room, the sheepish faces at breakfast. As if nothing had happened. As if the nightmare were over. As if the children didn't know, hadn't heard. As if the playwright weren't a madman with a single formula: Exit stage right, in a rage. Enter stage left, forgetful. Do it again, night after night, though your audience be numb, your critics seething.

Often, the true acting came between shows. The averted eye. The pretense that all was right in our cloven world. We went about school, Papi went about work, Mother went about the house, and our meals together were the essence of sobriety, the soul of civilization, the model of will.

How much power can anyone wield in a marriage? How could either of my parents change the other one's soul? I have pondered those questions all my life, it seems, even as I grew older and my own marriage faltered, fell in on itself, imploded at last with a hole in its heart. In the best of circumstances—in a good match between people of a single culture—merging two lives is an unruly task. It was hard to know whether Mother and Papi were merely struggling with contexts or were a bad match, period. We pondered their incompatibilities, cringed at their scuffles, wondered who would emerge victorious. I knew sooner or later one would prevail. A winner would force the hand. A loser would submit. It was the way of the world. The natural order of things.

IT WAS AT about this time that I learned something else about power: that try as you might, you didn't always know what was

up for the grabbing, you couldn't always be sure who your ene-
mies were.

George and I were in our lot one spring afternoon, whacking base-
balls with our bat, when we heard Papi's voice call for us over the retaining wall. He sounded cheerful, excited even. We ran to see why.

Next to him in the front of our walkway stood Juan Díaz, my
father's *pongo*, the messenger boy from Cartavio. His hair was
gummed down, his face splayed in a grin, his bicycle propped by
his side.

"Look who rode six hundred kilometers all the way from
Cartavio, Georgie!" Papi said with genuine warmth.

George dashed across the street, cut across the grass, and
leapt into the laughing man's arms. "Juan Díaz!" he yelled. "You
said you'd come see me someday!"

"*Sí, mi amigo,*" the man said. "I keep my word." He was small,
wiry. His lips were thin and wide, near purple; his cheekbones
angled and ruddy; his eyes tilted high like a puma's. He set
Georgie down and looked at me.

"*Hola, Juan Díaz,*" I said.

"Marisi." He nodded at me.

"You rode all the way from Cartavio?" I asked him.

"He said he would!" George crowed.

"*Sí.* It took me days, but I did it."

"You are like the *chasqui!*" Papi told him, planting a whop on
his shoulder. "Running messages for the Inca, from Cusco all the
way to the four corners of the Tahuantisuyo!"

"Juan Díaz," I said, a seed of hope rising in my chest, "is
Antonio coming, too?" I remembered that he and Antonio were
friends. Although it had been almost three years since I'd seen
Antonio, I loved him still.

"No, no," the small man shook his glue-slicked head. "Antonio
come to Lima? *No es posible.* Not if his big-bellied wife has anything to say about it."

"He's married now?" my father said, smiling. "Well, well. I guess he'll never leave Cartavio now."

"One child in his woman and one on his hip. He's not going anywhere soon," Díaz said, gloating.

"I'll leave you with the children, Juan," my father said. "I'm going inside to finish up some work. Stay, why don't you, for some *almuerzo*." He waved and went into the house.

George and Juan Díaz threw the baseball after that and spun around on the bicycle. I stood at the edge of the lot, trying to imagine Antonio with a wife and children, feeling the jealousy in my nine-year-old heart. George was at play with his own special friend; they had forgotten about me entirely. I drifted back to the house, dreaming idly, considering whether, if I couldn't have Antonio, Cousin Nub would consent to marry me someday. They both seemed so far away now.

At five o'clock, after a late-afternoon lunch, after Nora had served Juan Díaz a heaping plateful of *arroz con pollo* in the kitchen and the household had retired for a brief siesta, I wandered into the garage, where my father kept his electric train set. We were not allowed to touch the trains when he wasn't there, but we could turn on the light and look to our heart's content. I loved to study the idyll laid out on that table: green topiaries, arched bridges, tunneled hills. There was a red brick station with a platform, a glass pond, two plastic swans, a spired church, a green schoolhouse with a porch. Nothing in it looked Peruvian. Perhaps it was Swiss, buffed to a sleek perfection. There were no people to give us a clue. The town had the look of large-scale abandonment, as if all its souls had departed on an imperative so unequivocal, so swift, that it had not even begun to factor the absence. The doors to the church and the school were unlocked, and they swung open on hinges to admit any passerby, any thief. The chairs at the railroad station waited for travelers to nestle back into them, check their watches, worry their paper schedules. The park bench by the pond awaited the return of an old man who had sat there minutes ago before snatching up his newspaper and strolling out of view.

"Marisi."

I jumped back. The lightbulb that hung over the table did a poor job of illuminating the dank corners of the garage. I squinted to see who was there. Trunks and suitcases were stacked in one corner, rusted machinery in another, cardboard boxes lined the walls.

"*Psst*. Over here." It was a man's voice, calling at me from a shadow on the far side of the kitchen door. I leaned in and saw him.

"Juan Díaz," I said with relief. "You scared me. What are you doing there?"

"Can you see me?" *Me ves?*

"Yes. But where—"

"Why don't you come here, get a closer look?"

I walked along the table, skimming one hand along its smooth green edge. I could see his face and his shoulders. There was a dull glow in the back of his eyes. He did not blink.

"You saw me give your brother a ride on my bicycle?"

"Yes."

"I never got a chance to give you one, Marisi. You saw how Georgie laughed? You saw what a good time he had?" He looked stiff, unnatural, and there was an odd timbre to his voice. It was high. Higher than I remembered it, and buttery.

"Yes."

"Well, come here, *bebita*. I have something for you. Antonio told me you'd like it."

"Antonio did?" I came closer.

"Yes, *niñita*, Antonio. He told me about you. About how wise you are for your years. How old are you now, nine? Ten? *Qué in-teligente. Qué graciosa. Qué bonita. Ven acá, muñeca.*" Come here, dollface.

I saw what he had for me when I turned the corner and faced him. He was holding his man thing, moving it lazily in the palm of his hand. It sat there, insolent as a bullyboy: straight, thick, hard. It pointed at me the way a gun marks an arcade animal.

"You see my *caballito*?" My horsey? "Come, sit on it, *gordita*. Take a bouncy ride." His voice was light, but his face was stern, his neck tense, rigid as carved mahogany.

"No, Juan Díaz," I said.

"Come play with me, *niña*. Sit on me. How can you say no? You didn't say no to Antonio."

I shook my head and slid back along the outskirts of my father's town. My throat was dry, my knees soft.

Suddenly, he was hurtling toward me. He grabbed my shoulders and pushed me to the floor. "I don't want to play with you!" I screamed. The cement was cold. I could feel its grit under my skirt. He held me down and I struggled against him, pushing his knees with my feet. His lever was wagging in my face, a flailing part on a heavy machine. I reached up and took hold of it with both hands. He gasped.

And then I pulled down with all my might.

He bellowed and rolled over, clutching at his groin. I scooted back and brushed the hair out of my eyes. Then I scrambled up the steps to the kitchen door, pushed past, and shot through the house into my room.

⌒

I SAT ON my bed alone and trembled. I did not scream. I did not call for help. My brain inched forward, plowing through muck. What had Antonio told Juan Díaz? Had the truth, harmless as it was, done this to me? I had touched my friend once. I had shown him a place on my body. But that was all. Had a simple account of the facts been enough to send Juan Díaz after me? Or had Antonio embroidered the truth? Had he made our glancing encounter more than it was? Or, as I prefer to think, had Juan Díaz done the embroidering?

You didn't say no to Antonio. That was true. I hadn't. Antonio had told *me* no. Put it away, he had said, and then he had spoken of a greater force.

I kept my eyes on the door, expecting the messenger to burst in and wrestle me to the floor again. But time passed and nothing prowled the corridors save my own jangled mind. The toys George and I had played with that morning were still arrayed on the bed: a rifle, pink bullets, a bat. I stared at them, contemplating the message that had just been delivered. Had one man twisted another's words? Or had my friend woven a tale so distorted, so ugly, that the messenger had sat there for years, stunned by this freak of nature, this child, this apotheosis of perversion? Had the two just laughed and slapped the table? Can you believe it? *That* little elf?

There was another possibility: That an event that had seemed natural three years before, devoid of anything but the simplest curiosity, had multiplied of its own accord. That my curiosity—however innocent—had violated something so forbidden, so unfathomable, that a sick air would follow forever. Pandora's box. Lift that tiny top, stretch those baby fingers, pull that little skirt, then giggle and walk away. But what billows behind is toxic. What seems barely fleeting grows.

I had always known—from every scrap of myth and scripture that had been planted in my brain—that even seemingly inconsequential things had consequences. An apple could cast you from the garden. Not just you, but all your generations to follow.

Here, peek at this, let me peek at that, and the toxins flow, evil multiplying on evil, hunting you down three years later. A man on a bicycle comes to collect.

Who can say where children get their resilience? Who can say how we put terror behind us and move down the road? I claim no special quality here beyond a blessed numbness, a realization that life was well outside my control. Fathers took new jobs, grandmothers died, parents squabbled, houses shrank, energy bubbles collided, poisons oozed, Campbell turned out to be Clapp, lions slipped out of their cages. The gift was to carry on.

So it was that when George whacked open my door and said, "Come on, let's go!" I sighed and trotted after him, pulling our tin-pot armor behind. Juan Díaz was gone. He had left during the siesta. "Funny," my mother commented, shaking her head, "I was so sure he was going to ask your father for a job. It goes to show: The man is prouder than I realized."

I told nobody then or thereafter, curbing my tongue when Juan Díaz was referred to again and again for the rest of my childhood as the quintessence of old-fashioned loyalty: his bicycle ride of love. I did not want to reveal my complicity—the fact that I had showed myself to Antonio, the risk that Juan Díaz could expose me, the possibility that Antonio may have betrayed me—all those bits of a darker truth.

I put those complications behind me, did what any good warrior would do. I ran out to our vacant lot and marched into the battlefield again.

⁓

JUST AS LATIN America swung into an anti-capitalist, anti-*yanqui* era, George and I entered a new phase of our own: We insisted on playing American games only. We had no idea that the political climate in Peru was as inhospitable to the United States as it was. We didn't realize that Peru had had it with the colossus up north. Three years before, the Central Intelligence Agency had brought down a leftist government in Guatemala, and Peruvian intellectuals were seething about that. Two years before, Fidel Castro had led a band of revolutionaries into southeastern Cuba to gather popular support for an overthrow of U.S.-backed dictator Fulgencio Batista. America was getting too cocky for its Latin neighbors. Insurrection was in the air. In Mexico City, Che Guevara was whipping up a fervor, planning a guerrilla-led revolution against the capitalists, which he hoped would spread like wildfire from Central America down through the Andes to Argentina.

We knew nothing of this. It was odd, then, that we chose this moment to flex our American muscle, leave the Conquista behind, play cowboy. We had exercised, in our own fashion, considerable calculation in this change: We did it to throw our weight around, show our superiority. We were quite successful in this. We were more American than the Americans: more swaggering, more obstreperous, more cowboy than anyone who dared venture onto our little patch of Avenida Angamos. There is one more thing, so clear in retrospect, so unregistered then: I was playing two worlds off the middle. At the Roosevelt School, I was *muy Peruana*, careful not to speak English well, hooting at the lumbering Anglos. But once we hit the street, I was a yee-hawin' rodeo, playing Anglo for all I could get.

"I've chawed Big Red," I'd boast to Albertito Giesecke, the angel-faced boy who dreamed of becoming a priest. "I've chawed it and spit it. Real far. Betcha I could hit cow caca if it were a block away. I gotta cousin who larned me how!"

"Our grandpa's a cowboy," we'd crow at anyone who would listen. A cowboy *abuelo!* A living Doc Holliday! He owns a piece of *Norteamerica* that stretches out as far as the eye can see. He has cattle. He has horses. Drives a big shiny car. Wears a big broad hat. We're better than you.

Our arrogance flourished even as everything else seemed to fizzle: As my parents' feuds became more public, as Mother scolded Papi openly at parties, as he defied her by sloshing around another drink, as my abuelita grew weary of the *gringa porfiada*, as *yanquis* in general became pariahs, as Fidelismo began to rise, as the economy plummeted, as graffiti screamed from the wall of our empty lot—*The United States is a vampire nation!* A gun-slinging *pishtaco*, peddler of rock-and-cola, sucking its victims dry.

My mother, on the other hand, was getting more and more patriotic. On the morning of May 8, 1958, she woke us with a directive. "Children, get dressed. We're going to the airport. The Vice President of the United States is arriving today." I climbed into a dress with crinoline petticoats, as frilled and feminine as a tutu. Then George and I headed outside. Tang was there to take us.

"How do you know the vice president?" we asked Mother as we drove north along the coast.

"I don't," she said. "I just want you to see him. He's a person like you and me. I want you to be proud you are Americans."

The road was lined with Lima's poor. They had come out of their dusty *chacras* to see the capitalist gringo ride by in his motorcade with his red-white-and-blue to the wind. The airport was choked with people, jostling through halls like tots on carnival day, swilling *refrescos* and chewing on *chicharrón*. They eyed my mother as she trooped past in her tailored wool suit. I puffed out my chest to better display my frippery.

She elbowed her way to an open balcony and lined the three of us up at the rail. Vicki and George were on one side of her, I on the other. "There," she said, pointing. Then, shading her eyes like a general at a parade, she said it again. "There. That, children, is our Vice President Richard Milhous Nixon." A plane came into view.

It was a giant machine, highly glossed, brightly painted, sporting the stars and stripes on both sides. It wheeled over Lima, flew in, touched the tarmac without so much as a tremor, and glided to a stop before us. There was a roar in the crowd, as people pressed forward to see.

I stood on my toes and leaned over the rail as the airplane door opened and a man in uniform stepped out. Then two more Americans came through the door. The first was a man in a suit, his hairline a sharp, black V. *"Ves?"* shouted a woman behind me. *"El Gringo* Nixon!" The crowd surged forward again, and I marveled at the figure in the distance. The man was a fairer version of my father.

I felt myself bouncing against the rail as I stood there wondering at the likeness, a light bounce at first, then like a jib in high wind. Something was ramming me forward. I turned in time to see my mother raise her purse and slam it down on the person behind me. He was on his knees, a man in rags, thrusting himself into my crinoline, grinning poison into the sky.

"Vayate cholo!" she shrieked. Go away!

She pounded his head with her purse until he scudded back on his knees and scrambled to his feet. He was leering, pants open. The crowd backed away. A woman giggled nervously.

"Vayate, loco!" my mother screamed again. She was red in the face, wild.

"Gri-i-i-in-ga!" the man screeched back at her, leaning out like a gargoyle, then rearing and flaring like a cobra preparing to strike.

"Let's go!" Mother pulled us by the elbows and stormed away. "Let's get the hell out of here. Jesus God! I'm sick of this place."

As we sped to the safety of Tang, I looked back through the crowd. The man was babbling to himself, pulling up his trousers, paying the oglers no mind. People were laughing and pointing at the overheated gringa with her fancy, crestfallen children.

Instinctively, I began to cry. Being a girl had become dangerous work in my corner of the hemisphere.

Being American was perilous, too. That day we learned what Peru really thought about gringos. Wherever Richard Milhous Nixon went, he was menaced. My father's people came into the streets with stones in their pockets, empty Coca-Cola bottles, putrefying garbage. They spat on him, chased his big, black cars through the streets, flailed their fists, launched their Pachamama arsenals, filled the air with rage. One stone grazed his neck. Another hit one of his secret servicemen in the face. When he laid a wreath fashioned to look like the American flag at the monument of South America's liberator San Martín, jeering student demonstrators tore it up.

No one had to explain what that meant. George and I dragged into our dirt lot chastened. There was such a thing as too much power.

AS COOLER WEATHER approached, we saw the cement trucks come and go from our lot across the street. We weren't allowed to play in it anymore. They were digging out dirt, filling the hole with concrete, but they never finished the apartment tower that was pictured on the signboard. Techo Rex wasn't building much, either. The Arana brothers were finding precious little to do as the economy shriveled, socialism spiraled, and American business began pulling out of Peru. By now much of the Arana family had been recruited to make Techo Rex viable. Tía Eloísa was typing the correspondence. Tía Chaba was keeping the books. Tío Pedro began looking for projects in the hinterlands. Tío Víctor proposed they erect tract houses, because they were easily built, instantly rented. Papi approached his former bosses at Grace and eked out a contract to help build a dam.

In Abuelita's house, conversations turned more and more to

the hacienda my grandfather had just inherited from Tía Carmen. Owned originally by my great-grandfather Pedro Pablo Arana, the Hacienda Nogales was tucked into a far valley in Huancavelica, where the Andes began their ascent to the skies. The hacienda entered the lives of the Lima Aranas almost as a revelation, so little did they know about the secretive Pedro Pablo or about the history of the hacienda that had now come into their possession. Although it was assumed that it once had been the property of Pedro Pablo's wife, my reclusive and eccentric great-grandmother, Eloísa Sobrevilla Díaz de Arana, all that was really known was that it had been her refuge as Pedro Pablo traveled about the country, marshaling his political career, and that he had paid little attention to it during his lifetime. Nor had their children been much attached to it. Both my abuelito and Tía Carmen had been sent to school in Lima at very young ages and had returned to Nogales only at rare intervals. So when my great-grandmother died in 1912, the house with all its land and *peones* began an almost century-long decline. My great-grandfather, who preferred to live in the hustle and bustle of Lima, ignored it, and no one thought much about it until 1926, when Pedro Pablo died. Instead of bequeathing the hacienda to his son, however—to my abuelito, as was the custom—Pedro Pablo had willed it to his daughter, a spinster with no other prospect of an income. What he could not have foreseen is that Tía Carmen would marry a parasite who abused the *peones*, sold off whatever was valuable, and bled the hacienda dry. Now the question was, in the late '50s, could it be made into a productive enterprise again? Could it grow crops and boost the family coffers? It made for endless debate about what would be most profitable: Sugar? Asparagus? Cotton?

Try as they might, the brothers couldn't engage their father's attention on the question. He looked pleased momentarily when Tía Carmen's lawyer called on him to say the land was legally his, but once the man was done, Abuelito simply thanked him, turned, and mounted the stairs to his room. It did not really interest him.

One Sunday, we all came to wish Abuelita a happy birthday— even Mother was there. She hadn't called on the house in years, but we had been passing by and Papi had insisted she come in. In any case, the grown-ups were well into one of those conversations about the hacienda, when suddenly there was a slow thumping on the stairboards. They paused and turned around. To our shock, it was my grandfather coming down to join us. He descended cautiously, placing two feet on each step before he proceeded to the next. He gripped the banisters on either side, inching his mottled hands along, eyes fixed on his shoes. When he reached bottom, he headed for his wing-backed chair. He didn't look up, didn't say a word, but Tío Pedro jumped up to take an elbow and navigate him. He looked tired and small. Hair sprouted from around his ears.

He sat in his chair, put an elbow on each armrest, and carefully brought the fingertips of both hands together so that they met. He separated and touched them, opening and closing, as if he had something to say. But the dialogue continued its tinny course—*claro que hay una ventaja con caña, pero es difícil que de en la sierra; pues tiene un gran mercado; el asparrago también seria bueno, no?*—with my aunts and uncles working hard to make Abuelito's advent seem ordinary. Finally, my grandfather's hands stopped moving, and he looked over them into my mother's face. The room fell silent.

"Why do you despise me?" he said in a high, squeaky English, with a voice I seldom heard. My abuelita shot a look around the room. She had no idea what he had just said. No one translated.

My mother's eyes grew wide, and her face, which until that moment had been the picture of boredom, took on the color of a ripe guava. "I don't . . ." she sputtered. "But I don't . . ."

He lowered his eyes, clutched the sides of his chair, and, with great effort, drew himself to his feet. He turned and shuffled away.

"*Pero, hijito!*" Abuelita said, in her jolly tone, although the party had grown stone-cold sober. "You come all the way down here and then you say something in English—something none of us understands—and now you're going back up again? Stay, Victor! Have a little glass of sherry. Have some cake!"

He raised one hand and fluttered it, keeping his eyes on his shoes.

"Despise him?" my mother said in the car on the way home. "Despise him? How could I possibly despise him? How could anyone on this earth think your father despicable?"

"He's an old man," said my father. "Who knows what's on his mind."

I asked what *despicable* meant, but I needn't have. I soon met the word again, in a context that made its meaning abundantly clear.

I was in the house of Albertito Giesecke. I had developed a crush on the boy, had wangled my way into playing chess in his house one winter afternoon, when his mother invited me to tea. The Giesecke name was fairly well known in Lima for Albertito's grandfather. More than twenty years before, he had flown over Machu Picchu to confirm Hiram Bingham's "discovery" of that mystical mountain city.

Albertito's father seemed Peruvian in every respect to me, although I'd been told that the flying grandfather was an American and that he was famous for brave expeditions. Albertito's father had gone to Papi's preparatory school, Villa Maria. They had been friends. He indicated where I should sit at the table and then peered at me while he smoothed a napkin over his tie.

"So," he said, "you're Jorge's daughter?"

"*Sí, señor,*" I responded, and sank my teeth into an *alfajor*, savoring its sweet caramel center.

"*Claro, pues,* you look like an Arana," he said.

He studied me as his wife asked me about the Roosevelt School, as she chattered on about the *garúa*, about how it was impossible to breathe when fog locked in over the city. I thought perhaps he was admiring my good manners. I had had excellent lessons from Abuelita on how a lady should conduct herself at table, even if I didn't employ that training all the time. I was being a perfect little *señorita*.

Finally, *Señor* Giesecke wiped his thin lips on his napkin, leaned across the table toward me, and spoke in a clipped English. "You know, I've always wondered whether your father was related to the *cauchero*."

"The *cauchero*?" I said. "Oh, you mean the Arana who lived in the jungle? The rich one with all the rubber? People are always asking me that. My aunts and uncles say no."

He laughed merrily and took a long, noisy slurp from his cup. "Of course they would say no," he said then, clacking the cup back in the saucer. "I would say no myself, even if it were one hundred percent true. He was a nasty man, Julio César Arana. A monster. *Uy-uy-uy! Pedro, José, y Santa María!* He was totally *despicable*."

THAT SAME WINTER, I began ballet classes. Mother had noticed my tendency to exaggeration—"It's the soul of an artistic temperament!" she assured my father—and responded accordingly by enrolling me in the British Academy of Dance. As far as she was concerned, there would be no skimping on any form of education. It was a mansion with high ceilings on Calle Esquilache in San Isidro. There, I took to ballet as if I'd been born to dance, stretching out at the barre, growing thin as a whippet, gliding in mirrors, pausing in doorways like a haughty diva with a neck as long as a swan's. This was a new kind of power, a fine ammunition.

My teacher was a diminutive Englishwoman. On the first day, she waddled into class like an undernourished duck, toes pointing at opposite walls. But once music rippled up and slid into her limbs, she became agile as a nymph: smooth-browed, tulle-winged, all of her grammar in her bones. I ached to be like her, worked hard to imitate the sinews of her tiny body.

I returned from class one day filled with important news. I'd been cast as a bluebell in *The Nutcracker*'s Waltz of the Flowers. I pranced in the door, whipped a heel onto the dining room table, and spun *chaînés* through the hall. Mother laughed and clapped her hands. I went to bed more pleased with myself than I'd been in a long time.

But at two o'clock in the morning, Papi swung in through the front door, lit to the gills. Mother had been sitting in the living room waiting for him, her cigarette glowing in the dark. The crescendo of their exchange was what woke me—first came the Valkyrie, then came the *basso*. A two-part invention. With cymbals.

The first dish flew into the floor of the hallway. The second punched a hole in the living room wall. Vicki and I sat up. George came in, rubbing his eyes.

"They're at it again," he said.

"I know," said Vicki. "Don't worry. Sit here with us. It'll be over soon."

We sat there listening, watching the light flicker on the walls. Cars were moving along Avenida Angamos, even at that hour of the night.

"I'm fed up, Jorge! You know what that means? *Fed up!*" and the walls reverberated with another explosion.

"Ay, por Dios!" croaked the answer, and we heard the shards under his shoes.

But it didn't stop. The upstairs neighbors clomped down to complain. Mother stormed past into the street, flagged down a taxi, and directed the driver to my grandparents' house. *"Espérate,"* she told him as he gawped at her night clothes—wait—and then she stepped out of the cab and climbed onto the ledge under my uncle's window. "Víc-tor!" she sang into the night. *"Ayúdame."* Help.

The next thing we knew, Tío Víctor was standing in our bedroom doorway, his silhouette sharp against the blaze of the hallway. He was shaking his head.

The sight of him—black against the fulgor of light—is etched into memory like a chord before the key modulates, like a sign that the tempo must change. There was no fire, no corpse, no wounds, but I knew this time things had gone too far. Until then we children had been spectators at a private drama. We had seen curtains rise, curtains fall, costumes change, and then we had watched our players strut out again, slick back their hair. My uncle's silhouette changed everything. We were pathetic. We were disgusting. The pretense was pointless now. People knew.

Our parents scrambled to make the unfortunate scene up to us. One languid Sunday afternoon, Papi drove us out the bumpy Carretera Central to Peru's mecca of roast chicken, a ranch two hours outside Lima, La Granja Azul. With us was our cousin Cito. He was six foot two and buckram straight, a clone of his father, the distinguished and extravagantly mustachioed *comandante* Tío Salvador. We took a table in a tiled courtyard beside a flowering garden, under the crest of a looming mountain.

The chicken arrived in heaping rattan baskets, fragrant and steaming with cumin and achiote, flanked by crisp yucca fries and a piquant sauce of ají. The grown-ups drank Pilsen; the children, *chicha morada.* It was a lotus-eater's banquet, an orgy of forgetting. Peruvian style.

There was much to enchant us. Family stories wove their sultry magic, curling into our brains like a drug. It seemed that Tío Salvador, who was one of the most skilled sword fighters in all

Peru, had recently challenged someone to a duel and nicked someone with his *florete*. It was in all the newspapers. They were thrilled about this, brought up the story of the monkey and the anteater, and reminisced about Papi's godfather, an old roué who'd been shot in the back on his way into his mistress's house.

George and I were captivated by those stories and lingered long after lunch to hear them, but the conversation soon turned to subjects less interesting to us: how four new trucks with the Techo Rex logo were sitting idle in Lima. Bored, we decided to leave the adults to their lamentations. We hadn't been this close to Pachamama in a long time. We decided to head up the mountain behind us.

We trudged up the gray dirt, staring down at our feet, scouring the trail for evidence of a benevolent *apu*. The mountain was barren, a sullen hump of dust and stone. A futile walk, I thought. No trophies here, no tooth or bone. But I was wrong.

"Look over there!" George sang. "A skull!" He clambered after it, grinding stones as he tore up the steep incline. I swiveled around to see if I could spot a skull of my own. In the distance, I saw a glint of white. I decided to cut my own path after it.

I shinnied up the bald scarp with nothing to hold on to, no frazzled bush, no craggy rock. The ground was dry, and as I ascended, cascades of tiny stones crunched under my shoes and spilled behind. Dust puffed, circled my head, invaded my nostrils. I could taste grit on my tongue.

We didn't need to go far to find what we were looking for: a finger bone here, a link of spine there. I grabbed a protrusion as I passed, pulled out a jaw, wrenched out its teeth, and stuffed them into the pockets of my new yellow dress. "George! Three teeth!" I boomed. *Dientes!* Then I saw how high I'd come.

George was so far away he seemed to be on another mountain. He was small as a bluebottle, spindly black. He did not hear me call out.

He was almost at the top of his ridge. If I could just scrabble a little higher, I would reach mine first, peer over Olympus to the other side. I grew dizzy with the height, the dust, the sun at the back of my head, but I finally came to within feet of the crest. I turned to check George, could not find him, then scaled ahead, anxious to see.

I mounted the peak and looked over. No more than twenty feet away, rising out of the earth, was a white plaster Virgin, her hands spread out in welcome, a grave at her feet. There was a hole in her chest, and inside that, a heart pulsing blue. I staggered. Black stones shifted under me. One foot slid out. I pulled it back.

I turned to where La Granja Azul lay, as neat and as tidy as the scene in my father's garage. I could see the garden, I could see tables, but I couldn't see my parents. I leaned out to find them. Then the world started to spin.

I was falling. Tossed from that summit like a boned cat, I slid, bounced, plummeted, flipped onto my head, and skipped down the slope, skull against skulls, spraying bone into air. Halfway down, I landed on a ledge, flapping my arms helplessly, desperately scanning the garden below. My parents stood by their table, looking up at me, rigid as statues. But my footing was not firm, and, as I reeled again, I saw my mother's face for a fleeting instant. She turned her back and her gold head whirled from view.

There is little I recall after that. I know that Cito bounded up to lift my body out. I know Georgie screamed that it wasn't his fault. I know my father sped into Lima, swinging around to look at me again and again with tears sliding out of his eyes. I know my mother was bending over me when the anodyne lifted. "Look what you've done, Marisi," she said. "You've gone and ruined your dress."

I blinked and came to. I was in what looked to be a hospital room, wrapped like a mummy, skin tingling. I reached up to touch my head. It was clean as a cue ball, a swatch of gauze on top. My mother held up a scrap of yellow dress. It was shredded, brown with blood. "Look what you did," she said.

"The *apu*," I said, my tongue thick with narcotic. "And the Virgin Mary."

She tilted her head and focused her eyes on mine. "What do you mean?"

"George and I were hunting for teeth and bones. That's why the *apu* got angry. He made me fall." My legs ached; my head was throbbing.

Mother smiled and dropped the dress on the gurney. "So. Good. The doctor said you might have had a concussion, but I can see you're all there. If you're talking about George and bones and *apus,* you're the child I remember. Your noggin's working fine."

She paused, put one hand on my shoulder, and looked into my face earnestly. Even now, almost four decades later, I remember her words. She would repeat them again and again later: "Look, Marisi. That was no ghost. No evil spirit of the mountain. It was God: God did it. And, while we're on the subject, there's nothing wrong with your hunting for bones. Don't misunderstand me, I don't like it one bit. But there's a difference between my not liking what you do and what you do being wrong. It's what we creatures do, go digging in the dirt. What we've always done. We do it because we're part of it. You, me, your father, the doctor who put bandages on you, the birds in the trees, this hank of yellow dress. We've all come from a mountain, one way or another, and it's back to a mountain we'll go."

She paused a bit to let it sink in. "The mountain didn't do this to you, honey. The *indios* might tell you that, but it's not true. They say the *duendes* this, the *pishtacos* that. Listen to me: You fell because it was the will of God. Sometimes God knocks us back a bit to remind us we're not as big and mighty as we think."

I studied her face. "*Señor* Gonzalez said the *apus* would be mad if we dug up the dead. And Grandpa Doc said there were injuns on Elk Mountain who believed the same thing."

"Well, sometimes people say that for very good reasons. 'Don't touch the bones,' they say, 'or spirits will punish you.' The truth is that if I died, and you saw someone picking the teeth out of my head, you probably wouldn't like it very much. So we say, No, don't do that. And to make people really pay attention, we make threats. Shout it."

"Is that what you and Papi do?"

"Why?"

"Because you shout at each other all the time."

She looked at me hard. Then she bent down and kissed my forehead.

"I shout because something is bugging me. I'm not sure what. Your father drinks because he thinks it's *macho*. He's actually a very good man. We have trouble understanding each other sometimes, Mareezie. We're different people, with different heads."

"But you just said you're from the same mountain, and to the same mountain you'll go."

"Yes." And then she tipped back her head and laughed, her eyes like periwinkle petals. "That is true, my precious angel. We are. And we will."

Much after my fall, thirty years to the month to be exact, a gringo archaeologist dug an Inca princess out of the Nevado Ampato, a snowy peak twenty thousand feet high and one hundred thirty miles south of Cusco. The mummy was five hundred years old, but the girl had been no more than twelve when her family had carried her up and offered her to the mountain *apu*. She had long black hair, according to the man who found her, a ballerina's neck, a sun-dried brain. They found the frozen remains of a chicken lunch and *chicha* in her stomach. She was wearing a yellow *aksu*.

Juanita the Ice Maiden, they called her. Her flesh was freeze-dried to her bones. The gringo archaeologist brought her down, thawed her out, and one day she showed up under glass in Washington, D.C. Surely this would provoke the gods.

But nothing happened. The sun rose, the sun fell, moons came and went, and no retribution occurred. If ghosts were at work, they were taking their time. If God was at work, His mill hadn't finished the job. The girl was feeding museum revenues, not buds on the slope. God and the *duendes* were playing a game. Something had changed the course.

Lying in that hospital bed, looking at the ceiling, I understood my fall exactly in that way. Something had interfered; something had changed the course: The *apu* had caught sight of my mother probably at the very instant she had given me up for dead. I had flapped my arms like a rag doll; she had turned her back. But it was that very motion, her whirling around, that had stopped the *apu* cold.

He saw her hair spin out like a pinwheel. Presented with that evidence, he realized I was not some ordinary child whose sacrifice would have no consequence. I was special; I had power. He could see that from the light that radiated from my mother like a cloudless morning. Inca gods had always found the color of the sun irresistible, as yellow-haired Pizarro came to know so well. If, between God and the *apu*, I had been rolling toward some serious blood payment, Mother's gold had just bought me time.

⁓

LIES. I WAS getting very good at them. Making up stories to explain what I couldn't possibly know. Inventing excuses for my troubles in life. There is, after all, something indescribably rewarding in telling a good lie. You create your own truth. It is the essence of power. You do what you can.

I went back to school after a week's convalescence, attending

Nutcracker rehearsals with black stitches sprouting from my pate. "Maybe you can do something other than dance," said the English ballet mistress, eyeing my head with dismay. "Maybe you can play the piano?"

"I want to dance," I said adamantly. "I want to be onstage. I want to wear my costume."

"Then you shall," she said, and patted me on the head. "Fine."

"You can play the piano?" said a ball of a girl, her face filled with admiration. *Tocas?*

"Yes," I said grandly. "Call me and I'll play for you over the phone."

When she called that night, I was ready. "*Hola*, Cristina. I'm walking over to the piano now. I'm sitting down on the bench. I'm adjusting the sheet music. Chopin. *Valse, opus 64.* I'm flexing my fingers. Ready?"

"Ready," she squealed.

A record spun on our turntable. I lowered the arm. Arthur Rubenstein began to play.

"Hear me?" I said.

A brief silence in the receiver, and then her amazement gushed through the wire. "You can talk and play at the same time?"

"Sure. The *teléfono* is tucked in my shoulder. I do this all the time for my cousins in America."

"*Caramba*, Marisi. I had no idea you were so good."

I turned the dial up slightly, made the music *più mosso*. And then I lifted the arm off the album. "There, I can't play for long," I said. "My injuries, you know."

Lies. I was so good at them. More to the point, I loved them so. Why not? If I could slip from English to Spanish, from boys to ballet, from pledging American allegiance to swearing on life I was a Peruvian, from church to church, from Campbell to Clapp—why not from role to role, truth to truth? Lies. Thank you, God. You gave me a skill.

"My mother is pregnant," I told *Señora* Arellano's class. *Espera bebe*. Margarita had just announced that her mother was expecting, and the teacher was making happy cooing noises in her direction.

"Really?" *Señora* Arellano's sweet face turned to me and she leaned a large bosom into her desk. "*Qué maravilla*. We're expecting not just one baby in this class. But *two*."

The next Saturday morning, Margarita banged her skinny little fist against our door and my father answered.

"*Buenos días, señor*," she said, her eyes big as Ping-Pong balls. "Is the *señora* having a baby?"

"*Buenos días*, Margarita. Who told you that?"

"Marisi. She told us in school the other day. She said so in class."

"Well, then, Marisi did not tell you the truth."

"She lied?"

"If that's what she said, she lied."

After a stern lecture, Papi took me outside, called our friends over, and denounced me right there in our lot. "Listen, all of you. Marisi's mother is *not* having a baby, and I'll thank you to say so in school. When Marisi tells you something in the future, I want you to be skeptical. Tell her she can't be trusted. Tell her you're aware of her reputation. She needs to learn that lying doesn't pay."

I became the leper of Avenida Angamos. At first I was furious with Papi, but with the passing of every day I cared less. "See my sister?" Vicki announced to her friends in the school playground. "She lies. Don't you, Marisi? Isn't it so?"

"Yip," I said, and giggled inside, imagining I'd just told a lie. But no one else was laughing.

"*That* over there is not our *only* house," I whispered to the ambassador's son, standing under his fuchsia gateway and pointing down the street. "We have houses all over the world. One in

Cartavio, one in the United States of America, one in a little village in Switzerland. With swans. We just don't like to show off."

"Liar!" he screamed, and slammed the door.

"Marisita," my abuelita said, "what part are you dancing in *The Nutcracker*? I'm coming to see it, you know."

"The star," I said recklessly. "Clara." She'd bustle into the Teatro Municipal with red roses and a fancy box of chocolates and learn the truth soon enough.

I didn't see Abuelita as often as I wanted to. She and Mother were hardly on speaking terms, and Mother no longer attended family gatherings. After my grandfather had descended the staircase to pose his question about whether or not he was despicable, Abuelita had decided the gringa's presence was too hard on his nerves. But one day, after we'd been in the Lima house for almost two years, Abuelita showed up for George's birthday.

She appeared in a belted navy blue dress, a single strand of pearls around her neck. Her shoes were pointed and high, her nails a deep claret. She walked in on a cloud of jasmine, handed Georgie her present, dropped into the chair closest to Mother, slipped her dark glasses into her purse, and squeezed the clasp shut with an annunciatory *snap*.

"You know," she said in a low voice to Mother, "a woman I know got into a brawl with her husband. He'd been out having drinks with his friends. (Men are like that, Marie. Especially if they have *sangre ligera*. Especially if they're people of a certain class, accustomed to light hearts and a certain gregariousness. Even Alexander the Great got a little *borracho* between the wars.) Well, the woman was unreasonably angry, frustrated with her marriage, fed up *hasta aquí*. So she threw a plate across the room. You know what happened? It hit him in the head. The next thing she knew, her husband was dead." Abuelita opened her purse and rummaged around in it. "All because of a few nips," she added. *Unas copitas*.

My mother watched the older woman draw out a handkerchief, unfold it, shake it into the air like a frail wing, refold it, and set it on her lap.

"That will not happen to your son," Mother assured her. "I might throw a dish at a wall if he makes me angry, I might leave him, I might take the children and run away, I might do a million things. But I am not a stupid woman, Rosa. I will not kill him."

My grandmother looked into her eyes for a very long time, sighed deeply, and shook her head up and down, indicating that she believed her.

Less than a week later—after I forced Margarita to snitch a can of ham from Sandra's bomb shelter, after a skinny brown Santa Claus ran by sweating in the December heat, after Drosselmeyer tucked a nutcracker under his arm and went to a party, after the Mouse King was chased across stage at the Teatro Municipal, after I waltzed through the starring girl's dreams in my blue petal costume—Mother proved that what she had told Abuelita was true.

Her arsenal was not pointing at my father. It was pointed away.

It happened like this: Papi stumbled in after an all-night bender with the *hombres*. Mother took her battle station by the Christmas tree, a flashing, revolving colossus of electrical wizardry he had fashioned from graduated Hula Hoops. At the very moment when porcelain might otherwise fly, she drew back and kicked the thing over. When the twenty-five hoops scattered their red and green across the floor—when the crash-bang clitterclatter had won his undivided attention—she set down her terms. "That's it, Jorge. I've been in your country fourteen long years. No more. I'm going home."

INDEPENDENCE

Sueños Norteños

I<small>T WASN'T UNTIL</small> I'd been in the United States awhile that I understood how stifling Peru had been for my mother: a closed world, our *mundo mesquino*, which, as a Peruvian, I thrived in and loved. There were family rules I'd always understood instinctively: Mind tradition, go into business with siblings, give preferential treatment to relatives, stay in the neighborhood, call on your grandparents every Sunday for tea. Eccentrics were forgiven—sword fighters, recluses, extroverts, wayward sons with illegitimate children. But neglect was inexcusable. A wife was supposed to look up to her mother-in-law, seek advice about children, plead for assistance if her man became unruly. Not mark her own turf, as my mother had done.

Crossing to Mother's side of America, on the other hand, we encountered no family at all. The Clapps, Brooks, Reeds, and Adamses were nowhere to be seen when we flew into Miami that spring of 1959. They were not alerted, and they were not there. They stayed in far corners of the country, unmindful of our existence. If I had arrived on these shores expecting warm ties to my northern relations, I'd soon discover how different family life could be. I would never set foot on Grandpa Doc's land again. I would never set eyes on Mother's sisters again. I would never meet the full complement of her siblings, never really know who the gringo half of my family were. We emigrated to America in quintessentially American fashion: declaring our independence, reshuffling the deck.

Papi had yielded to Mother entirely. "The *señora* is making him do it," I heard Nora say to the maid upstairs as the movers took our things from Avenida Angamos. Men were trooping to the curb with our furniture on their heads. The blond dining room table, the carved consoles, the portraits by Sir Joshua Reynolds copied by indigenous hands: All our worldly goods promenaded by for the United States ambassador, the next-door soldier, and the upstairs electrocutioner to see. Mother's piano, an antique too delicate for sea voyage, was hauled to my grandparents' house and wedged into the *sala*. All that was left of our material Peru was packed and wrapped and fitted into a wooden container, then nailed shut and ferried away.

Tío Víctor and Tío Pedro came around to watch the enormous crate lurch away in a flat truck. They stood on the *avenida*, wrinkling their foreheads, rubbing their temples, chewing on cigarettes, wondering how Techo Rex would survive. "Don't worry," my father told them. "I'll do what I can from there." But *there* meant New York City. He had gone back to his bosses at W. R. Grace, taken a job in Manhattan. He'd be planning large-scale engineering projects for a number of Latin American countries, but he'd be sitting a hemisphere away.

"Watch out for those giants up north, Marisi," Tío Víctor told me, sweeping me up and letting me kiss his lavender-scented chin. "They'll step on you, you're so small." *Cuidado. Te pueden pisar.*

Mother bustled about energetically, issuing promises at every turn. We could eat off the floors once we got there, her side of America was so clean. Water would course from the spigots. Milk would not be contaminated. Everything would come tucked in boxes with colorful pictures on top. We could eat berries from bushes. We could swim streams with our mouths open. A germ-free country! With perfect roads and tidy houses, just like the village in Papi's garage.

I took my last look down Avenida Angamos and saw the uppity ambassador's son peering out his gate at us. "Will we have swans?" I asked.

"We will," she confirmed gaily. "Or geese or ducks or pelicans or anything else your little heart desires."

THERE WERE NO swans at the Dutch Maid Motel on Route 22 in Springfield, New Jersey. The discount emporia rose up beside it like floats in a carnival day parade. MOTHER GOOSE SHOES, said one billboard, and behind it—as though to deliver on an uncle's warning—a giant's shoe, big as a building, with smiling gringos streaming through its doors. BIG BOY LUMBER, said another sign, and looming above it, a musclebound Gog in a red plaid shirt with his head shaved clean as a tub.

The Dutch Maid Motel was shell pink with white lace in its windows, a picket fence leading the way. Two yellow-haired dolls in frilled aprons framed the front lawn marquee, cocking their wooden toes and bending over so that their underpants showed. In the back garden, freshly planted shrubs stood at attention, and white lawn chairs waited for swimmers to clamber out of the pool. It was the antithesis of anything we had ever known in Wyoming. We'd never seen a highway so busy, with so many people and such enormous stores. We had never seen such shiny

long cars, such a webwork of roads. We looked around for the familiar: open prairie, cattle, horses, and boots. But none of these
was in evidence. This America was different.

We had come to New Jersey for the public schools. Not because it would be the most convenient commute for my father. It
was not. It took nearly an hour for the hulking Erie-Lackawanna
to cart a clamoring army of worsted wool to the Hudson River
every weekday morning. Nor were we there, as far as we could
tell, because of my mother. She didn't have a relative within a
five-state radius.

"Because of the public schools?" said Papi, scratching his head
with wonder. To him, the notion of building a life around children was alien, bizarre, inexplicable. In Peru, it had been the
other way around: children built lives around their parents. The
elders defined the world.

While Papi traveled to Hoboken on the lurching, squealing
Erie-Lackawanna, then ferried across the Hudson to Fulton
Street, snapping a newspaper as smartly as any itinerant company man, Mother sallied forth with school ratings and a real-
estate map in hand.

George and I headed for the Dutch Maid's lobby, where we'd
discovered how well we were going to fare in these United
States. "See that?" I said to George, pointing a finger at Lucy and
Desi in the lobby's box. "She's the wife, and her husband speaks
Spanish. Their family's just like us!" "See that?" said my brother,
as Hoss Cartwright swung a leg over a horse. "He's a guy with a
ranch, just like Grandpa. This place is gonna be great!" Only
Vicki reserved opinion, peering at us from a far corner, seeing
that those lambent shadows bore no resemblance to the trawl of
highway outside.

"Ey! *Mangia, mangia!*" crowed an Italian waitress with high
hair in the Howard Johnson across the road from the lumber

giant. Her lips were beige patent, her eyes winged like Nefertiti's, her black hairdo leaning like a tower about to crash. "You people *paesan'*? You just get hee or what?"

"No, no," said Papi, flashing a smile and flirting. "That's Spanish you're hearing."

"Zat right?" She stared at us for a while, cracking her gum, thinking it over. "Don't hee mucha that around hee. I don't speak Italian myself, but for a minute, you sounded like *paesan'*." She walked away, keeling against the cant of her hair, wiping her hands on her hips.

I was living on strawberry milk shakes. Was there a nectar so silky, so sweet on the tongue, so satisfying to the eye in its prettily tapered glass? Afternoons would come and Mother would bring hot dogs and french fries wrapped in wax paper, with mustard and relish on the side. George tore in happily. He was pudgy now, constantly eating. The yellow pills he'd been taking ever since Boston had made him jolly and fat. He polished off his frankfurters, praising their tidy ingenuity, but I could hardly take more than a bite. It would take time before I could eat from cardboard, sitting on the edge of a bed, with paper spread out on my knees. I longed for fragrant *sopa de albahaca* from my abuelita's table, with her well-ironed napkins and oversize spoons. As it was, I consumed very little in that wholesale paradise. I sat in the pink motel, awaited my fluted shakes, checked on Desi's progress in his wife's country, listened to the thrum of the road, and read neon messages that squiggled from the giant's chest like fortunes down a *bruja*'s braid. *Shop here, America. We build you.*

⁓

NOT PARAMONGA, NOT Cartavio, not Rawlins could have prepared me for Summit, New Jersey. Mother chose it for the excellence of its schools, but she might as well have chosen it for its polarity to everything we'd known. Moving from Lima to Summit was like wandering into Belgrade from Bombay, the differences were so marked.

It was a small-town suburb of New York City, bedroom community for company presidents and businessmen. Split between Anglos and Italians, the residents were largely prosperous, but there was a hierarchy to that prosperity I was slow to see. The rich were the commuters, WASPs who had graduated from the Ivy League, played golf at the Beacon Hill Country Club, shopped at Brooks Brothers, and sent their children to prep schools nearby: Pingry, Lawrenceville, Kent Place. The less rich were the Italians—merchants, landscapers, restaurateurs, mechanics—who serviced the town. There was another notable category: scientists who worked in nearby Bell Labs or Ciba-Geigy, and their brainy, musical children. But there were no indigents: no beggars in the streets, no *señoras* hawking fruit.

Ours was the only Hispanic family. There were few Jews. The relative sizes of the town's churches told the story. Summit Presbyterian was the largest, most prestigious. That imposing stone structure sat squarely in the middle of town, and the rich could be seen strutting in and out of it in their finery. The Catholic Church of St. Theresa, with steps sweeping up to its portals as if they led to salvation itself, was situated several blocks away, next to its own school. The Episcopal, Methodist, and Baptist churches were scattered about town, signaling lesser lights.

By June we were in Troy Court, a cluster of brick apartment buildings on New England Avenue. It was a modest district, on the other side of town from the mansions, and it would have been clear to anyone but us children that it was home to people on the fringes of society. There were strings of apartments up and down the avenue, where transients came and went, and old ramshackle houses, where nurses and waitresses lived.

Mother had her eye on a house in the middle range of the Summit spectrum, but it would be months before the owners vacated it. She had decided we would be wise to wait. When we moved into the apartment, it was empty save for an upright piano, the one thing we had bought on Route 22. We took our meals on it, plinking while we chewed, sleeping on the floor, waiting for our crate to arrive.

Within a week, we had recreated Lima on New England Avenue—*huacos* on the shelves, llama skins draped through the rooms. The display looked odd, even to us. The Lima we had come from had been a jumble, a place where Spanish and indigenous objects mixed freely—where modern and ancient accompanied each other, where a rich man's house might be flanked by a tenement—but here, in this quiet, suburban setting, our possessions looked out of place. When the truck finally pulled away, two neighbors came over to see.

They were ten and eight, as sunny and frisky as Dutch maids on a roadside billboard. "You new?" said the older one. "*We're* new. We just moved in a few days ago."

They were from Westfield, a few towns over. George and I told them we were from Peru, but they puckered their mouths, rolled their eyes, and allowed as how they didn't know where that was.

"Your parents are Westfieldian people?" I asked, trying to make conversation, figuring Westfield to be a country, like Peru.

"Were," the tall one said. "Our mother got married last week."

I was taking that information in, but she sailed ahead breezily. "My name is Suzi Hess. This is my sister, Sara. My mother used to be called Hess, too. Like us. But she's Mrs. Loeb now."

There it was. The gringo roulette.

"Oh, I know all about that," I said, flaunting my urbanity. "My mother has a different name, too."

"Different from you?"

"No." I rushed to explain. "But different from her parents."

"Well, of course, silly. Every married woman has a different name from her parents."

My head felt fat as a blowfish. I needed to say that in Peru women strung their married and maiden names together, and that when my mother did that, her maiden name had turned out to be married, too, but it was going to take so much explanation. It was more complicated than I was willing to say: I was ashamed of my mother; ashamed that she was ashamed. In Peru, divorce was unthinkable. These girls, on the other hand, spoke of it so freely. I wanted them to be my friends. I burbled, dithered, stared down my nose, pulled on my ear. It didn't take long for Suzi to take pity. "Okay, let's see now. Your mother is divorced like ours, right?" she said, trying to help me along.

"Unh, yeah," I said, and my head filled with the miracle that we might have this great flaw in common.

"So she has children by another marriage?" she said.

"Unh, yeah. I dunno."

"You don't know? You don't know whether or not you have sisters or brothers somewhere else?"

"I dunno," I repeated.

"You mean they could be walking around and you wouldn't have any idea they're there?"

I hadn't thought of that. Now I genuinely tried to squeeze that possibility into my brain. "No idea," I responded.

"Jee-zee-kew-zee. They do things crazy in Pay-roo," Suzi said. She laughed merrily, a tinkly, high titter as sweet as a canary's. Freckly Sara flashed her big, buck teeth and put out a hand. "Friends?"

"Yip. Sure."

While George and I were running up and down the driveway behind those apartments, working to seal a friendship with these girls, Mother was humming through our rooms, settling into the life she had dreamed of for so long. She'd whisk outside from time to time, smoothing her hair, trotting to a cab, pointing to our big sister's face in the window. "You mind Vicki, you hear?" When we asked where she was going, she'd reply, "To Summit Food Market!" Or "Off to your school!" Or "Off to see about the house!" Off!

She seemed enraptured with her new life, was a bundle of energy. I watched her cook meals, wash dishes, scrub floors—do tasks I had never seen her do before—but she dug in with relish, singing as she went, looking up joyfully when I walked in, pushing the hair from her eyes.

If it had never been clear before, it was crystal clear now: My mother had been a sad woman in Peru. There was nothing sad about her now. It didn't seem to matter that she wasn't with the Clapps. She did not visit them, nor did she call or write them, as far as I knew. She didn't seem to need them at all. It began to dawn on me that it wasn't *them* she had missed in Peru; she'd missed these American streets and her freedom to roam around in them.

Papi was another story: He dragged out to the train station earlier and earlier in the morning, shuffled home beat at the end of the day. He grew more and more disengaged. He missed his Peruvian family and his *compadres*. You could see it in the way he slumped through the door, headed for his chair, heaved himself down with a sigh. "Write to your abuelita," he'd tell me day after day, pointing to the stack of letters from her. "She wants to know how you are."

In town, he had trouble understanding the fast-talking, slang-slinging suburbanites; he'd cast a weary look my way to signal me to translate. At first, I was as puzzled by accents as he was. But his reliance on me made an impression. In Peru I had always thought he and I were similar, that Mother was the different one. But here in Summit, I felt more kinship with my mother, my father the odd one out. "You kids are turning into gringos," he'd say, staring at us in amazement. But I knew our mother was the only gringo among us; she was it a full hundred percent. My father was the only Peruvian; he, too, was one hundred percent. They were wholes. They were complete. They were who they were. They would never *become* anything like the other. We children, on the other hand, were becoming others all the time, shuttling back and forth. We were the fifty-fifties. We were the cobbled ones.

SUMMIT WAS NOTHING like Mother, really, nor was it anything like the American school in Lima, nor like Rawlins, Wyoming, whose lingo we heard in our dreams. At first, we swaggered around, George and I, like cowboys, a-yawin' and a-struttin', thinking we knew what America was. But when Easterners looked at us, they drew their chins into their necks, pocketed their hands, and sidled away. We trotted down Springfield Avenue, hiking our jeans, jiggling our heels, only to find that the places that drew these gringos were Roots haberdashery and Summit Athletic. Not bars with decapitated fauna. Not general stores with buckshot and beans. There were men in hats, plenty of them, but they were scurrying out of the Summit train station with their faces pulled down and their collars pulled up, repairing to Brookdale Liquors, then tearing home with their wives behind the wheel. On weekends, a different breed swept down Main Street: in pastel cardigans, with bags of charcoal briquets, golf clubs, and Roots merchandise dangling from their hands, pennies winking out of their shoes.

It was the way they spoke that was most puzzling. Why didn't it sound like English we'd heard before? It certainly didn't sound like Nub, or Grandpa Doc, or Old Joe Krozier. "Ah'll

take a pack uh this here Juicy Fruit, mister," I drawled to
Summit's version of a corner-store Wong, a scrubbed little man
in a white jacket and spectacles behind the counter at Liss
Pharmacy.

"Beg your pardon, miss?"

I cleared my throat and tried again, raising my voice this
time. "This here Jee-you-see Fah-root, mister. How much yew
want?"

"Oh, ho! No need to shout, my dear. That'll cost you...a
nickel."

"Nekel? *Qué quiere decir* nekel?" I whispered to George.

"That big *moneda* there," he hissed, pointing into my palm.
"The five-cent one."

"Oh." I surrendered it to the man. He pursed his lips.

"Y'ever chaw weed?" I asked Suzi, sitting on the stair step of
our apartment, looking out at the pristine grass where children
were not to go.

"Chaw weed?"

"Yip. My cousin Nub, he's a cowboy, and he larned me how."

"Taught me how."

"O-keh, o-keh. Taught me how. Have you ever done it?"

"No, I haven't. Gee, Marie, you gotta stop talking weird.
You say things all wrong. And I don't know why. I hear your
mother talking just like everybody else. If you don't talk right
you'll never fit in school. Kids are gonna make fun of you, for
sure."

Suzi and Sara became our tutors, whiling away summer
days until fireflies bumped our faces, teaching us what to say.
You said *okay*, not *o-keh*. You went to a *movie*, not a *cinema*.
You caught *colds*, not *constipations*. You wrote on a clean,
spanking new *sheet* of paper. Not a fresh *shit*. It was clear we
had entered a new phase, far from our dirt-lot hankerings on

Avenida Angamos. We weren't hoping to be thought of as better. We just hoped we wouldn't be made "fun of." We hoped not to be noticed at all.

~

BRAYTON WAS A school fit for giants. Its bricks rose high as the Rawlins Penitentiary's that first Monday in September when Mother shooed us up the concrete stairs into the principal's office. He was bending over the windowsill, clanking metal with a ruler, talking to himself.

"Mr. Nelson?" my mother ventured.

The man whirled around with his ruler in the air. He was large, bald, like the lumbergog at Big Boy, with a face as bright as a toy's. "Come in! Come in! Day one, and this thingamajig's giving me trouble. Whew! Hot in here, don't you think?"

"What *is* it?" I whispered to George.

"Heater," he whispered back. "For when it gets cold." I studied the iron serpent. I'd never seen anything quite like it before.

This world is filled with all manner of signs, Antonio once taught me. If we only have the wisdom to see them. The ruler on the radiator was one. I was going to be colder than I'd ever thought possible, an arctic wind piercing my bones. I'd freeze by the time I had a best friend, before my teacher thought to look at me, before I'd counted forty days at my desk. Fall rolled in like a torrent, tempering leaves with frost. Freezing them hard so that branches disowned them and they clicked to earth one by one. George and I scampered down Tulip Street like two caracaras in an ice storm, shivering and chattering all the way to Mr. Nelson's overworked coils.

There were no other Latinos at school. Nor were there any as far as we could see in the whole of that leafless town in the fall of '59. Vicki was the junior-high Hispanic. The only face like mine in the elementary school's corridors was my brother's round, sunny one.

My first best friend was Kit, a pale, black-Irish beauty, wan as the tragic heroine that hung on my grandmother's wall. She was big-brained and cameo-delicate. Musical. Wicked. And she shared my passion for a scare.

"Have you read Poe?" she asked me, leaning her chair toward mine in Mr. Schwartz's fifth-grade English class.

"Only once upon a midnight dreary," I replied, sealing a fiendish bond.

We staged catatonic fits, saw apparitions in the windows, channeled spirits in the playground, held witches' séances, plotted to steal Johnny Britt's soul. Before long, Suzi and Sara Hess were eyeing me nervously, crossing the street to walk on the other side.

One winter day, as I strolled home alone, I heard the sound of feet smacking the pavement behind me. I turned and saw gangly Kelly O'Neill coming at me, face red, hair whipping her splotchy cheeks. I stopped and waited.

"You know what you are?" she said, puffing and panting her way toward me.

"What?"

"You're a pain. You've brought nothing but trouble."

"Trouble?"

"Yes, trouble. All that voodoo. You've poisoned Kit, and now you're trying to poison everybody else. Devil worshiper! You're disgusting!"

"I'm not...I'm a...You mean on the playground? Our games? It's just fun, Kelly. We do it for fun."

"You're gonna burn in purgatory, you are, you...Spic! You call yourselves Christians? My dad says you're a buncha dirty creeps. You come here with your—"

"Hey!" I said in a thin little voice. "I'm an American! My grandpa has a—"

"You are *not* an American. Don't *lie!*" she screeched at me. "No American talks the way you do. You say words all wrong. Don't you see us laughing at you? You make me vomit! Didn't you hear what we were saying about you this morning?" She stopped and put her finger to her lip, trying to remember what it was. "Meat man," she said finally, enunciating each syllable sharply and wagging her hand like a metronome. "How do you say the word for the man who sells the meat?"

I frowned at her, but decided to take the test. "You mean botcher?"

"Baw-tcher! Ha!" she exploded. "Do you hear how you say that? Baw-tcher! It's butcher, you idiot. Buh-buh-buh-tcher!"

"Baw-baw-baw-tcher," I said, nodding my head in agreement. It sounded the same to me.

"Wait . . ." she said, putting her finger to her lip again, and then she barked out another command: "How do you say the thing you read from? The thing like the ones you're carrying there—the stuff you check out of a library?"

"Bucks!" I yelled triumphantly.

"Bucks!" she yelled back. "Listen to you! It's *books*! Buh-buh-buh-book!"

"Kelly," I said in a tiny, trembly voice, my chin shaking uncontrollably. "You listen to me . . . you listen to . . ."

But Kelly was not listening. She was snarling, her spittle flicking the cold air between us. "That dopey way you talk! And all your *stoo*-pid witch stuff. You know what you do? You make this neighborhood *stink*. Stink!" She pulled her books into her chest and stomped past me, her red kilt swinging about her big red knees. Then she whirled around and . . . *Squeet!* A gob of foamy saliva hit my coat and hung there, heavy as a question.

I wanted to throw my books down, march up, grab her by

her greasy yellow hair and pull out her brain. But I stood my ground and felt my face quiver. My eyes began to fill. Against all instincts, I lowered my head and felt heat rise to my ears.

"So," she said. "You're a crybaby." Then she turned on her heel and took herself down the road.

I watched her lumber away, my throat tight with the effort to keep from bawling. Then I drew myself up and stormed home, plotting revenge. How had she dared talk to me like that? I was just as American as anyone; my mother had told me so. Spit at me? I fumed. But then the thought of her spittle made me stop in my tracks. Spit. I knew something about that. I recognized a sign when I saw one. The next day—my fortieth at an American government desk, and Halloween Day besides—I swiped a Peruvian blow dart from our wall, smeared green paint on my cheeks, put feathers in my hair, and ran to school in an improvised costume. The instant O'Neill sat down in the front of the class, I shot a wet spitball into the back of her skull. *Thwap*, you die. The giant shrieked. My little green face sniggered. Mr. Schwartz's head jerked up and saw me.

To Mr. Schwartz I had probably seemed a placid child until then. A good girl, an unremarkable pupil, a gray little thing, neither here nor there. But in that one act performed in that Amazon getup, I showed him the two-face I really was—the pretender par excellence.

Many years later, when I was studying at the British University of Hong Kong—linguistics to be precise, after I'd studied Chinese, after I'd studied Russian and French, trying on languages like so many dresses—I came across a theory claiming that bilingualism can hurt you. This was not one of those theories about the educational process or the capacities of the brain. It was a slender little monograph, not particularly well written, which claimed that in operating as two distinct personalities with two distinct tongues, a bicultural person will be highly suspect to those who have only one culture. The bicultural person seems so thoroughly one way in one language, so thoroughly different in another. Only an impostor would hide that other half so well. A liar.

An African-American friend of mine, Carol, once told me that this happens to blacks in a white culture, too: You talk like a white in the workplace, like a black in your neighborhood. You use two dialects, two personalities, two senses of humor, two ways of shaking a hand, two ways of saying hello—one for the world you're trying to make a way in, another when you're home with your kin. Now, Carol was a very sedate woman—elegant in bearing, cautious with words. I came upon her unexpectedly one day as I elbowed my way through a party: There she was, in a group of black women, swiveling her hips, flinging her hands, carrying on in another lingo, so that I hardly recognized her. She laughed about it later, but I could see it was nervous laughter. She confided that she'd always thought that whites who saw her in her other context wouldn't understand it. She worried they wouldn't trust her when she resumed standard English, they might conclude she was insincere. I mentioned the linguist's monograph. She and I agreed that, however different our backgrounds were, the fear of being called a faker, an impostor, had meaning for both of us.

But the monograph doesn't begin to tell the story. The truth about biculturalism is more complicated. That others doubt you is not the point. The doubt creeps into you, too. What Carol was saying was that not only did she fear people would think her a two-face, she was confessing that *she* was afraid she was. I understood it, because I, too, had doubted my own trustworthiness. I had been fooling people for years. Slip into my American skin,

and the playground would never know I was really Peruvian. Slip
into the Latina, and Peruvians wouldn't suspect I was a Yank.
But even by the age of ten, I had gone one giant step past Carol:
I was flitting from one identity to another so deftly that it was
just as easy to affect a third. I could lie, I could fake, I could act.
It was a way for a newcomer to cope in America. You can't quite
sound like your schoolmates? Never mind! Make it up, fashion a
whole new person. *Act the part*, says the quote under my school
photo, *and you can become whatever you wish to become*.
Invention. It was a new kind of independence.

MOTHER WAS IN such a festive mood, settling into our new
home on Tulip Street, that she didn't seem to mind that I had
been made to stay after school and write *Halloween costumes are
not supposed to harm my friends* one hundred times on the blackboard. She was so cheerful about the three floors of rooms, the
two-piano salon, our part-time cook, even the piles of frozen apples in our backyard, that she dismissed O'Neill's venom as little
more than a schoolyard spat. She read my teacher's note about
the importance of a safe Halloween, slipped it into a drawer,
turned to my painted face, and asked where the blow dart was.
"Here," I said, drawing the bamboo quiver from inside my pon-
cho. She hung it back on the wall.

"What you did was wrong, very very wrong, but I think you've
had all the flogging a green-cheeked jungle girl can stand," she
said. "Come, I want to give you some pie." I whooped, threw my
arms around her waist, and dragged her into a tango until she giggled so breathlessly I had to steady her with the kitchen counter.

I spent a winter trying to do things the O'Neill way, although I
never would have admitted it. I studiously avoided words like
book or *butcher*, gorged on Wonder Bread, wailed with Chubby
Checker, wheedled a pair of loafers, scored a perfect attendance

at Calvary Episcopal's Sunday school, made sure I could Peppermint Twist. But when no one was looking, Kit and I sharpened our dark arts, and I fed my best friend a bundle of lies.

"You know what this is?" I said one day, waving a little flask in her face.

"Perfume?" she ventured, and quite reasonably, since a golden liquid was in it and the image of a blossom on its side.

"Wrong!" I said. "It only looks like perfume. It's a magic potion. My father brought it from Peru. One drink of this stuff and I have special powers. I can summon ghosts, witches, spirits. Anyone you'd like me to bring back from the dead?"

"How about Edgar Allan Poe?" she said excitedly.

"Poe, it is," I said, and smacked my lips in anticipation.

"How will I know you've summoned him?" Kit asked, superbly rational creature that she was. "Will I get to see him?"

"Oh," I said, rolling my eyes and thumping the bedspread under me, "believe me, you'll know when I see him. Trrrrrrrust me, you'll know. This is powerful stuff. Straight from the jungle. My father went down the Amazon to get it. In a canoe! Bought it himself from a cannibal." I think she believed me. I could see it in the wide black of her eyes.

It was true that my father had bought it for me. He had wandered into a little Latino *mercado* in Manhattan. Orange-blossom perfume. *Agua de azahar.*

I twisted off the tiny gold cap and raised the vial to my lips. An intense sweetness flooded my nostrils. I put my tongue to the rim. It was bitter. I thought twice about taking the lie too far, but then the romance of my remarkable powers overtook me. I squeezed my eyes shut and guzzled the contents down.

"Oh!" Kit said, and her hand flew to her throat.

"Oh!" I said, and flung the bottle onto the bed. The liquid was burning its way down my gullet; I had no problem pretending convulsions. I clutched the bedspread behind me and arched my back in a serpentine curve. When I snapped to, I bounced on my haunches like a demented monkey. I bared my teeth, growled, and goggled maniacally over the top of Kit's head. "It's him!"

"Where?" she screeched, and jumped around to face the wall behind her.

"No!" I cried. "Over there! In the window!" and I stumbled my way there from the bed.

As I went past her, I could see that Kit's face was red, her eyes terrified. She staggered back.

"Do you see?" I screamed, and, somehow, I actually pictured Poe's sallow face hovering outside my window, his hair in wild disarray. "Aaaaayeeeeee!" I wailed, and pointed to the disembodied head. "It's coming in!"

Suddenly, Kit bolted from the room, and, paralyzed with fear, I chased after. We scurried downstairs, squealing and jumping, throwing our arms around each other in the radiant light of the hall. "Did you see him?" I panted, my trachea burning from the full ounce of perfume that had wended its way through it.

"I think so," said Kit. "Yes, I saw him. I did."

"Oh, Mareezie," my mother said, coming out from the living room, smiling and shaking her head. "I can see you two have been housebound too long. You're playing your ghost games, aren't you? Why don't you bundle up and I'll take you to the rink, let you air out awhile?" We shook our flushed faces vigorously and ran to pack up our skates. If there was one thing better than a scare, it was speeding like a demon over ice.

Hard water. My first time on it, I'd been gawky as a toucan on marble, my knees splaying out over my blades. But before long, I had straightened my cap, pushed off the chain-link, swung my arms out, and sailed the ice free, making my mother's eyes dance. She loved to watch me skate. That night, while we spun around the rink, she sat in the car, elbows propped on the steering wheel—a cigarette in her hand, a grin on her face—her collar pulled high to her ears. I watched her watch me, turning to see her over my shoulder, feeling the pride and alcohol in me, thinking my chest would burst.

One evening not too long after that, we were driving home from the rink alone, when Mother pointed to the side of the road. A woman was navigating the curb on her toes, hugging her body, waving at us to stop. She had no purse, no keys, no bag: nothing at all in her hands. "Look at that," Mother said, "a thin little tunic on a freezing night like this. What's that poor woman up to?" She pulled the car over, cranked down the window, and offered her a ride. I'd never seen her do anything remotely like that in Lima. She had always been wary of strangers there.

The woman was older, graying, her hair swept up off her face. "Thank you, yes," she said, and hopped in, nimble as a bird. She shivered and chattered in the back, perched on the edge of her seat, hanging on to the front, motioning where to go. "Look at you, child," she said to me, but she wasn't looking at all. "Your nose is crisp as a radish!" Then she waved a frantic finger at the windshield. "I'm just down here on Prospect. Off Tulip. Very close now! Very close!" Her voice was high and wobbly, as if she'd been laughing too long.

Mother peered at the rearview mirror. "You look very cold," she said.

"Not so!" the woman chirped. "Here we are. Here's the driveway. Turn here."

FAIR OAKS, the sign said. We were just around the corner from our house, yards away from our apple trees, but I had never noticed this place before. It was hidden by pines, set off the road. Mother steered the car up the driveway and finally pulled to a stop. A massive building was in front of us, with bright lights blazing within. *Patient Registration*, one door said. *Staff Only,* said another. The woman sprang from the car and wordlessly darted inside.

"I wonder," Mother said as we turned back onto the road, "what the poor soul was doing wandering down Tulip Street like that. Did you see, Mareezie? Do you realize what this is?" She was half awed, half alarmed. I shook my head no. "A nuthouse, honey. That's what." She looked at me sideways and issued a little laugh.

We were living by the loony bin. The *loco* depository. Behind our garden. Near as the berry bush.

George and I patrolled the other side of our apple trees routinely after that, half expecting ghouls to lurch out, drooling and clawing at our eyes. But all we saw were heads with vacant faces, staring from windows, working their hands with their hands. In the evenings at times, I thought I could hear keening, as woeful as a wolf's on Elk Mountain. "That's a dog," Mother would rush to say. But I knew otherwise. It was a woman in a cotton tunic, standing on her toes, scanning the night for home.

⁓

IF SUMMIT WASN'T everything Mother had ever hoped for, she was fooling us well. She was radiant, steaming up and down Springfield Avenue, with a strong wind in her sail. She was doing things we'd never imagined could make her happy: going to market, hustling to the discount stores, speeding forgotten things to school for us with pin curls against her scalp. Even with a once-a-week maid to help her, there was plenty of work to do. She was tired and high-strung and driven, but there were no furrows in her brow.

As for Papi, he was coming and going in the dark now—leaving before dawn and arriving long past dusk—collapsing onto the sofa. He spent weekends behind a typewriter, writing long missives to Peru. *You should see how the children are growing,* he'd plick-plack, but he himself was seeing less and less of us by the day.

His life was unfolding in Manhattan, up a crowded elevator, behind a littered desk, over papers sketched with imagined columns of steel. If work culminated in a belching factory, a carmine furnace, a caroming machine part—if there were *pishtacos* snapping hands off at the wrists—he did not see them. His days were long white sheets of paper, coiled tight, stamped blue.

He was a Peruvian in New York City: a gray hat, gray wool straphanger, roaming the labyrinth, his heart in another land. In all our years in Peru, not one week had passed that the man did not greet his father, receive the blessings of his mother, stretch his legs under a table with a friend. Now he was one bewildered face in a line that trudged from the station. "There he is! I see him!" I'd sing from the back of the car, pointing into the dark of a New Jersey winter. But it was hardly the father I'd known. He'd waft through the house like a wisp over embers, clap his Smith-Corona on a table, roll the onionskin through, fill a glass, tamp an ashtray with a butt, and peck out wistful dispatches from the North.

Gringo life perplexed him, with its golf-cart weekends, Monday morning ball talk, barbecue aprons and hats. Suits moved through offices disparaging "the Third World," speaking of us as if we were the back end of civilization, as if he were an invisible man. "Hey, Freddy! Be sure to take gum and cigs when you go down to bananaland. Those *cholos* will kiss your ass!"

There was a frayed edge to his days on Tulip Street, a slow corrosion of the soul. Long, barren weeks were made bearable by the prospect of Peruvian interludes: The Ariases had invited us to dinner in a suburb two hours away. Carmen Cunningham, who now lived in Irvington, was bringing ceviche, made with *corvina* she had discovered in some tucked-away fish market. One of Papi's cousins was coming to town. No *Señor* de los

Milagros, no Santa Rosa de Lima, no *apu* of San Cristóbal could bless him with greater gifts.

But there were times he'd ride in on a late train and clump upstairs in the wee hours of a Saturday morning, smelling of rum and smoke. In Peru, the bottle had been for *simpático* men—for high-living *gente lijera*, as my grandmother had said. In this country it was for the forlorn.

The day finally came when he realized he had to break free from that golf-shirt internment, from the wing-toed chain gang of the 7:25. It happened one Friday night in February. Kit and I had just received a mail-order package from the North Carolina Biological Supply Company: two tree frogs, a lamb's heart, two lizards, one spotted king snake. (Pickled in formaldehyde. Suspended in clear plastic. Only in America! A middleman ships the remains!) We laid the lamb's heart out on a wood slab in the basement, poked it with our scalpels, imagined the lamb's blood coursing through it, then wrapped it back up and stuck it outside in a steep snowy bank between the back stoop and the garage. I smoothed over the snow, said good-bye to Kit, and we left our dissections for another day.

Hours after I went to bed, I awoke to the sounds of Mother moving from door to door, securing the latches from the inside. *Thwock. Thwock. Thwock.* I figured Papi had come home, and so I pulled up my alpaca blanket and nuzzled into its warmth. In truth, at that very moment, he was riding into the station. The Erie-Lackawanna's last train chugged in from Hoboken, disgorged him and a few stragglers, then hissed off into the black.

It was still dark when I reawoke to a howl that sounded as if it were rising from a vault under my floorboards. *Bah-eeeee!* High and urgent, like the wail of a snared animal. Or a *loco* on the far side of loose.

I shot out of bed and ran to my window. The back-porch light was on, and a yellow bulb threw its lemon glow over the snow. Out where the apple trees marked the frontiers of our garden, out by the hand-wringers of Fair Oaks, there was no trace of a footprint. If a *loco* were under my room, he had flown there. I peered at the big brown house on my left: No sign of movement there. Then I checked the one on the other side: pitch dark.

Whonk! Whonk! Two loud bangs shook my room and shivered out along the walls of the corridor. I grabbed the sides of my window frame. Was an earthquake shaking the bedrock of New Jersey? I strained to see over the peaked gable, but it blocked my view of the porch. Nothing trembled. Nothing stirred. There was only a terrible silence, and a sulfurous light, like the gleam of a feral eye.

Suddenly, something gray bobbed out from under the gable and pulled in again. It was fast, small, quiet, like the hindquarter of an animal. I hiked myself up to get a better angle, but the overhang prevented me from seeing more. All I could make out were three porch steps, the packed snow on the driveway, the round white shoulder where the laboratory lamb heart lay, and the still of the garden beyond.

Then came a sight that will never leave me. The gray object slid out from under the gable again. All at once, I was looking down at my father, moving in the dreamy glissade of a dancer, as if I were watching from the rafters of a stage. His feet were skating on ice, and the calves of his gray wool pants legs were sliding out from under him. Back and forth, back and forth, struggling for purchase on that one treacherous step. His head hovered beneath me: a dark crest, black as a winter's crow.

It was a simple thing. Over soon. He must have grabbed hold of something, for I no longer saw him. There was a long pause, and then the whack of fists against the door.

"Hoh-nee!" he bellowed. His voice reverberated through my toes, up my legs, and into my gut. "Oh-pen the door!" He took hold of the knob, pulled at it, and shook the door so that the tiny panes of glass rattled in their frames.

"Hoh-nee bay-bee!" he yelled, and then staggered back to give me a bird's-eye perspective on his head.

I looked out beyond him, into the night. One by one, lights were going on in our neighbors' houses. I imagined their faces at the windows, talking over their shoulders. No dear, it's fine, nothing serious. Only the alien next door.

HE WENT OFF to Peru after that. It was to be a single trip, a field visit to Paramonga, just like the visits the New York gringos made when we lived in that hacienda, putting up at the guest house for months at a time. He left in February and said he'd be back in early April, when buds were jutting from trees. Mother seemed to carry on fine without him. There was little the woman couldn't do. She shoveled the driveway, drove me to play rehearsals, stayed long into the night reading with Vicki. She was reveling in freedom now, as if she didn't need a man.

As for us children, we were Americans now. We hardly thought of our pasts; we hardly spoke Spanish. As the months went by, I shucked Peru entirely, referring to it only when I thought it would give me a moment's advantage, a teacher's attention. When Papi returned, I wished he wouldn't speak Spanish to me in front of the neighbors; I hoped he wouldn't reveal to my friends that I was a faker; I prayed he wouldn't show up on our door stoop high.

But he went off more and more after that. It began with two months, and then, before we knew it, it was six. By the time summer warmed our apple trees to life again, Papi was off on a long-term engineering project somewhere in Colombia. Then it was eight months in Mexico. He would leave Mother presigned checks so that she could handle the family finances; he would sign off complete power of attorney. By the time my own frame pushed forth cautious blossoms, he was gone nine months at a time, returning only long enough to gasp at us as we mutated into other forms of life.

George had shot up well past him: a confident, lanky boy. Vicki had chewed through whole libraries, feeding her polymathic brain. Marisi had become Marie, a molting I first saw in a mirror on the sixth floor of the Carnegie Hall building, where my body had metamorphosed under the spandex of leotards. I was twelve years old, taking ballet classes in New York two afternoons every week now, catching the bus to Port Authority at Forty-second Street, or taking a train to Grand Central, skipping through midtown past the Biltmore Hotel, navigating my way to Carnegie Hall. "There's nothing you can't do, Mareezie," Mother would tell me. "Decide what you want, don't be afraid, go after it. There is *nothing* you cannot do."

When Mother's car wended its way down Tulip Street to pick me up after school one day, I looked across the playground and saw a black head of hair sitting where she should be. Could it be? My father had not been home in almost a year. I ran to the fence to be sure. He got out of the car and stood by the gringos, searching for his offspring in the crowded field. His eyes swept past me three times before I leapt up and screamed out, "Papi! Papi! *Aquí!*"

"You've changed," he said to me, laughing. "I hardly know you anymore," and then he handed me a fuzzy white llama toy, stuffed and smiling, with a spangle around its neck.

Mornings would come and I would wake to the sound of my parents' voices, chatting on the other side of my wall. They were scrolling through lives each was living, sharing events after the fact. He had his subjects. She had hers.

"Papi," I said to him, during one of his longer visits, "I'm writing a report on the Andes, for my seventh-grade social studies class."

"On the Andes? Why?" He looked up from the living room sofa and lowered *The New York Times*.

"Because." I stopped there, stymied. His face was awaiting my answer, open in genuine surprise. "Because I'm *Peruana*, Papi," I said.

"You?" he said. "A Peruvian?" And then he laughed, shaking his head, long and hard. "No, Marisi. You're a gringa, like your mother. You're not a Peruvian anymore."

I went off and thought about that, my heart a little smaller for his words. Had Peru fallen out of me? Like a leaf in a winter wind?

What of my language, my patrimony, the power of my *qosqo*? Was that gone, too? I looked down at the copper money winking out from my loafers. I loved my mother's country, pledged it allegiance every day, dreamed its golden dreams, bought its daily lotteries of the soul. But I was sure that somewhere inside me I was also Peruvian.

It was Lucilla who reminded me of that.

Lucilla was black as Antonio's stone, a cocky, junior-high-school girl who chose her friends by the color of their skin. She was sassy, funny, filled with dislike for much about Summit, and part of that much was me.

"Hurry up, girl!" she'd yell as we scooted from one class to another, and then she'd give me a kick in the can.

"Git! Git! Can't be late!" And then—*foomp!*—her pointy shoe would connect with my tail.

It had started in gym class, where the lineup put her behind me. She was ahead of me in one significant way: superior in every sinew of her body. If I could pound out a hundred sit-ups, she could pound out a hundred fifty-five. One day—who knew why?—she decided to stick her foot into my life. She tripped me on the playing fields, kicked me down corridors, slapped a boot up against the door of my bathroom stall and kept me there until the bell rang, until I begged her for mercy. Then Lucilla and her girls would holler and slap their knees as I flitted, panicked, down the hall.

Once, when she was standing alone on the hockey field, away from her gang of girls, I decided to risk the question. "Lucilla," I said, "why do you want to get me in trouble?"

"You're already there, girl," she said, and bugged her eyes.

"What?"

"You a wiggle-butt wetback," she added. "You nothing *but* trouble. You oughta go back where you belong."

There it was. Lucilla's proof. The Truth, whether or not my father could factor it. His children had not gone from any first thing to a second. We were the "neither-here-nor-there people": one thing when here, the other when there. Or forever from some other place. We were neither; we were both.

Funny that it was a black who reminded me of that. I've often thought of Lucilla as I sit in my corner of Washington now, seeing how this country has changed since I was a girl. There were days I felt George, Vicki, and I were the only Latinos in the United States; I certainly did not see any others around. I knew we were the only ones in the Summit school system. But I've returned to Summit often over the years and watched its subtle transformations. Today, you cannot walk down a main street in New Jersey and not hear Spanish, or pass a Latin grocery, or see a Latino face. The last time I checked, there was a child with my surname—no relation—in the corridors of Summit High School. There are thousands of families with Spanish surnames in the American capital. There are nearly forty million of us in your country now, Lucilla. We belong here. Just like you.

BY THE TIME I settled into junior high school, my parents had
bought into North American soil for good. We never imagined
they wouldn't stay together. They cared for each other deeply,
that much was written on their faces every time Papi walked
through the front door and they saw each other for the first time.
She would wait for him nervously, running upstairs to fix her
makeup, spraying perfume under her blouse. Somehow, as
years went by, the separations became the norm for us. We
learned to live without our father; we were happy to see him
when he came back, happy to be handed so many presents, and
then, as he grew restless to return to Lima, we were happy to see
him go.

We moved from the rental on Tulip Street to ownership on
Parkview Terrace. The new house was crawling with vines.
Creepers sprang from the flower beds, working their way up brick.
The sun would vault the sky, and Mother would still be outside,
hacking back foliage, digging into the loam. I would sit and watch
her work silently, wondering why she wouldn't talk to me about
herself. Why was she so unwilling to tell me the details of her
childhood, pour out her stories to me as Antonio the gardener had
done? I marveled that I had watched Antonio's hands do the same
labor. My mother's violinist fingers were just as strong.

Antonio: I remembered every *historia* he'd taught me, but the
man seemed like ancient history now. "What were those belly
button stories you used to tell?" my mother would ask me. I'd
shrug my shoulders and grin. My *qosqo* was powerless now.
Unplugged. Deactivated. Dead.

I laughed when I recalled the *bruja*'s prophesy. A vine was to
mount my house and grab me by the throat? It seemed so foolish
now in my Episcopalian maturity, in my confirmed membership
in the Calvary Church. Mother's faith had won my soul. No talk

about black light, no sorcery from a crone in braids could bobble my God or the machinery of an observable world.

Trees did not mourn. Skies did not weep. Vines did not leap through your window in revenge.

❧

"WHY DO YOUR mother and father live apart?" asked Kit one day. "Are they divorced?" She was polite when she said it, quaint and Victorian, as she tended to be.

"No. They're not divorced," I said. "My father lives in Peru, my mother lives in the United States, that's all. He lives there because he works there. She lives here because we go to school here." It made all the sense in the world to me.

"Oh," said Kit, and ended it there. Her father was a scientist; her mother, a viola player. They were functional versions of my parents, but they lived in one house, spoke one language, visited their in-laws within one hundred miles of one another, stared at each other's faces every day.

"Why do your mother and father live apart?" A German girl who lived behind our new house asked the same question on another day.

I gave her the same answer. "Oh," she said, but her reaction was more interesting than Kit's. "That makes things better, doesn't it? That way you have two homes, not one. Two languages. Two totally different lives." Her name was Erika, and she'd been born in Frankfurt during the Allied Occupation. Her mother had been a dancer; her father, a British military man. Erika had never seen her father except in a photograph album. He was in England somewhere, alive. On paper, he seemed a stiff man, oddly handsome, with Erika's blond locks and her dimple in his chin. He'd been posted to Germany to help piece the country together, but he'd clearly left chaos behind. Unanswered questions hovered over Erika. Questions about names, marriages, nationalities. Her mother had left Germany to escape them. We had our alien origins in common, but there was something else, too, about our mothers, about their burdens from the past.

"Heil Hitler!" the boys would shout as we strolled down to Memorial Field arm in arm.

"Hey, cut it out!" I'd call back over my shoulder. "I'm not German!"

"Remember the Alamo, then!"

They'd yuk about that, pumping their shoulders like vultures.

It was the idea of Erika's two-ness that attracted me. Half German, half English. She was an exotic in the suburban landscape, an indisputably eccentric girl. The idiom we shared was ballet. There was not much else we had in common. She was plump, whereas I had grown scrawny. She was honey, where I was mahogany. Her mother made pastries and sewed fancy dresses, whereas mine knew only the rudiments of housekeeping. I sat in her family room watching Adolf Eichmann on trial, hearing her mother spit German in his face. I looked at the stacks of magazines with inexplicable photographs of mass graves, my friend's fingers dancing across pages, pointing out heart-stopping details. I played piano when she and her mother asked me, Beethoven after Mozart after Brahms, until they leaned back and stared at the ceiling like dolls.

Erika's mother, Minna, had been rounded up during the war and made to work in a Frankfurt munitions plant. That bit of information sprang from her lips one day as she taught me to make sauerbraten. It wasn't clear—she couldn't say—why the Nazis had singled her out on the street and marched her to the machines. (Was she Jewish, like the dead in the photographs? She was dark-haired, dark-eyed, nothing like Erika. But she wore crosses and kept a rosary in her purse.) As bombers climbed the air from the runways of Germany, she polished steel instruments, dancing away nights in a cabaret on the lively side of town.

Unbidden admissions would spring from her as we sat, heads down, rolling dough or pinning a pattern onto cloth. These were things she did not tell her own daughter, but she would blurt them to me, unpacking the burdens of her heart, as if I were a priest in a confessional.

Erika would be somewhere else, belting a song into a mirror or shimmying to some idiocy in the box, and Minna would pour her history into my twelve-year-old ears, doing what I longed for my mother to do. There was much about our families that was different: They had a television, whereas my parents most intentionally did not. They were willfully frivolous—in dress, entertainments, and dreams—whereas my family most assuredly was not. There was a Pentecostalist stepfather, Minna's husband: a rangy, red-haired American who had taken in the immigrants the way a vestryman takes up a cause. He came and went, consuming his meals in silence, hardly denting a pillow, hardly touching their lives. Going to visit Erika and Minna was like flying into foreign territory. There was always something new there: When I studied my hands like a gringo, another secret would come my way.

Minna had spent a lifetime pulling her mother's head out of an oven. It had started when she was a girl of six. One gray winter weekend, as we puttered about her sewing room, she received a telephone call from Frankfurt: The mother was at it again.

That was hardly the half of it. If Minna knew who her father was, she never said so. Her world was staunchly female, and the males—even the fathers and husbands—in it incidental. They were largely incomprehensible, sometimes irresistible, but ultimately expendable. In Minna's life story, they came and went like brisk winds.

During the war, she had lived in a Bohemian quarter of Frankfurt. Prostitutes lived in the apartments above. Night after night, she could hear the clump of Nazi boots as officers made their bibulous way upstairs to savor the retail charms. They were twisted, those Nazis, perpetrators of the unnatural, forcing the women to treat them like animals, roaring their pleasure through walls. One day, as I carefully pinned a facing to a perfectly round collar, she told me about one of them—one of Hitler's generals, no less—who demanded to be served his hostess's feces in Dresden porcelain, with her urine in crystal on the side. How Minna had extracted that information from the upstairs neighbor, it did not occur to me to ask.

I staggered from those confessions into the glare of a suburban landscape, hopping the fence, into my tidy brick house. "Mareezie?" my mother called as I came in the back door. "Did you finish your sewing?" When she noted my pale face slipping past to my room, her voice would rise in alarm: "What goes on in that house anyway?"

I was afraid to tell Minna's stories, just as I'd been afraid to tell about Antonio's spirit world. These were tales of dark forces, best kept to myself. Minna was of another dimension, from another side, a *bruja* who spoke terrible truths. If I relayed her words to my mother, she would surely be swept from my life.

As it was, I was in thrall to the ghosts of Minna's past. I told my mother I was going to her house to sew, to cook, to talk about ballet, but what I really did there was listen. Her stories would never disappoint me. In the cabaret where she had danced, she told me, the Nazis came for their revels, demanding a single performance from her every night. "I was beautiful then," she made a point of saying, "dark and different; that's why they came." She told me about a body stocking of sheerest silk, how she would trail long skeins of perfumed chiffon and dance barefoot, hair coiled down her spine. A scarf masked the lower half of her face. Her eyes were rimmed black as an Egyptian's. "It was fascina-a-a-tion!" she rasped at me in her deep, husky voice, and I could imagine her silk-hung pulchritude shivering the night, filling the monsters with desire.

"I'm going to Erika's," I said to my mother. "If that's all right with you."

"What for?" Mother asked, narrowing her eyes.

"Her mother is teaching me a dance. You know, she was a ballerina once."

"Really? I didn't know that. What's the music you're dancing to?"

"'It Was Fascination,'" I replied, and hummed a few bars.

"Oh, I know that tune," Mother said. "It was popular during the war. Fine. Go right ahead." I left her chirping the song.

Minna and Erika never asked about my father. They had no curiosity about him whatsoever. When he pulled up in a taxi with his suitcases bulging with gifts, they understood they would see me less for a while. Minna was more interested in my mother, asking me questions I could not answer. What had *she* done during the war?

One day when Papi had been on a long assignment in the interior of Peru, Minna parted the bushes and saw my mother on her knees in our yard. Mother's hair was tied back in a cotton bandanna; sweat dripped from her chin to the soil; she was jabbing the earth with a spade. Minna watched her work for a while, then stepped to the fence to ask, "Everything okay?" Mother looked up, startled. "You're digging so hard in one place there," she commented in her thick German accent. "Is something wrong? Are you all right?"

As it happened, things were not right at all. My father had not written in months. Bills were stacked in a kitchen drawer, unpaid.

"I'm fine," said Mother, pulling herself to her feet and dusting her knees. "Thank you very much." But when she came in and recounted that brief exchange, quizzing me about what in God's name I'd been spilling to the neighbors, I deduced that Minna's powers did in fact go beyond normal. She'd seen into my mother's heart.

~

I LEARNED MANY things from Erika and Minna, but chief among them was that I was no foreigner. I did not have the requisite distance, the emotional remove. There was much about me that may have looked different, felt different, but I was deeply and indelibly American, from this hemisphere, taught Americanness from infancy, ready to defend it with my soul.

"How can you eat that gummy stuff they call bread here," Erika said to me, piquing me with her arrogance.

"Get off it, Erika. It's not as bad as you say."

"It's awful! You should taste German bread. They have so many kinds there: black, white, rye, egg, salty, sweet, big loaves with seeds on top, flaky little rolls that melt in your mouth. It's *real* bread. Not like here."

I recalled the street vendors in Peru, with their mounds of fragrant bread: hard golden crusts, feathery soft centers, baked fresh and brought to your door. But I defended the supermarket variety.

"You can't possibly like it!" Erika argued. "You're not even from here!"

"Yes, I *am*," I said. "I'm an American from way back. My great-great-great-great-grandfather was born here! One of my ancestors was a president!"

"Oh, yeah?" she said. "Then why are you living in that dump?"

I could have lived in a palace, and Erika would have said it wasn't as good as the German kind. Everything German was better. The chocolate was deeper. The milk was creamier. The sausages more savory. The dresses more elegant. The homes cozier. Soaps, shoes, perfume. There was no material commodity in all these United States of America that could compare with its counterpart in Frankfurt.

We argued this as we trudged to and from school, dodging the neighborhood boys. "German dolls are prettiest!" she would shout. "German Christmases are fanciest!" "German underwear's most comfortable!" and a bank of boys' arms flew up as we passed, in rigid Nazi salutes. George was among them, grinning at me, slicing the air at Erika—a rosy-cheeked American boy.

"Lay off!" I'd bark. "Stop that! She's my friend!" And they'd laugh themselves red in the face.

But I had my own battles to fight in those early 1960s. I could no sooner stand criticism of the United States than I could stand ill to be said of Peru. The truth was that I was getting it on both sides. Peruvians who came to visit forgot I was also a gringa, launching verbal salvos about *Estadounidenses* who chanced by on the streets: "They're gawky, aren't they! Clowns! And dullwitted! Cross an idiot with a bully and what do you get? *Un norteamericano!*"

Americans, on the other hand, would forget I was Peruvian, disparaging my roots to my face. "Latin Americans are a poor, indolent people," my teacher droned to the class, "beset by ignorance and disease." All I could do was stare at his mouth, at the spittle that danced on his lips.

"I'd rather have a Nih-gro maid than a Mexican," a suburbanite said to her dashboard. Her daughter and I sat in the backseat, listening to her well-lacquered head. "At least you can trust the black girls. The Mexicans steal you blind."

If there were other hybrids in Summit, they were too subtle for us. We did not know them. Erika, I discovered eventually,

was as different from me as anyone I had ever met. Her foreignness had seemed familiar, but a true sisterhood did not exist for
us. She was German. There was no two-ness in her. The British
father had given her his face but not a smidgen more. When she
came to the United States from Germany, she came as an immi-
grant, in a straight voyage from A to B. I, on the other hand, was
an American twice over; I had the palsy of a double soul.

~

WE HADN'T HEARD from Papi in such a long time that I began
to wonder if I'd been wrong about their marriage being inde-
structible, if it was possible that he had forgotten us entirely. The
checks he usually sent signed in advance to Mother had not
come for the third month in a row. The bill drawer was overflow-
ing now, and, at Vassar, Vicki needed to buy books. George was
outgrowing his clothes. There was the question of my ballet lessons. Mother went out and got herself a job.

It was work that my father would never have approved of, had
he been around to have any say. She walked into a dress shop on
Springfield Avenue and asked if any positions were available.
The woman behind the counter hired her on the spot. She was
to begin the following week as the most junior of three
salesladies. On her first day, I strolled by after school to look in
the window. She was sweeping the floors.

It was at about this time, when I was thirteen years old, that
Abuelita suddenly reappeared in our lives. She flew into New
York's Idlewild Airport on a September day with Tío Víctor and
Rosita, his new bride. Abuelita was accompanying them on their
honeymoon. They taxied to Manhattan, checked into the
Biltmore Hotel. When Tío Víctor called and said they were
there, I made my way on a Saturday morning and rapped on her
room door, listening for the click of her shoes. When I saw her, I
buried my face in her hair.

"*Ay*, Marisita," she said, after she'd held me at arm's length and taken a good, long look. "You're so big." She straightened her dress, reached for her gloves. "Come, let's go and have breakfast together." We headed downstairs, alone.

We walked several blocks of Forty-eighth Street with our elbows entwined before I realized that I was towering over my grandmother. She ticked down the concrete in her high-polish, sling-back Chanel shoes, looking about nervously, clutching an alligator purse. "Ugly city," she said. "So much unhappiness. *No es un Paris.*" Nothing like Paris, no.

I laughed at that. It had never occurred to me that New York could be anything but enchanting just as it was. I loved its gray glass, its whirligig humanity, its surly ruckus. I'd been commuting to the city since before my twelfth birthday. At first I'd go from school to the train to the Hoboken tubes, to Thirty-third Street and then take a bus up Eighth Avenue. Eventually I took the bus all the way from New Jersey to Port Authority, which was the simpler way to go, and then I'd walk uptown, swinging my ballet bag over one shoulder. I had begged Mother to let me study ballet and voice in New York. It was not her idea. But when she saw how resourceful I was in calling up studios, inquiring about fees, scheduling auditions, she supported me. The first few times, she went with me, but when she saw that I was the one doing the navigating, she decided I could commute alone. New York may well have looked daunting to my grandmother, but it was a city that knew my feet. I said so. She threw me a wary glance.

We took a table in a bustling coffee shop. After the waiter had listened to our order, after I had translated all her desires, Abuelita turned to me and unfurled a napkin into her lap. One of her well-defined eyebrows was arched high, in the direction of the waiter. "*Así que eres coqueta, Marisi,*" she said. So, I see you're a flirt.

I was nothing of the kind, I insisted. I had simply read food off a menu to the man.

"You smiled," she said.

"*Sí.* I was polite. I smiled. That's what people—"

"Young ladies do not smile at waiters," she said with finality. "Someone should be teaching you that."

There was no point arguing it with her. I let the subject go.

"Vicki is at university," she started, placing her wrists on the table carefully. "*Quién sabe* where Georgie is. Your father is off on some project. And your mother and I, for some reason, can't have a civil conversation. I want this time alone with you, Marisi," she said. "I have something to say." Her face churned briefly, then sank with gravity. She looked up, swallowing me with her eyes.

"This has nothing to do with how I feel about your mother," she began, uttering words I cannot forget. "It has nothing to do with how she feels about me. It has little to do with our discomforts, one way or the other. It has everything to do with love." She stopped there, allowing the waiter to plink plates on the table, defying me to smile my gratitude, holding me with her gaze.

"Love," she said it again, once he was gone. *El amor.* "You know by now, *mi'jita,* how different some countries can be. The ways we live, the things we do, what we believe. But there's one thing that stays the same. That one thing, Marisi, is love."

I wagged my head like a perfect little jackass, thinking she was referring to her fondness for me, ready to tell her that I loved her, too. "I'm speaking, of course," she said, "about your mother and father.

"How long," she asked, "has it been since you've seen him, Marisi?" It had been months since I'd seen Papi; I didn't know how many. "That is precisely what I mean," she said. "Not because he doesn't love you, you know. This is not between you and him. I'm talking about something else."

She paused, set down her fork, and continued. "Please don't say to me that your mother is not with your father because that is how married people in this country behave. Even I know a few things about the *yanquis*. If they're in love, they're together. They make it a point to be together. *Punto*. That is all. For years I've tried to understand this about your mother, until I realized there was nothing to understand. Love does not slice differently depending on nationality. It's always one and the same."

I had nothing to say. I chewed on my toast, wondering where this conversation would go. She launched ahead without any encouragement from me. "We have something in common, your mother and I. When I married your grandfather, I knew nothing about the Aranas. They were a mystery to me. In many ways they still are. A foreign land. You know, I've always suspected there is good reason why your abuelito is the way he is. Something that explains why he's so taciturn, so unwilling to deal with people, so removed from the rest of the world. But in the end, his little peculiarities don't really matter. My life isn't particularly easy, but I gave my life over to one man, and the strength of our family is my reward. When men are left to their own devices, Marisi—I don't care whether they're from Piccadilly or the Ucayali—when women are not at men's sides, things fall apart. Other women worm in. Other opportunities unfold. It's only natural. I wonder sometimes if your mother understands this. If she cares about it at all. Why does she insist on living in one place, if her husband is someplace else? Does she want an end to this marriage? Is that what she wants?"

I was staggered by what she was saying to me. This was a real-life conversation, and she was talking about taboos freely, in a way I'd heard only Erika's mother do. She was looking at me expectantly, as if I were a full-grown woman with important opinions to share. I struggled to find the words to respond to her. "She's happy here, Abuelita. This is her country. She likes that we go to school here, that we're learning to be like her." Two pallid eggs stared up from my plate.

She sighed and leaned back in her chair. Her shoulders were limp in her dress. "I want you to do something for me, Marisita. I want you to tell your mother that if she loves your father, she will make an effort to be with him. Tell her this: Living apart will not solve their differences. It will only make them grow. Love cannot possibly survive with a hemisphere in between.

"I want you to do something more, one more thing. When you tell her that, don't say that I asked you to say it. That will add confusion, muddle my meaning. I want this message to reach her in its simplest possible form."

That evening, Mother came to the Biltmore Hotel to call on Abuelita. She was exhausted from spending days on her feet—I could see that in her swollen ankles—but she did not tell Abuelita about the dress shop. They conversed stiffly in Spanish: how much we'd grown, how well we were doing in school. It was an awkward truce of sorts. The next morning, my grandmother visited Summit. She toured my mother's garden, circled the flower beds, insisted she couldn't stay. "Your home is pleasant, Marie," she said, reaching for her daughter-in-law's hands and squeezing them into her own. *Muy acogedor.* "I can see why you love your country." Then she left me to say the rest.

~

FOR DAYS I wondered how to relay my grandmother's message to Mother. I was not good at diplomacy. In those days of my prodigality, the mouth outran the head, blurting substituted for frankness, too often I went too far. I worried that I would reveal

my source or—at the very least—provoke renewed hostilities between the women I most admired. How to counsel a grown-up
about love?

Love seemed to have so little to do with it. Although my father
said he cared for this country, he seemed to be an utter misfit in
it, just as Mother had been a misfit in his. The question, as far as
I could tell, was one of logistics. But of love? It seemed a wheel-
work so remote, so abstract, that I could not even imagine the
contours of the machine.

If she loves your father, she will make an effort to be with him.
That meant one thing only: If there was love between my mother
and father, we would all be living in Peru. Could love be so dicta-
torial, so unilateral as all that?

I decided to wait and watch until the right moment for my de-
livery of the secret dispatch. But days passed, then weeks and
months, and the hugger-mugger never got done. It wasn't because I was avoiding the mission; it was because a ray of deduc-
tive reasoning had lit my brain.

The evidence appeared—as I have since learned important
things do—in a small way. My father came home that fall, lavish-
ing us with gifts, beaming on our accomplishments, registering
our adolescent habits with alarm. His first week home was the
easiest. The bills all got paid. Mother arranged for a vacation
from the dress shop, and the two of them took to the kitchen to
turn out *criollo* feasts. By the second week, she was back at
work, and he was angry that his wife was waiting on other
women in such a common establishment. The indignity of it.
The insult. No woman in his family had ever had to do that.
Never mind that she liked having her own money, that she was
savoring the freedoms it gave her. He was plunking the Johnnie
Walker on the table, cursing America's crudeness, prowling the
house like a jaguar in a cage. By the second month, they were
bickering about new bills, about Peruvian versus American

mores, about how each of them misused the other language's preterite past. By the third month, Papi's bags were packed. Before winter was hard upon us, a bitter wind would blow him out the door again.

He'd be back. The cycle was nothing new. It had happened the year Castro took Cuba. It had happened the spring a spy plane was shot down over Russia. It had happened the autumn of the first Catholic President. It had happened the summer East Germany built a wall. It had happened just after we watched our chief executive's head explode into the streets of Dallas.

But the evidence, as I say, was in the details. I was looking for love with a grandmother's charge on my shoulders, and it was finally in still, small voices that I found it. I heard it in the mornings when he came home, in the everyday pitter-patter on the other side of my wall. At dawn, when my parents were alone in their room, when the world had not encroached with its borders and geographies and biases and resentments, they would talk for hours. It was a light chatter, filled with dreams and amusements and a mutual concern about us. Mother would tell of her life, Papi would tell about his, and each would listen to the other, with little exclamations of delight. There was nothing earthshaking about this. They were stark polarities, my parents: irrepressibly different, adamantly themselves, but ardently, irrefutably in love. Abuelita had not been right about them. She hadn't had any experience by which to judge their hard-won union. I didn't have to tell them they should live together. They were who they were—nonconformists, independent. Doing fine with a hemisphere in between.

So have they been for well over half a century of marriage, for day after day of their turbulent fusion. Long after Abuelita's plea in the coffee shop, my parents have chased each other from America to America, pursuing their love along the corridors of time: As Grandpa Doc flew into the blue after Grandma Lo. As pairs of eagles wheeled through the sky to remind me of them. As the dust of my abuelitos moved through God's mill. As Antonio spawned future generations in the cane fields of Cartavio. As Juan Díaz disappeared into the hills of Pachamama. As Vicki became a professor of literature and big sister to thousands. As George became a psychiatrist, mender of broken minds. As I sprang capriciously from ballet to opera to books. The two halves of my parents stayed together.

That is the wonder of this tale.

EPILOGUE

VENICE MAY HAVE its Bridge of Sighs, but there is another one in Lima—*Puente de los Suspiros*—and every time I return to Peru, I find myself drawn to it, as if it holds some secret, some deeper meaning about life and love. It is not the imposing suspension bridge my father so admires: the kind of steel colossus that makes him slam on the brakes, pull the car over, get out and stare. Nothing like the Verrazano, Golden Gate, or Chesapeake Bay. And certainly nothing like that intricately wrought, melancholy structure that juts between palace and dungeon over the northeastern waters of Italy. This is a modest trestle, spanning a dry little gorge in the historic district of Barranco. Cut from wood a hundred years or so ago, it is short and square and simple. It was not built to inspire voyagers to nobler ground or brave new worlds. It is where the lovers go.

What is it about a bridge that draws me? Perhaps it is the way it arches up, launches out, leaps for new ground. Perhaps it is the way even the most modest—an Andean bridge woven from osier, a slim ladder of slats—can swing out over an abyss, defy nature's will to divide. Even a vine—thrown from one cliff to another—is a miracle. It connects points that might never have touched. Perhaps it is simply that a bridge depends on two sides to support it, that it is a promise, a commitment to two.

I love to walk a bridge and feel that split second when I am neither here nor there, when I am between going and coming, when I am God's being in transit, suspended between ground and ground. You could say it's because I'm an engineer's daughter and curious about solid structures. I've always been fascinated by the fit of a joint, the balance in trestles, the strength of a plinth. Or you could say it's because I'm a musician's daughter, who knows something about the architecture of instruments. I've pulled string over a bridge on a violin, stretched it tight, anticipated sound.

It could be, perhaps, because I am neither engineer nor musician. Because I'm neither gringa nor Latina. Because I'm not any one thing. The reality is I am a mongrel. I live on bridges; I've earned my place on them, stand comfortably when I'm on one, content with betwixt and between.

I've spent a lifetime contemplating my mother and father, studying their differences. I count both their cultures as my own. But I'm happy to be who I am, strung between identities, shuttling from one to another, switching from brain to brain. I am the product of people who launched from one land to another, who slipped into other skins, lived by other rules—yet never put their cultures behind them.

What they *did* put behind them were pasts. My father was running from history. He didn't know its particulars but had lived with its consequences. The Aranas had become good at avoidance, deft with excuses, masters of contortion. We couldn't see—didn't *try* to find out—what was at the bottom of my grandfather's strangeness: We wove veils of subterfuge, refused to see things as they were. With time, we looked upon my abuelito with a certain petulance. Had we admitted the truth about our connection to Julio César, we might have turned petulances against *him* instead.

Who knows? Perhaps even if we'd acknowledged our connection to the Casa Arana, we still would have displaced the blame. We might have pointed fingers at the gringos: They'd been the ones starved for rubber, their roads gaping in anticipation, their factories ready to whirl. As the *indios* in Cartavio would say, the *pishtacos* were loose in the rain forest: the machine ghosts were hungry, and the grease of dark people was required.

As it turned out, it didn't much matter where the dark people were. After the English crushed Julio César, they transplanted Peru's rubber trees to Malaya, thereby plunging the curse into the far side of the planet, and the afflicted welcomed the disease. The Malayans bore the hardships of their rubber trade valiantly. The British pocketed the cash.

As fate had it, I, too, was transplanted to Malaya. I was twenty-three at the time: the docile bride of an American banker. I hit ground in Kuala Lumpur as unsuspectingly as a pilfered little sprout of Para fine hard. By then, Malaya had become Malaysia, and the country was no longer British. The rubber industry had gone not only from Peru to Malaysia, but from trees to chemical vats, and the old curing posts had turned into tourist stops.

I moved with my first husband into a house above the jungle, to a place that stood on a hill. It was a colonial stucco structure with frangipani nodding by the balcony, monkeys screeching and coupling on the blacktop, papayas dangling in the heat. A Malay woman drove me up the driveway and deposited me at the door. "This was the home of an English rubber baron," she said. "A powerful tycoon. He built it high, so that he could look out at the jungle canopy." I went up to the porch and looked out over a magnificent sea of trees. I smiled at their greenness. I breathed in their air. I brought a child into the world to look at them with me—a little gringa with her grandmother's hair of gold. I didn't know we were staring at trees from Julio César Arana's hellhole. I didn't know the *apus* had meant me to study the foliage. I had forgotten about the *bruja* and the vine.

Signs are everywhere, Antonio used to tell me. *Marisi, you must learn to look.*

The connections have not always been easy to follow. But they are there when I look for them. They are there.

The lie that we were not related to the jungle Aranas took its toll slowly, but it ate souls one by one. My grandfather became a hermit. My grandmother had to be satisfied to look at the world through her children, clacking through their lives in high heels and perfume. Her social nature curbed, she moved through Lima crimped as a widow, then died in her chair, her feet too disfigured to walk. My father could never understand why his father stayed upstairs day after day, hid himself in his study, shirked a man's responsibilities, failed his wife. Little wonder that Papi catapulted himself to a new life. Little wonder that he needed a little alcohol to fuel himself into it. Little wonder there was a bit of jetsam along the way.

The history from which my mother was escaping was different—writ not over a century, but in a handful of years—very hasty, very gringo. In one night, her life exploded. She left her parents' house on a lark with her big sister and awoke the next morning as the sixteen-year-old wife of a brute. She was trapped, abused, then decided to quit that marriage altogether. When she found love with a Canadian, it was snatched away soon—in a faraway place, in another country's war. All she could do was box the pain, bury it into some deep corner of consciousness. She got on a train looking to put the past behind her. When she got off, she met the man to put her in another part of the world.

Papi extracted himself from the Arana welter. He returned to Peru regularly and looked after his parents. But he did it from afar, removed from the charade of denial. When his father died during one of his visits, he couldn't bring himself to sit wake with the body; he couldn't bear to mount the staircase to say farewell.

My mother reinvented herself completely. I never saw the Clapps after that one spring in Wyoming. Much, much later, I learned that Nub, my chaw-lovin' cousin, had put a bullet through his brain. I met two of twelve other American cousins when they were already grandparents; I tracked them down in order to write this book. I never saw my mother's sisters again, never even met two of them. Of my parents, my mother remains the exotic creature, the far more mysterious one. I often marvel that these two are still together, still drawn by each other's attractions, still shuttling between the United States and Peru.

If two opposing energy bubbles meet, Antonio used to say, there is a natural conflict. If they lock, they rise to a higher plane. Call it enlightenment. Call it love. Call it the start of a twice-blessed soul.

I often think how fortunate I've been: Here I am, after all, the product of a chance meeting, in chance circumstances. Then I remind myself how little chance had to do with it. I was meant to go between the *apus* and Elk Mountain, meant to sit on a crate with Antonio, meant to play conquistadors with Georgie, meant to watch sunsets with Grandpa Doc, meant to weave dreams about my mother, meant to plumb the Arana past.

Sometimes when I sit alone on my porch in the springtime, when light enters my garden at a certain angle, I think I see the black and yellow heliconia butterflies that used to skim the floripondio bushes of my childhood. I see Amazon hummingbirds darting in and out of my buddleia. I see flocks of lime-green parakeets swoop down East Capitol Street, then bank swiftly, up and away. I see Antonio shaking a dirty finger at me.

Qué te dice, Marisi? he is asking me. What does this book tell you about the connections, the *historias*, the love that resulted in you? But as soon as I imagine him asking, he's gone.

Come on, little fool, I say to myself as I sit in my wicker rocker—think. There is a man who is all science, from a culture that points him in. There is a woman who is all music, from a culture that drives her out. There's a jungle, a war, a marriage passing through time. And then...there is *me*. Is that it, Antonio? Am I the point of this *historia*? The pivot, the midway crossing?

I, a Latina, who—to this day—burns incense, prays on her knees to the Virgin, feels auras, listens for spirits of the dead.

I, an Anglo, who snaps her out of it, snuffs candles, faces reality, sweeps ash into the ash can, works at a newspaper every day.

I, a north–south collision, a New World fusion. An American *chica*. A bridge.

ACKNOWLEDGMENTS

THIS BOOK IS the product of a communal memory. I have been fortunate to have had the participation of many family members who helped me recall scenes and exchanges from my early life. None should be blamed for inaccuracies, for if there are errors on these pages, they are entirely mine. Nevertheless, I owe an enormous debt of gratitude to my relatives for their willingness to revisit the past with me—even the difficult parts—and add texture and color to my memories. They are: Jorge Arana Cisneros, Marie Clapp Arana, Rosa Victoria (Vicki) Arana, George Winston Arana, Maria Isabel (Chaba) Arana Cisneros, Eloísa Arana Cisneros, Víctor Arana Cisneros, Robert Hugh (Huey) Loseman, Erma Jean Grise, and Joyce Loseman-Wheeler.

An author who is steered toward truth is fortunate, and I was indeed fortunate to be steered there by historians Roger Rumrill Garcia of Lima, Umberto Morey of Iquitos, and Juan M. Cravero Tirado, former senator from Ayacucho, all of whom assisted me in reconstructing the connection between my great-grandfather Pedro Pablo Arana and the *cauchero* Julio César Arana.

Leonard Downie, Robert Kaiser, and Nina King granted me time away from my job at *The Washington Post* to write. The Hoover Institution on War, Revolution and Peace at Stanford University gave me a month's fellowship, an office next to the Stanford Library, and then left me alone to think.

When I pecked out five vaguely worded pages of a proposal and faxed them with humble apologies to Amanda Urban, it was she who convinced me that I might have a book there. I thank Binky not only for the many years of friendship she has given me, but for her laser-true antennae, rock-hard faith, and great good humor. She is the engine that made this possible.

I've been in the book business for a long time, first on the publishing side and now in the reviewer's corner, but I have never encountered anyone like Susan Kamil. For all those skeptics who say good editors exited this world with Maxwell Perkins, I would ask them to consider mine: the hardest nose, biggest heart, keenest mind in the industry. Susan saw the forest for the trees as I struggled to distinguish what was and was not important about endless recollections. She drew me a road map, then nudged me along. I couldn't have done it without her.

I owe considerable gratitude, too, to my daughter, Hilary (Lalo) Walsh, who read the first draft and gave me the benefit of her nimble brain and wicked wit. Thanks to my son, the inimitable Adam Williamson Ward, who has always been generous, not only with his love, but with his computer skills. Thanks also to my children's father, Wendell (Nick) B. Ward, Jr., for support and encouragement.

There are others who helped me: Mary Hadar, by telling me I was as much a writer as an editor. Kathy Lord, whose careful line-editing is rare and much to be valued. Jamie Alcabes, who corrected numerous typographical errors in the original. Jane and John Amos, who offered a quiet house in West Virginia when there was rewriting to do. Steve Coll, managing editor of *The Washington Post*, and my colleagues at *Book World*, who give me continuing support.

But all said and done, this book simply would not be if it weren't for my husband, Jonathan Yardley. He told me I had a story to tell in the first place, offered kind words as I completed each chapter, and then read every version, with patience and gallantry and love. He is as deeply etched into my life and work as the memories on these pages. I owe him more than I can possibly say.

ABOUT THE AUTHOR

MARIE ARANA is the editor of *The Washington Post's Book World*. She has served on the boards of directors of the National Association of Hispanic Journalists and the National Book Critics Circle. Formerly a book editor at Harcourt Brace Jovanovich and vice president at Simon & Schuster, she joined *The Washington Post* in 1992. Apart from her editorial work, she has also done feature writing for *The Post*. She lives on Capitol Hill in Washington, D.C., with her son, Adam Ward, and her husband, Jonathan Yardley.